THE WORKS OF WILLIAM SHAKESPEARE

VOLUME EIGHT

WILLIAM SHAKESPEARE

From the Statue by Lord Ronald Gower in the Grounds of The
Memorial Theatre at Stratford-on-Avon

THE WORKS OF WILLIAM SHAKESPEARE

VOLUME EIGHT

Troilus and Cressida
Twelfth Night or What You Will
The Two Gentlemen of Verona
The Winter's Tale

THE PEEBLES CLASSIC LIBRARY
SANDY LESBERG, *Editor*

Published by Peebles Press International
U.S.A.: 10 Columbus Circle, New York, NY 10019
U.K.: 12 Thayer Street, London W1M 5LD

Distributed by WHS Distributors

PRINTED AND BOUND IN THE U.S.A.

CONTENTS

TROILUS AND CRESSIDA

DRAMATIS PERSONÆ

PRIAM, *king of Troy*

HECTOR
TROILUS
PARIS } *his sons*
DEIPHOBUS
HELENUS

ÆNEAS } *Trojan commanders*
ANTENOR

CALCHAS, *a Trojan priest, taking part with the Greeks*
PANDARUS, *uncle to Cressida*
MARGARELON, *a bastard son of Priam*
AGAMEMNON, *the Grecian general*
MENELAUS, *his brother*

ACHILLES,
AJAX
ULYSSES } *Grecian commanders*
NESTOR
DIOMEDES
PATROCLUS

THERSITES, *a deformed and scurrilous Grecian*
ALEXANDER, *servant to Cressida*
Servant to Troilus
Servant to Paris
Servant to Diomedes

HELEN, *wife of Menelaus*
ANDROMACHE, *wife of Hector*
CASSANDRA, *daughter of Priam, a prophetess*
CRESSIDA, *daughter of Calchas*

Trojan and Greek Soldiers, and Attendants

SCENE.—*Troy, and the Grecian Camp before it.*

12

TROILUS AND CRESSIDA

PROLOGUE

In Troy there lies the scene.   From Isles of Greece
The princes orgulous, their high blood chafed,
Have to the port of Athens sent their ships,
Fraught with the ministers and instruments
Of cruel war: sixty and nine, that wore
Their crownets regal, from the Athenian bay
Put forth toward Phrygia; and their vow is made
To ransack Troy, within whose strong immures
The ravished Helen, Menelaus' queen,
With wanton Paris sleeps: and that 's the quarrel.
To Tenedos they come;
And the deep-drawing barks do there disgorge
Their warlike fraughtage: now on Dardan plains
The fresh and yet unbruiséd Greeks do pitch
Their brave pavilions; Priam's six-gated city,
Dardan, and Thymbria, Helias, Chetas, Troien,
And Antenorides, with massy staples
And corresponsive and fulfilling bolts,
Sperr up the sons of Troy.
Now expectation, tickling skittish spirits
On one and other side, Trojan and Greek,
Sets all on hazard.   Hither am I come
A prologue arméd, not in confidence
Of author's pen or actor's voice, but suited
In like conditions as our argument,
To tell you, fair beholders, that our play
Leaps o'er the vaunt and firstlings of those broils,
Beginning in the middle; thence away
To what may be digested in a play.
Like, or find fault; do as your pleasures are;
Now good or bad, 't is but the chance of war.

ACT ONE

Scene I.—Troy.   Before Priam's Palace

Enter Troilus *armed, and* Pandarus

Tro.   Call here my varlet, I 'll unarm again:
Why should I war without the walls of Troy,
That find such cruel battle here within?

Each Trojan that is master of his heart,
Let him to field; Troilus, alas, hath none.
 Pan. Will this gear ne'er be mended?
 Tro. The Greeks are strong, and skilful to their strength,
Fierce to their skill, and to their fierceness valiant;
But I am weaker than a woman's tear,
Tamer than sleep, fonder than ignorance,
Less valiant than the virgin in the night,
And skilless as unpractised infancy.
 Pan. Well, I have told you enough of this: for my
part, I 'll not meddle nor make no further. He that will
have a cake out of the wheat must needs tarry the grinding.
 Tro. Have I not tarried?
 Pan. Ay, the grinding; but you must tarry the bolting.
 Tro. Have I not tarried?
 Pan. Ay, the bolting; but you must tarry the leavening.
 Tro. Still have I tarried.
 Pan. Ay, to the leavening; but here 's yet in the word
'hereafter' the kneading, the making of the cake, the
heating of the oven, and the baking; nay, you must stay
the cooling too, or you may chance to burn your lips.
 Tro. Patience herself, what goddess e'er she be,
Doth lesser blench at sufferance than I do.
At Priam's royal table do I sit;
And when fair Cressid comes into my thoughts,—
So, traitor!—'when she comes'!—When is she thence?
 Pan. Well, she looked yesternight fairer than ever
I saw her look, or any woman else.
 Tro. I was about to tell thee—when my heart,
As wedgéd with a sigh, would rive in twain;
Lest Hector or my father should perceive me
I have—as when the sun doth light a storm—
Buried this sigh in wrinkle of a smile,
But sorrow that is couched in seeming gladness
Is like that mirth fate turns to sudden sadness.
 Pan. An her hair were not somewhat darker than
Helen's,—well, go to,—there were no more comparison
between the women;—but, for my part, she is my kins-
woman; I would not, as they term it, praise her;—but I
would somebody had heard her talk yesterday, as I did.
I will not dispraise your sister Cassandra's wit, but—
 Tro. O Pandarus! I tell thee, Pandarus,—
When I do tell thee there my hopes lie drowned,
Reply not in how many fathoms deep
They lie indrenched. I tell thee, I am mad
In Cressid's love; thou answer'st, 'she is fair';
Pour'st in the open ulcer of my heart
Her eyes, her hair, her cheek, her gait, her voice;
Handlest in thy discourse,—O, that; her hand!

In whose comparison all whites are ink
Writing their own reproach; to whose soft seizure
The cygnet's down is harsh, and spirit of sense
Hard as the palm of ploughman!—this thou tell'st me,
As true thou tell'st me when I say I love her;
But, saying thus, instead of oil and balm,
Thou lay'st in every gash that love hath given me
The knife that made it.
    Pan. I speak no more than truth.
    Tro. Thou dost not speak so much.
    Pan. 'Faith, I 'll not meddle in 't. Let her be as she
is: if she be fair, 't is the better for her; an she be not,
she has the mends in her own hands.
    Tro. Good Pandarus,—how now, Pandarus?
    Pan. I have had my labour for my travail; ill-thought
on of her, and ill-thought on of you; gone between and
between, but small thanks for my labour.
    Tro. What, art thou angry, Pandarus? what, with me?
    Pan. Because she 's kin to me, therefore she 's not so
fair as Helen: an she were not kin to me, she would be as
fair on Friday as Helen is on Sunday. But what care I?
I care not, an she were a black-a-moor; 't is all one to
me.
    Tro. Say I, she is not fair?
    Pan. I do not care whether you do or not. She 's a
fool to stay behind her father; let her to the Greeks; and
so I'll tell her the next time I see her: for my part, I 'll
meddle nor make no more i' the matter.
    Tro. Pandarus,—
    Pan. Not I.
    Tro. Sweet Pandarus,—
    Pan. Pray you, speak no more to me: I will leave all as I
found it, and there an end.

                              [*Exit Pandarus. Alarum*
    Tro. Peace, you ungracious clamours! peace, rude
            sounds!
Fools on both sides! Helen must needs be fair,
When with your blood you daily paint her thus.
I cannot fight upon this argument;
It is too starved a subject for my sword.
But Pandarus—O gods, how do you rogue me!
I cannot come to Cressid but by Pandar;
And he 's as tetchy to be woo'd to woo
As she is stubborn-chaste against all suit.
Tell me, Apollo, for thy Daphne's love,
What Cressid is, what Pandar, and what we?
Her bed is India; there she lies, a pearl:
Between our Ilium and where she resides,
Let it be called the wild and wandering flood;

                              15

Ourself the merchant; and this sailing Pandar,
Our doubtful hope, our convoy, and our bark.

Alarum.   Enter ÆNEAS

  Æne.   How now, Prince Troilus? wherefore not afield?
  Tro.   Because not there: this woman's answer sorts,
For womanish it is to be from thence.
What news, Æneas, from the field to-day?
  Æne.   That Paris is returnéd home, and hurt.
  Tro.   By whom, Æneas?
  Æne.   Troilus, by Menelaus.
  Tro.   Let Paris bleed: 't is but a scar to scorn;
Paris is gored with Menelaus' horn.   [*Alarum*
  Æne.   Hark, what good sport is out of town to-day!
  Tro.   Better at home, if 'would I might' were 'may.'—
But to the sport abroad:—are you bound thither?
  Æne.   In all swift haste.
  Tro.   Come, go we, then, together.   [*Exeunt*

SCENE II.—The same.   A Street

Enter CRESSIDA and ALEXANDER

  Cres.   Who were those went by?
  Alex.   Queen Hecuba, and Helen.
  Cres.   And whither go they?
  Alex.   Up to the eastern tower,
Whose height commands as subject all the vale,
To see the battle.   Hector, whose patience
Is as a virtue, fixed, to-day was moved:
He chid Andromache, and struck his armourer;
And, like as there were husbandry in war,
Before the sun rose, he was harnessed light,
And to the field goes he; where every flower
Did, as a prophet, weep what it foresaw
In Hector's wrath.
  Cres.   What was his cause of anger?
  Alex.   The noise goes, this: there is among the Greeks
A lord of Trojan blood, nephew to Hector;
They call him Ajax.
  Cres.   Good; and what of him?
  Alex.   They say he is a very man *per se,*
And stands alone.
  Cres.   So do all men; unless they are drunk, sick, or
have no legs.
  Alex.   This man, lady, hath robbed many beasts of
their particular additions; he is as valiant as the lion,
churlish as the bear, slow as the elephant: a man into
whom nature hath so crowded humours, that his valour is

crushed into folly, his folly sauced with discretion: there is no man hath a virtue that he hath not a glimpse of; nor any man an attaint but he carries some stain of it. He is melancholy without cause, and merry against the hair: he hath the joints of everything; but everything so out of joint, that he is a gouty Briareus, many hands and no use; or purblinded Argus, all eyes and no sight.

Cres. But how should this man, that makes me smile, make Hector angry?

Alex. They say he yesterday coped Hector in the battle, and struck him down; the disdain and shame whereof hath ever since kept Hector fasting and waking.

Cres. Who comes here?

Alex. Madam, your uncle Pandarus.

Enter PANDARUS

Cres. Hector's a gallant man.

Alex. As may be in the world, lady.

Pan. What 's that? what 's that?

Cres. Good morrow, uncle Pandarus.

Pan. Good morrow, cousin Cressid. What do you talk of?—Good morrow, Alexander.—How do you, cousin? When were you at Ilium?

Cres. This morning, uncle.

Pan. What were you talking of, when I came? Was Hector armed and gone, ere ye came to Ilium? Helen was not up, was she?

Cres. Hector was gone; but Helen was not up.

Pan. E'en so: Hector was stirring early.

Cres. That were we talking of, and of his anger.

Pan. Was he angry?

Cres. So he says here.

Pan. True, he was so; I know the cause too; he'll lay about him to-day, I can tell them that: and there's Troilus will not come far behind him. Let them take heed of Troilus, I can tell them that too.

Cres. What, is he angry too?

Pan. Who, Troilus? Troilus is the better man of the two.

Cres. O Jupiter! there's no comparison.

Pan. What, not between Troilus and Hector? Do you know a man if you see him?

Cres. Ay; if I ever saw him before, and knew him.

Pan. Well, I say, Troilus is Troilus.

Cres. Then you say as I say; for I am sure he is not Hector.

Pan. No, nor Hector is not Troilus, in some degrees.

Cres. 'T is just to each of them; he is himself.

17

Pan.   Himself?   Alas, poor Troilus!   I would he were.

Cres.   So he is.

Pan.   Condition, I had gone bare-foot to India.

Cres.   He is not Hector.

Pan.   Himself? no, he 's not himself.—'Would 'a were himself!   Well, the gods are above; time must friend, or end; well, Troilus, well,—I would, my heart were in her body!—No, Hector is not a better man than Troilus.

Cres.   Excuse me.

Pan.   He is elder.

Cres.   Pardon me, pardon me.

Pan.   The other 's not come to 't; you shall tell me another tale, when the other 's come to 't.   Hector shall not have his wit, this year.—

Cres.   He shall not need it, if he have his own.

Pan.   Nor his qualities,—

Cres.   No matter.

Pan.   Nor his beauty.

Cres.   'Twould not become him; his own 's better.

Pan.   You have no judgment, niece; Helen herself swore the other day, that Troilus, for a brown favour—for so 't is, I must confess—not brown neither—

Cres.   No, but brown,—

Pan.   'Faith, to say truth, brown and not brown—

Cres.   To say the truth, true and not true—

Pan.   She praised his complexion above Paris.

Cres.   Why, Paris hath colour enough.

Pan.   So he has.

Cres.   Then Troilus should have too much: if she praised him above, his complexion is higher than his: he having colour enough, and the other higher, is too flaming a praise for a good complexion.   I had as lief Helen's golden tongue had commended Troilus for a copper nose.

Pan.   I swear to you, I think Helen loves him better than Paris.

Cres.   Then she 's a merry Greek, indeed.

Pan.   Nay, I am sure she does.   She came to him the other day into the compassed window,—and, you know, he has not passed three or four hairs on his chin—

Cres.   Indeed, a tapster's arithmetic may soon bring his particulars therein to a total.

Pan.   Why, he is very young: and yet will he, within three pound, lift as much as his brother Hector.

Cres.   Is he so young a man, and so old a lifter?

Pan.   But, to prove to you that Helen loves him,—she came, and puts me her white hand to his cloven chin,—

Cres.   Juno have mercy! how came it cloven?

18

Pan. Why, you know, 't is dimpled: I think his smiling becomes him better than any man in all Phrygia.

Cres. O, he smiles valiantly.

Pan. Does he not?

Cres. O, yes, an 't were a cloud in autumn.

Pan. Why, go to then.—But to prove to you that Helen loves Troilus,—

Cres. Troilus will stand to the proof, if you 'll prove it so.—

Pan. Troilus! why, he esteems her no more than I esteem an addle egg.

Cres. If you love an addle egg as well as you love an idle head, you would eat chickens i' the shell.—

Pan. I cannot choose but laugh, to think how she tickled his chin;—indeed, she has a marvellous white hand, I must needs confess,—

Cres. Without the rack.—

Pan. And she takes upon her to spy a white hair on his chin.

Cres. Alas, poor chin! many a wart is richer.

Pan. But there was such laughing! Queen Hecuba laughed, that her eyes ran o'er,—

Cres. With millstones.—

Pan. And Cassandra laughed,—

Cres. But there was more temperate fire under the pot of her eyes:—did her eyes run o'er too?—

Pan. And Hector laughed.

Cres. At what was all this laughing?

Pan. Marry, at the white hair that Helen spied on Troilus' chin.

Cres. An 't had been a green hair, I should have laughed too.

Pan. They laughed not so much at the hair, as at his pretty answer.

Cres. What was his answer?

Pan. Quoth she, 'Here's but one-and-fifty hairs on your chin, and one of them is white.'

Cres. This is her question.

Pan. That 's true; make no question of that. 'One and-fifty hairs,' quoth he, 'and one white: that white hair is my father, and all the rest are his sons.'—'Jupiter!' quoth she, 'which of these hairs is Paris, my husband?'—'The forked one,' quoth he; 'pluck 't out, and give it him.' But there was such laughing! and Helen so blushed, and Paris so chafed, and all the rest so laughed, that it passed.

Cres. So let it now, for it has been a great while going by.

Pan. Well, cousin, I told you a thing yesterday; think on 't.

19

Cres. So I do.

Pan. I'll be sworn, 't is true; he will weep you, an 't were a man born in April.

Cres. And I'll spring up in his tears, an 't were a nettle against May.   [*A retreat sounded*

Pan. Hark! they are coming from the field. Shall we stand up here, and see them as they pass toward Ilium? good niece, do,—sweet niece Cressida.

Cres. At your pleasure.

Pan. Here, here, here 's an excellent place; here we may see most bravely; I'll tell you them all by their names, as they pass by; but mark Troilus above the rest.

Cres. Speak not so loud.

ÆNEAS *passes*

Pan. That 's Æneas. Is not that a brave man? he's one of the flowers of Troy, I can tell you: but mark Troilus; you shall see anon.

ANTENOR *passes*

Cres. Who 's that?

Pan. That 's Antenor; he has a shrewd wit, I can tell you, and he 's a man good enough: he 's one o' the soundest judgments in Troy, whosoever, and a proper man of person. When comes Troilus?—I 'll show you Troilus anon: if he see me, you shall see him nod at me.

Cres. Will he give you the nod?

Pan. You shall see.

Cres. If he do, the rich shall have more.

HECTOR *passes*

Pan. That 's Hector, that, that, look you, that; there 's a fellow!—Go thy way, Hector.—There 's a brave man, niece—O brave Hector!—Look how he looks; there 's a countenance! Is 't not a brave man?

Cres. O, a brave man.

Pan. Is 'a not? It does a man's heart good:—look you what hacks are on his helmet! look you yonder, do you see? look you there: there 's no jesting; there 's laying on; take 't off who will, as they say: there be hacks!

Cres. Be those with swords?

Pan. Swords? anything, he cares not; an the devil come to him, it 's all one: by God's lid, it does one's heart good.—Yonder comes Paris; yonder comes Paris: look ye yonder, niece: is 't not a gallant man too, is 't not?—[PARIS *passes*]—Why, this is brave now.—Who said he came hurt home to-day? he 's not hurt: why, this will do Helen's heart good now, ha! Would I could see Troilus now!—You shall see Troilus anon.

20

HELENUS *passes*

Cres. Who 's that?
Pan. That's Helenus:—I marvel, where Troilus is:—
that 's Helenus:—I think he went not forth to-day:—
that 's Helenus.
Cres. Can Helenus fight, uncle?
Pan. Helenus! no,—yes,—he 'll fight indifferent well.—
I marvel, where Troilus is.—Hark! do you not hear the
people cry, 'Troilus'?—Helenus is a priest.
Cres. What sneaking fellow comes yonder?

TROILUS *passes*

Pan. Where? yonder? that 's Deiphobus:—'t is
Troilus! there 's a man, niece!—Hem!—Brave Troilus,
the prince of chivalry!
Cres. Peace, for shame, peace!
Pan. Mark him; note him:—O brave Troilus!—look
well upon him, niece: look you, how his sword is bloodied,
and his helm more hacked than Hector's; and how he
looks, and how he goes!—O admirable youth! he ne'er saw
three-and-twenty.—Go thy way, Troilus, go thy way!—
Had I a sister were a grace, or a daughter goddess, he
should take his choice. O admirable man! Paris?—Paris
is dirt to him; and, I warrant, Helen, to change, would
give an eye to boot.

Warriors pass

Cres. Here come more.
Pan. Asses, fools, dolts! chaff and bran, chaff and
bran! porridge after meat!—I could live and die i' the
eyes of Troilus.—Ne'er look, ne'er look;—the eagles are
gone: crows and daws, crows and daws!—I had rather be
such a man as Troilus than Agamemnon and all Greece.
Cres. There is among the Greeks Achilles, a better man
than Troilus.
Pan. Achilles! a drayman, a porter, a very camel.
Cres. Well, well!
Pan. Well, well!—Why, have you any discretion?
have you any eyes? Do you know what a man is?
Is not birth, beauty, good shape, discourse, manhood,
learning, gentleness, virtue, youth, liberality, and so forth,
the spice and salt that season a man?
Cres. Ay, a minced man: and then to be baked with
no date in the pie,—for then the man's date 's out.
Pan. You are such a woman! one knows not at what
ward you lie.
Cres. Upon my back, to defend my belly; upon my
wit, to defend my wiles; upon my secrecy, to defend mine

honesty; my mask, to defend my beauty; and you, to
defend all these: and at all these wards I lie, at a thousand watches.

Pan. Say one of your watches.

Cres. Nay, I'll watch you for that; and that's one of
the chiefest of them too: if I cannot ward what I would
not have hit, I can watch you for telling how I took the
blow; unless it swell past hiding, and then it's past watching.

Pan. You are such another!

Enter TROILUS' BOY

Boy. Sir, my lord would instantly speak with you.

Pan. Where?

Boy. At your own house, there he unarms him.

Pan. Good boy, tell him I come.   [*Exit Boy*
I doubt he be hurt.—Fare ye well, good niece.

Cres. Adieu, uncle.

Pan. I'll be with you, niece, by-and-by.

Cres. To bring, uncle?

Pan. Ay, a token from Troilus.

Cres. By the same token—you are a bawd.—
                                        [*Exit Pandarus*
Words, vows, gifts, tears, and love's full sacrifice,
He offers in another's enterprise:
But more in Troilus thousand-fold I see
Than in the glass of Pandar's praise may be;
Yet I hold off. Women are angels, wooing:
Things won are done, joy's soul dies in the doing:
That She beloved knows nought that knows not this,—
Men prize the thing ungained more than it is:
That She was never yet that ever knew
Love got so sweet as when desire did sue.
Therefore this maxim out of love I teach,—
Achievement is command; ungained, beseech:
Then though my heart's content firm love doth bear,
Nothing of that shall from mine eyes appear.   [*Exit*

SCENE III.—The Grecian Camp. Before AGAMEMNON'S Tent

Sennet. Enter AGAMEMNON, NESTOR, ULYSSES, MENELAUS, *and others*

Agam. Princes,
What grief hath set the jaundice on your cheeks?
The ample proposition that hope makes
In all designs begun on earth below

22

Fails in the promised largeness: checks and disasters
Grow in the veins of actions highest reared;
As knots, by the conflux of meeting sap,
Infect the sound pine and divert his grain
Tortive and errant from his course of growth.
Nor princes, is it matter new to us,
That we come short of our suppose so far,
That, after seven years' siege, yet Troy walls stand;
Sith every action that hath gone before
Whereof we have record, trial did draw
Bias and thwart, not answering the aim
And that unbodied figure of the thought
That gave 't surmiséd shape.   Why then, you princes,
Do you with cheeks abashed behold our wrecks
And think them shames, which are, indeed, nought else
But the protractive trials of great Jove
To find persistive constancy in men?
The fineness of which metal is not found
In fortune's love; for then the bold and coward,
The wise and fool, the artist and unread,
The hard and soft, seem all affined and kin:
But, in the wind and tempest of her frown,
Distinction, with a broad and powerful fan,
Puffing at all, winnows the light away;
And what hath mass or matter, by itself
Lies rich in virtue and unmingléd.
     Nest.   With due observance of thy godlike seat,
Great Agamemnon, Nestor shall apply
Thy latest words.   In the reproof of chance
Lies the true proof of men: the sea being smooth,
How many shallow bauble boats dare sail
Upon her patient breast, making their way
With those of nobler bulk!
But let the ruffian Boreas once enrage
The gentle Thetis, and, anon, behold
The strong-ribbed bark through liquid mountains cut,
Bounding between the two moist elements,
Like Perseus' horse: where 's then the saucy boat,
Whose weak untimbered sides but even now
Co-rivalled greatness? either to harbour fled,
Or made a toast for Neptune.   Even so
Doth valour's show and valour's worth divide
In storms of fortune: for in her ray and brightness
The herd hath more annoyance by the brize
Than by the tiger; but when the splitting wind
Makes flexible the knees of knotted oaks,
And flies fled under shade, why, then the thing of courage,
As roused with rage, with rage doth sympathise,
And with an accent tuned in selfsame key

Retorts to chiding fortune.
   Ulyss.   Agamemnon,—
Thou great commander, nerve and bone of Greece,
Heart of our numbers, soul and holy spirit,
In whom the tempers and the minds of all
Should be shut up,—hear what Ulysses speaks.
Besides the applause and approbation
The which,—[*To Agamemnon*] most mighty for thy place
        and sway,—
[*To Nestor*] And thou most reverend for thy stretched-
        out life,—
I give to both your speeches, which were such
As Agamemnon and the hand of Greece
Should hold up high in brass; and such again,
As venerable Nestor, hatched in silver,
Should with a bond of air strong as the axle-tree
On which heaven rides knit all the Greekish ears
To his experienced tongue,—yet let it please both,
Thou great,—and wise,—to hear Ulysses speak.
   Agam. Speak, Prince of Ithaca; and be't of less
        expect
That matter needless of importless burden
Divide thy lips, than we are confident
When rank Thersites opes his mastiff jaws
We shall hear music, wit, and oracle.
   Ulyss. Troy, yet upon his basis, had been down,
And the great Hector's sword had lacked a master,
But for these instances:
The speciality of rule hath been neglected:
And, look, how many Grecian tents do stand
Hollow on this plain so many hollow factions.
When that the general is not like the hive
To whom the foragers shall all repair,
What honey is expected?   Degree being vizarded,
The unworthiest shows as fairly in the mask.
The heavens themselves, the planets, and this centre,
Observe degree, priority, and place,
Insisture, course, proportion, season, form,
Office, and custom, in all line of order:
And therefore in the glorious planet Sol
In noble eminence enthroned and sphered
Amidst the other; whose med'cinable eye
Corrects the ill aspécts of planets evil,
And posts, like the commandment of a king,
Sans check, to good and bad: but when the planets,
In evil mixture, to disorder wander,
What plagues, and what portents, what mutiny,
What raging of the sea, shaking of earth,
Commotion in the winds, frights, changes, horrors,

Divert and crack, rend and deracinate
The unity and married calm of states
Quite from their fixture!   O, when degree is shaked,
Which is the ladder to all high designs,
The enterprise is sick.   How could communities,
Degrees in schools and brotherhoods in cities,
Peaceful commérce from dividable shores,
The primogenity and due of birth,
Prerogative of age, crowns, sceptres, laurels,
But by degree, stand in authentic place?
Take but degree away, untune that string,
And, hark, what discord follows! each thing meets
In mere oppugnancy: the bounded waters
Should lift their bosoms higher than the shores,
And make a sop of all this solid globe:
Strength should be lord of imbecility,
And the rude son should strike his father dead:
Force should be right; or, rather, right and wrong—
Between whose endless jar justice resides—
Should lose their names, and so should justice too.
Then everything includes itself in power,
Power into will, will into appetite;
And appetite, an universal wolf,
So doubly seconded with will and power,
Must make perforce an universal prey,
And last eat up himself.   Great Agamemnon,
This chaos, when degree is suffocate,
Follows the choking.
And this neglection of degree it is,
That by a pace goes backward in a purpose
It hath to climb.   The general 's disdained
By him one step below; he, by the next;
That next, by him beneath: so, every step,
Exampled by the first pace that is sick
Of his superior, grows to an envious fever
Of pale and bloodless emulation:
And 't is this fever that keeps Troy on foot,
Not her own sinews.   To end a tale of length,
Troy in our weakness stands, not in her strength.
     Nest.   Most wisely hath Ulysses here discovered
The fever whereof all our power is sick.
     Agam.   The nature of this sickness found, Ulysses,
What is the remedy?
     Ulyss.   The great Achilles, whom opinion crowns
The sinew and the forehand of our host,
Having his ear full of his airy fame,
Grows dainty of his worth, and in his tent
Lies mocking our designs.   With him Patroclus,
Upon a lazy bed, the livelong day

Breaks scurril jests;
And with ridiculous and awkward action—
Which, slanderer, he imitation calls—
He pageants us.   Sometime, great Agamemnon,
Thy topless deputation he puts on;
And, like a strutting player,—whose conceit
Lies in his hamstring, and doth think it rich
To hear the wooden dialogue and sound
'Twixt his stretched footing and the scaffoldage,—
Such to-be-pitied and o'er-wrested seeming
He acts thy greatness in: and when he speaks,
'T is like a chime a-mending; with terms unsquared
Which from the tongue of roaring Typhon dropped
Would seem hyperboles.   At this fusty stuff
The large Achilles, on his pressed bed lolling,
From his deep chest laughs out a loud applause;
Cries—'Excellent!—'t is Agamemnon just.
Now play me Nestor;—hem, and stroke thy beard,
As he, being drest to some oration.'
That 's done: as near as the extremest ends
Of parallels;—as like as Vulcan and his wife:
Yet good Achilles still cries, 'Excellent!
'T is Nestor right!   Now play him me, Patroclus,
Arming to answer in a night alarm.'
And then, forsooth, the faint defects of age
Must be the scene of mirth; to cough and spit,
And with a palsy-fumbling on his gorget
Shake in and out the rivet:—and at this sport.
Sir Valour dies; cries, 'O!—enough, Patroclus;
Or give me ribs of steel!   I shall split all
In pleasure of my spleen.'   And in this fashion,
All our abilities, gifts, natures, shapes,
Severals and generals of grace exact,
Achievements, plots, orders, preventions,
Excitements to the field, or speech for truce,
Success or loss, what is or is not, serves
As stuff for these two to make paradoxes.
   Nest.   And in the imitation of these twain—
Who, as Ulysses says, opinion crowns
With an imperial voice—many are infect.
Ajax is grown self-willed; and bears his head
In such a rein, in full as proud a pace
As broad Achilles; keeps his tent like him;
Makes factious feasts; rails on our state of war,
Bold as an oracle; and sets Thersites—
A slave whose gall coins slanders like a mint—
To match us in comparisons with dirt,
To weaken and discredit our exposure,
How rank soever rounded in with danger.

 Ulyss. They tax our policy, and call it cowardice;
Count wisdom as no member of the war;
Forestall prescience, and esteem no act
But that of hand: the still and mental parts
That do contrive how many hands shall strike
When fitness calls them on, and know, by measure
Of their observant toil, the enemies' weight,
Why, this hath not a finger's dignity:
They call this bed-work, mappery, closet-war;
So that the ram that batters down the wall,
For the great swing and rudeness of his poise,
They place before his hand that made the engine,
Or those that with the fineness of their souls
By reason guide his execution.
 Nest. Let this be granted, and Achilles' horse
Makes many Thetis sons.   *[A tucket*
 Agam.   What trumpet? look, Menelaus.
 Men. From Troy.

Enter ÆNEAS

 Agam. What would you 'fore our tent?
 Æne. Is this great Agamemnon's tent, I pray you?
 Agam. Even this.
 Æne. May one, that is a herald and a prince,
Do a fair message to his kingly ears?
 Agam. With surety stronger than Achilles' arm,
'Fore all the Greekish heads which with one voice
Call Agamemnon head and general.
 Æne. Fair leave, and large security. How may
A stranger to those most imperial looks
Know them from eyes of other mortals?
 Agam.   How!
 Æne. Ay;
I ask, that I might waken reverence,
And bid the cheek be ready with a blush
Modest as morning when she coldly eyes
The youthful Phœbus:
Which is that god in office, guiding men?
Which is the high and mighty Agamemnon?
 Agam. This Trojan scorns us; or the men of Troy
Are ceremonious courtiers.
 Æne. Courtiers as free, as debonair, unarmed,
As bending angels: that's their fame in peace:
But when they would seem soldiers, they have galls,
Good arms, strong joints, true swords,—in Jove's recórd
Nothing so full of heart. But peace, Æneas,
Peace, Trojan, lay thy finger on thy lips.
The worthiness of praise disdains his worth

If that the praised himself bring the praise forth;
But what the repining enemy commends,
That breath fame blows; that praise, sole pure, transcends.
    Agam.   Sir, you of Troy, call you yourself Æneas;
    Æne.   Ay, Greek, that is my name.
    Agam.   What's your affair, I pray you?
    Æne.   Sir, pardon, 'tis for Agamemnon's ears.
    Agam.   He hears nought privately that comes from
        Troy.
    Æne.   Nor I from Troy came not to whisper him:
I bring a trumpet to awake his ear;
To set his sense on the attentive bent,
And then to speak.
    Agam.   Speak frankly as the wind;
It is not Agamemnon's sleeping hour:
That thou shalt know, Trojan, he is awake,
He tells thee so himself.
    Æne.   Trumpet, blow loud,
Send thy brass voice through all these lazy tents;
And every Greek of mettle, let him know,
What Troy means fairly shall be spoke aloud.
                                  [Trumpet sounds
We have, great Agamemnon, here in Troy,
A prince called Hector,—Priam is his father,—
Who in this dull and long-continued truce
Is rusty grown: he bade me take a trumpet,
And to this purpose speak.—Kings, princes, lords!
If there be one among the fair'st of Greece,
That holds his honour higher than his ease;
That seeks his praise more than he fears his peril;
That knows his valour, and knows not his fear;
That loves his mistress more than in confession
With truant vows to her own lips he loves,
And dare avow her beauty and her worth
In other arms than hers,—to him this challenge:
Hector, in view of Trojans and of Greeks,
Shall make it good, or do his best to do it.
He hath a lady, wiser, fairer, truer,
Than ever Greek did compass in his arms;
And will to-morrow with his trumpet call,
Midway between your tents and walls of Troy,
To rouse a Grecian that is true in love:
If any come, Hector shall honour him;
If none, he'll say in Troy, when he retires,
The Grecian dames are sun-burnt, and not worth
The splinter of a lance. Even so much.
    Agam.   This shall be told our lovers, Lord Æneas;
If none of them have soul in such a kind,
We left them all at home: but we are soldiers;

And may that soldier a mere recreant prove,
That means not, hath not, or is not in love!
If then one is, or hath, or means to be,
That one meets Hector; if none else, I am he.
 Nest. Tell him of Nestor, one that was a man
When Hector's grandsire sucked: he is old now;
But if there be not in our Grecian host
One noble man that hath one spark of fire
To answer for his love, tell him from me,
I 'll hide my silver beard in a gold beaver,
And in my vantbrace put this withered brawn;
And, meeting him, will tell him, that my lady
Was fairer than his grandam, and as chaste
As may be in the world. His youth in flood,
I 'll prove this truth, with my three drops of blood.
 Æne. Now heavens forbid such scarcity of youth!—
 Ulyss. Amen.
 Agam. Fair Lord Æneas, let me touch your hand;
To our pavilion shall I lead you, sir.
Achilles shall have word of this intent;
So shall each lord of Greece, from tent to tent;
Yourself shall feast with us before you go,
And find the welcome of a noble foe.
      [*Exeunt all but Ulysses and Nestor*
 Ulyss. Nestor,—
 Nest. What says Ulysses?
 Ulyss. I have a young conception in my brain;
Be you my Time to bring it to some shape.
 Nest. What is 't?
 Ulyss. This 't is:—
Blunt wedges rive hard knots: the seeded pride
That hath to this maturity blown up
In rank Achilles must or now be cropped,
Or, shedding, breed a nursery of like evil,
To overbulk us all.
 Nest.   Well, and how?
 Ulyss. This challenge that the gallant Hector sends,
However it is spread in general name,
Relates in purpose only to Achilles.
 Nest. The purpose is perspicuous even as substance
Whose grossness little characters sum up:
And, in the publication, make no strain
But that Achilles, were his brain as barren
As banks of Libya—though, Apollo knows,
'T is dry enough—will, with great speed of judgment,
Ay, with celerity, find Hector's purpose
Pointing on him.
 Ulyss. And wake him to the answer, think you?
 Nest. Yes, it is most meet: who may you else oppose

That can from Hector bring his honour off,
If not Achilles?   Though 't be a sportful combat,
Yet in the trial much opinion dwells;
For here the Trojans taste our dear'st repute
With their fin'st palate: and trust to me, Ulysses,
Our imputation shall be oddly poised
In this wild action; for the success,
Although particular, shall give a scantling
Of good or bad unto the general;
And in such indexes, although small pricks
To their subséquent volumes, there is seen
The baby figure of the giant mass
Of things to come at large.   It is supposed,
He that meets Hector issues from our choice:
And choice, being mutual act of all our souls,
Makes merit her election; and doth boil
As 't were from forth us all a man distilled
Out of her virtues; who miscarrying,
What heart receives from hence the conquering part,
To steel a strong opinion to themselves?
Which entertained, limbs are his instruments,
In no less working than are swords and bows
Directive by the limbs.
    Ulyss.   Give pardon to my speech;—
Therefore 't is meet Achilles meet not Hector.
Let us like merchants show our foulest wares,
And think, perchance, that they will sell; if not,
The lustre of the better yet to show,
Shall show the better.   Do not, then, consent
That ever Hector and Achilles meet;
For both our honour and our shame in this
Are dogged with two strange followers.
    Nest.   I see them not with my old eyes: what are they?
    Ulyss.   What glory our Achilles shares from Hector,
Were he not proud, we all should wear with him:
But he already is too insolent;
And we were better parch in Afric sun
Than in the pride and salt scorn of his eyes,
Should he 'scape Hector fair: if he were foiled,
Why, then we did our main opinion crush
In taint of our best man.   No; make a lottery;
And, by device, let blockish Ajax draw
The sort to fight with Hector: 'mong ourselves,
Give him allowance as the worthier man,
For that will physic the great Myrmidon
Who broils in loud applause, and make him fall
His crest that prouder than blue Iris bends.
If the dull brainless Ajax come safe off,
We'll dress him up in voices: if he fail,

Yet go we under our opinion still
That we have better men. But, hit or miss,
Our project's life this shape of sense assumes,—
Ajax employed, plucks down Achilles' plumes.
    Nest. Ulysses,
Now I begin to relish thy advice;
And I will give a taste of it forthwith
To Agamemnon: go we to him straight.
Two curs shall tame each other: pride alone
Must tarre the mastiffs on, as 't were their bone.

                        [Exeunt

ACT TWO

Scene I.—Another Part of the Grecian Camp

Enter Ajax *and* Thersites

    Ajax. Thersites,—
    Ther. Agamemnon—how if he had boils,—full all over, generally?—
    Ajax. Thersites!
    Ther. And those boils did run?—Say so,—did not the general run then? were not that a botchy core?—
    Ajax. Dog!
    Ther. Then would come some matter from him; I see none now.
    Ajax. Thou bitch-wolf's son, canst thou not hear? Feel then.   *[Beating him*
    Ther. The plague of Greece upon thee, thou mongrel beef-witted lord!
    Ajax. Speak then, thou unsalted leaven, speak: I will beat thee into handsomeness.
    Ther. I shall sooner rail thee into wit and holiness; but, I think, thy horse will sooner con an oration than thou learn a prayer without book. Thou canst strike, canst thou? a red murrain o' thy jade's tricks!
    Ajax. Toadstool, learn me the proclamation!
    Ther. Dost thou think I have no sense, thou strikest me thus?
    Ajax. The proclamation!
    Ther. Thou art proclaimed a fool, I think.
    Ajax. Do not, porpentine, do not: my fingers itch.
    Ther. I would thou didst itch from head to foot, and I had the scratching of thee; I would make thee the loathsomest scab in Greece. When thou art forth in the incursions, thou strikest as slow as another.
    Ajax. I say, the proclamation!

Ther. Thou grumblest and railest every hour on Achilles; and thou art as full of envy at his greatness, as Cerberus is at Proserpina's beauty, ay, that thou barkest at him.

Ajax. Mistress Thersites!

Ther. Thou shouldst strike him.

Ajax. Cobloaf!

Ther. He would pun thee into shivers with his fist, as a sailor breaks a biscuit.

Ajax. You whoreson cur!   [*Beating him*

Ther. Do, do.

Ajax. Thou stool for a witch!

Ther. Ay, do, do; thou sodden-witted lord! thou hast no more brain than I have in mine elbows; an assinico may tutor thee: thou scurvy-valiant ass! thou art here but to thrash Trojans; and thou art bought and sold among those of any wit, like a barbarian slave. If thou use to beat me, I will begin at thy heel, and tell what thou art by inches, thou thing of no bowels, thou!

Ajax. You dog!

Ther. You scurvy lord!

Ajax. You cur!   [*Beating him*

Ther. Mars his idiot! do, rudeness; do, camel, do, do.

Enter ACHILLES *and* PATROCLUS

Achil. Why, how now, Ajax? wherefore do you thus? How now, Thersites? what 's the matter, man?

Ther. You see him there, do you?

Achil. Ay what 's the matter?

Ther. Nay, look upon him.

Achil. So I do: what's the matter?

Ther. Nay, but regard him well.

Achil. Well! why, so I do.

Ther. But yet you look not well upon him; for whosoever you take him to be, he is Ajax.

Achil. I know that, fool.

Ther. Ay, but that fool knows not himself.

Ajax. Therefore I beat thee.

Ther. Lo, lo, lo, lo, what modicums of wit he utters! his evasions have ears thus long. I have bobbed his brain more than he has beat my bones: I will buy nine sparrows for a penny, and his *pia mater* is not worth the ninth part of a sparrow. This lord, Achilles,—Ajax, who wears his wit in his belly, and his guts in his head,—I 'll tell you what I say of him.

Achil. What?

Ther. I say, this Ajax—

[*Ajax offers to strike him, Achilles interposes*

32

Achil. Nay, good Ajax.

Ther. Has not so much wit—

Achil. Nay, I must hold you.

Ther. As will stop the eye of Helen's needle for whom he comes to fight.

Achil. Peace, fool!

Ther. I would have peace and quietness, but the fool will not: he there; that he, look you, there.

Ajax. O thou damned cur! I shall—

Achil. Will you set your wit to a fool's?

Ther. No, I warrant you; for a fool's will shame it.

Patr. Good words, Thersites.

Achil. What 's the quarrel?

Ajax. I bade the vile owl go learn me the tenor of the proclamation, and he rails upon me.

Ther. I serve thee not.

Ajax. Well, go to, go to.

Ther. I serve here voluntary.

Achil. Your last service was sufferance, 't was not voluntary; no man is beaten voluntary: Ajax was here the voluntary, and you as under an impress.

Ther. E'en so;—a great deal of your wit too lies in your sinews, or else there be liars. Hector shall have a great catch, if he knock out either of your brains: 'a were as good crack a fusty nut with no kernel.

Achil. What, with me too, Thersites?

Ther. There's Ulysses, and old Nestor,—whose wit was mouldy ere your grandsires had nails on their toes,— yoke you like a draught-oxen, and make you plough up the wars.

Achil. What? what?

Ther. Yes, good sooth: to, Achilles! to, Ajax! to!

Ajax. I shall cut out your tongue.

Ther. 'T is no matter; I shall speak as much as thou, afterwards.

Patr. No more words, Thersites, peace!

Ther. I will hold my peace when Achilles' brach bids me, shall I?

Achil. There 's for you, Patroclus.

Ther. I will see you hanged, like clotpoles, ere I come any more to your tents: I will keep where there is wit stirring, and leave the faction of fools.   [*Exit*

Patr. A good riddance.

Achil. Marry, this, sir, is proclaimed through all our host:—

That Hector, by the fifth hour of the sun,
Will, with a trumpet, 'twixt our tents and Troy,
To-morrow morning call some knight to arms
That hath a stomach; and such a one that dare

Maintain—I know not what: 't is trash. Farewell.
   Ajax. Farewell. Who shall answer him?
   Achil.   I know not,—it is put to lottery; otherwise,
He knew his man.
                              [*Exeunt Achilles and Patroclus*
   Ajax. O, meaning you.—I will go learn more of it.
                                                        [*Exit*

SCENE II.—Troy. A Room in PRIAM's Palace

Enter PRIAM, HECTOR, TROILUS, PARIS, *and* HELENUS

   Pri.   After so many hours, lives, speeches spent,
Thus once again says Nestor from the Greeks:
'Deliver Helen, and all damage else—
As honour, loss of time, travail, expense,
Wounds, friends, and what else dear that is consumed
In hot digestion cf this cormorant war—
Shall be struck off.'—Hector, what say you to 't?
   Hect.   Though no man lesser fears the Greeks than I
As far as toucheth my particular, yet
Dread Priam,
There is no lady of more softer bowels,
More spungy to suck in the sense of fear,
More ready to cry out, 'Who knows what follows?'
Than Hector is. The wound of peace is surety,
Surety secure; but modest doubt is called
The beacon of the wise, the tent that searches
To the bottom of the worst. Let Helen go;
Since the first sword was drawn about this question,
Every tithe soul 'mongst many thousand dismes
Hath been as dear as Helen,—I mean, of ours:
If we have lost so many tenths of ours
To guard a thing not ours, nor worth to us,
Had it our name, the value of one ten,—
What merit 's in that reason which denies
The yielding of her up?
   Tro.   Fie, fie, my brother!
Weigh you the worth and honour of a king
So great as our dread father in a scale
Of common ounces? will you with counters sum
The vast proportion of his infinite?
And buckle in a waist most fathomless
With spans and inches so diminutive
As fears and reasons? fie, for godly shame!
   Hel.   No marvel, though you bite so sharp at reasons,
You are so empty of them. Should not our father

Bear the great sway of his affairs with reasons,
Because your speech hath none that tells him so?
   Tro.   You are for dreams and slumbers, brother priest;
You fur your gloves with reason. Here are your reasons:
You know, an enemy intends you harm;
You know, a sword employed is perilous;
And reason flies the object of all harm.
Who marvels then, when Helenus beholds
A Grecian and his sword, if he do set
The very wings of reason to his heels,
And fly like chidden Mercury from Jove,
Or like a star disorbed!—Nay, if we talk of reason,
Let 's shut our gates and sleep: manhood and honour
Should have hare-hearts, would they but fat their thoughts
With this crammed reason: reason and respect
Make livers pale and lustihood deject.
   Hect.   Brother, she is not worth what she doth cost
The holding.
   Tro.   What is aught but as 't is valued?
   Hect.   But value dwells not in particular will;
It holds his estimate and dignity
As well wherein 't is precious of itself
As in the prizer. 'T is mad idolatry
To make the service greater than the god;
And the will dotes, that is inclinable
To what infectiously itself affects,
Without some image of the affected merit.
   Tro.   I take to-day a wife, and my election
Is led on in the conduct of my will:
My will enkindled by mine eyes and ears,
Two traded pilots 'twixt the dangerous shores
Of will and judgment: how may I avoid,
Although my will distaste what it elected,
The wife I chose? there can be no evasion
To blench from this, and to stand firm by honour.
We turn not back the silks upon the merchant,
When we have soiled them; nor the remainder viands
We do not throw in unrespective sieve,
Because we now are full. It was thought meet
Paris should do some vengeance on the Greeks:
Your breath of full consent bellied his sails;
The seas and winds, old wranglers, took a truce,
And did him service: he touched the ports desired;
And, for an old aunt whom the Greeks held captive,
He brought a Grecian queen whose youth and freshness
Wrinkles Apollo, and makes stale the morning.
Why keep we her? the Grecians keep our aunt.
Is she worth keeping? why, she is a pearl,
Whose price hath launched above a thousand ships,

And turned crowned kings to merchants.
If you 'll avouch 't was wisdom Paris went—
As you must needs, for you all cried—'Go, Go'—
If you 'll confess he brought home noble prize—
As you must needs, for you all clapped your hands,
And cried—'Inestimable!'—why do you now
The issue of your proper wisdoms rate,
And do a deed that fortune never did,
Beggar the estimation which you prized
Richer than sea and land? O theft most base,
That we have stolen what we do fear to keep:
But thieves unworthy of a thing so stolen,
That in their country did them that disgrace
We fear to warrant in our native place!

> *Cas.*   [*Within*] Cry, Trojans, cry!
> *Pri.*   What noise? what shriek is this?
> *Tro.*   'T is our mad sister, I do know her voice.
> *Cas.*   [*Within*] Cry, Trojans!
> *Hect.* It is Cassandra.

Enter CASSANDRA, *raving*

> *Cas.*   Cry, Trojans, cry! lend me ten thousand eyes,
> And I will fill them with prophetic tears.
> *Hect.* Peace, sister, peace!
> *Cas.*   Virgins and boys, mid-age and wrinkled eld,
> Soft infancy, that nothing canst but cry,
> Add to my clamours! let us pay betimes
> A moiety of that mass of moan to come.
> Cry, Trojans, cry! practise your eyes with tears!
> Troy must not be, nor goodly Ilion stand;
> Our firebrand brother, Paris, burns us all.
> Cry, Trojans, cry! a Helen and a woe!
> Cry, cry! Troy burns, or else let Helen go.   [*Exit*
> *Hect.* Now, youthful Troilus, do not these high strains
> Of divination in our sister work
> Some touches of remorse? or is your blood
> So madly hot, that no discourse of reason
> Nor fear of bad success in a bad cause
> Can qualify the same?
> *Tro.*   Why, brother Hector,
> We may not think the justness of each act
> Such and no other than event doth form it;
> Nor once deject the courage of our minds
> Because Cassandra 's mad: her brain-sick raptures
> Cannot distaste the goodness of a quarrel
> Which hath our several honours all engaged
> To make it gracious.   For my private part,
> I am no more touched than all Priam's sons;

And Jove forbid there should be done amongst us
Such things as might offend the weakest spleen
To fight for and maintain.
   Par.   Else might the world convince of levity
As well my undertakings as your counsels;
But, I attest the gods, your full consent
Gave wings to my propension, and cut off
All fears attending on so dire a project:
For what, alas, can these my single arms?
What propugnation is in one man's valour,
To stand the push and enmity of those
This quarrel would excite?   Yet, I protest,
Were I alone to pass the difficulties,
And had as ample power as I have will,
Paris should ne'er retract what he hath done,
Nor faint in the pursuit.
   Pri.   Paris, you speak
Like one besotted on your sweet delights:
You have the honey still, but these the gall;
So to be valiant is no praise at all.
   Par.   Sir, I propose not merely to myself
The pleasures such a beauty brings with it:
But I would have the soil of her fair rape
Wiped off in honourable keeping her.
What treason were it to the ransacked queen,
Disgrace to your great worths, and shame to me,
Now to deliver her possession up,
On terms of base compulsion?   Can it be,
That so degenerate a strain as this
Should once set footing in your generous bosoms?
There's not the meanest spirit on our party
Without a heart to dare or sword to draw,
When Helen is defended; nor none so noble,
Whose life were ill bestowed, or death unfamed,
Where Helen is the subject: then, I say,
Well may we fight for her whom, we know well,
The world's large spaces cannot parallel.
   Hect.   Paris, and Troilus, you have both said well;
And on the cause and question now in hand
Have glozed,—but superficially; not much
Unlike young men, whom Aristotle thought
Unfit to hear moral philosophy.
The reasons you allege do more conduce
To the hot passion of distempered blood
Than to make up a free determination
'Twixt right and wrong; for pleasure and revenge
Have ears more deaf than adders to the voice
Of any true decision.   Nature craves
All dues be rendered to their owners: now

What nearer debt in all humanity
Than wife is to the husband?   If this law
Of nature be corrupted through affection,
And that great minds, of partial indulgence
To their benumbéd wills, resist the same,
There is a law in each well-ordered nation
To curb those raging appetites that are
Most disobedient and refractory.
If Helen then be wife to Sparta's king,
As it is known she is, these moral laws
Of nature and of nation speak aloud
To have her back returned; thus to persist
In doing wrong extenuates not wrong,
But makes it much more heavy.   Hector's opinion
Is this, in way of truth: yet, ne'ertheless,
My spritely brethren, I propend to you
In resolution to keep Helen still;
For 't is a cause that hath no mean dependence
Upon our joint and several dignities.
   Tro.   Why, there you touched the life of our design:
Were it not glory that we more affected
Than the performance of our heaving spleens,
I would not wish a drop of Trojan blood
Spent more in her defence.   But, worthy Hector,
She is a theme of honour and renown,
A spur to valiant and magnanimous deeds
Whose present courage may beat down our foes,
And fame in time to come canónise us:
For, I presume, brave Hector would not lose
So rich advantage of a promised glory
As smiles upon the forehead of this action,
For the wide world's revenue.
   Hect.   I am yours,
You valiant offspring of great Priamus.—
I have a roisting challenge sent amongst
The dull and factious nobles of the Greeks
Will strike amazement to their drowsy spirits.
I was advértised, their great general slept,
Whilst emulation in the army crept:
This, I presume, will wake him.
                                [Exeunt

SCENE III.—The Grecian Camp.   Before ACHILLES' Tent

Enter THERSITES

   Ther.   How now, Thersites? what, lost in the labyrinth
of thy fury! Shall the elephant Ajax carry it thus?
he beats me, and I rail at him: O worthy satisfaction!

would it were otherwise, that I could beat him, whilst he railed at me: 'sfoot, I'll learn to conjure and raise devils, but I'll see some issue of my spiteful execrations. Then, there's Achilles,—a rare enginer. If Troy be not taken till these two undermine it, the walls will stand till they fall of themselves. O thou great thunder-darter of Olympus, forget that thou art Jove the king of gods; and, Mercury, lose all the serpentine craft of thy caduceus; if ye take not that little, little, less-than-little wit from them that they have! which short-aimed ignorance itself knows is so abundant scarce, it will not in circumvention deliver a fly from a spider without drawing their massy irons and cutting the web. After this, the vengeance on the whole camp! or rather, the boneache, for that, methinks, is the curse dependent on those that war for a placket. I have said my prayers; and the devil Envy, say Amen. What, ho! my Lord Achilles!

Enter PATROCLUS

Patr. Who 's there? Thersites? Good Thersites, come in and rail.
Ther. If I could have remembered a gilt counterfeit, thou wouldst not have slipped out of my contemplation; but it is no matter: thyself upon thyself! The common curse of mankind, folly and ignorance, be thine in great revenue! heaven bless thee from a tutor, and discipline come not near thee! Let thy blood be thy direction till thy death! then, if she that lays thee out says thou art a fair corse, I'll be sworn and sworn upon 't she never shrouded any but lazars. Amen.—Where's Achilles?
Patr. What, art thou devout? wast thou in prayer?
Ther. Ay; the heavens hear me!

Enter ACHILLES

Achil. Who's there?
Patr. Thersites, my lord.
Achil. Where, where?—Art thou come? Why, my cheese, my digestion, why hast thou not served thyself in to my table so many meals? Come,—what's Agamemnon?
Ther. Thy commander, Achilles.—Then tell me, Patroclus, what's Achilles?
Patr. Thy lord, Thersites. Then tell me, I pray thee, what's thyself?
Ther. Thy knower, Patroclus. Then tell me, Patroclus, what art thou?
Patr. Thou may'st tell that knowest.
Achil. O! tell, tell.

Ther. I'll decline the whole question:—Agamemnon commands Achilles; Achilles is my lord; I am Patroclus' knower; and Patroclus is a fool.

Patr. You rascal!

Ther. Peace, fool! I have not done.

Achil. He is a privileged man.—Proceed, Thersites.

Ther. Agamemnon is a fool; Achilles is a fool; Thersites is a fool; and, as aforesaid, Patroclus is a fool.

Achil. Derive this, come.

Ther. Agamemnon is a fool to offer to command Achilles; Achilles is a fool to be commanded of Agamemnon; Thersites is a fool to serve such a fool; and Patroclus is a fool positive.

Patr. Why am I a fool?

Ther. Make that demand to the Creator. It suffices me thou art. Look you, who comes here?

Enter AGAMEMNON, ULYSSES, NESTOR, DIOMEDES, *and* AJAX

Achil. Patroclus, I'll speak with nobody.—Come in with me, Thersites.   [*Exit*

Ther. Here is such patchery, such juggling, and such knavery! All the argument is, a cuckold and a whore; a good quarrel, to draw emulous factions and bleed to death upon. Now, the dry serpigo on the subject, and war and lechery confound all!   [*Exit*

Agam. Where's Achilles?

Patr. Within his tent; but ill-disposed, my lord.

Agam. Let it be known to him that we are here.
He shent our messengers; and we lay by
Our appertainments, visiting of him:
Let him be told so; lest, perchance, he think
We dare not move the question of our place,
Or know not what we are.

Patr.   I shall say so to him.
                                                       [*Exit*

Ulyss. We saw him at the opening of his tent:
He is not sick.

Ajax. Yes, lion-sick, sick of proud heart: you may call it melancholy, if you will favour the man; but, by my head, 't is pride: but why? why? let him show us a cause.—A word, my lord.
                              [*Taking Agamemnon aside*

Nest. What moves Ajax thus to bay at him?

Ulyss. Achilles hath inveigled his fool from him.

Nest. Who? Thersites?

Ulyss. He.

Nest. Then will Ajax lack matter, if he have lost his argument.

Ulyss. No, you see, he is his argument that has his argument,—Achilles.

Nest. All the better; their fraction is more our wish than their faction; but it was a strong composure, a fool could disunite.

Ulyss. The amity that wisdom knits not, folly may easily untie. Here comes Patroclus.

Nest. No Achilles with him?

Ulyss. The elephant hath joints, but none for courtesy: his legs are legs for necessity, not for flexure.

Re-enter PATROCLUS

Patr. Achilles bids me say, he is much sorry
If anything more than your sport and pleasure
Did move your greatness and this noble state
To call upon him; he hopes it is no other
But, for your health and your digestion sake,
An after-dinner's breath.

Agam.   Hear you, Patroclus.
We are too well acquainted with these answers;
But his evasion, winged thus swift with scorn,
Cannot outfly our apprehensions.
Much attribute he hath, and much the reason
Why we ascribe it to him; yet all his virtues,
Not virtuously on his own part beheld,
Do in our eyes begin to lose their gloss;
Yea, like fair fruit in an unwholesome dish,
Are like to rot untasted. Go and tell him,
We come to speak with him; and you shall not sin
If you do say we think him over-proud
And under-honest; in self-assumption greater
Than in the note of judgment; and worthier than himself
Here tend the savage strangeness he puts on,
Disguise the holy strength of their command,
And underwrite in an observing kind
His humorous predominance; yea, watch
His pettish lunes, his ebbs, his flows, as if
The passage and whole carriage of this action
Rode on his tide. Go, tell him this; and add
That, if he overhold his price so much,
We'll none of him; but let him, like an engine
Not portable, lie under this report,—
Bring action hither, this cannot go to war;
A stirring dwarf we do allowance give
Before a sleeping giant:—tell him so.

Patr. I shall; and bring his answer presently.   [*Exit*

41

Agam.   In second voice we'll not be satisfied;
We come to speak with him.—Ulysses, enter you.
                                        [*Exit Ulysses*
    Ajax.   What is he more than another?
    Agam.   No more than what he thinks he is.
    Ajax.   Is he so much? Do you not think, he thinks
himself a better man than I am?
    Agam.   No question.
    Ajax.   Will you subscribe his thought, and say he is?
    Agam.   No, noble Ajax; you are as strong, as valiant,
as wise, no less noble, much more gentle, and altogether
more tractable.
    Ajax.   Why should a man be proud? How doth pride
grow? I know not what pride is.
    Agam.   Your mind is the clearer, Ajax, and your virtues
the fairer. He that is proud eats up himself: pride is his
own glass, his own trumpet, his own chronicle, and whatever praises itself but in the deed, devours the deed in the
praise.
    Ajax.   I do hate a proud man, as I hate the engendering
of toads.
    Nest.   [*Aside*] Yet he loves himself: is't not strange?

Re-enter ULYSSES

    Ulyss.   Achilles will not to the field to-morrow.
    Agam.   What's his excuse?
    Ulyss.   He doth rely on none;
But carries on the stream of his dispose,
Without observance or respect of any,
In will peculiar and in self-admission.
    Agam.   Why will he not, upon our fair request.
Untent his person and share the air with us?
    Ulyss.   Things small as nothing, for request's sake only,
He makes important. Possessed he is with greatness;
And speaks not to himself but with a pride
That quarrels at self-breath: imagined worth
Holds in his blood such swoln and hot discourse,
That, 'twixt his mental and his active parts,
Kingdomed Achilles in commotion rages,
And batters 'gainst itself: what should I say?
He is so plaguy proud, that the death-tokens of 't
Cry—'No recovery.'
    Agam.   Let Ajax go to him.—
Dear lord, go you and greet him in his tent;
'T is said he holds you well, and will be led,
At your request, a little from himself.
    Ulyss.   O Agamemnon! let it not be so.
We 'd consecrate the steps that Ajax makes

When they go from Achilles: shall the proud lord
That bastes his arrogance with his own seam,
And never suffers matter of the world
Enter his thoughts, save such as doth revolve
And ruminate himself,—shall he be worshipped
Of that we hold an idol more than he?
No, this thrice-worthy and right valiant lord
Must not so stale his palm, nobly acquired;
Nor, by my will, assubjugate his merit,
As amply titled as Achilles is,
By going to Achilles:
That were to inlard his fat-already pride;
And add more coals to Cancer when he burns
With entertaining great Hyperion.
This lord go to him! Jupiter forbid,
And say in thunder—'Achilles, go to him.'
   Nest. [*Aside*] O, this is well: he rubs the vein of him.
   Dio. [*Aside*] And how his silence drinks up this
       applause!
   Ajax. If I go to him, with my arméd fist
I'll pash him o'er the face.
   Agam. O, no, you shall not go.
   Ajax. An 'a be proud with me, I 'll pheese his pride:
Let me go to him.
   Ulyss. Not for the worth that hangs upon our quarrel.
   Ajax. A paltry, insolent fellow!
   Nest. [*Aside*] How he describes himself!
   Ajax. Can he not be sociable?
   Ulyss. [*Aside*] The raven chides blackness.
   Ajax. I 'll let his humours blood.
   Agam. [*Aside*] He will be the physician, that should
be the patient.
   Ajax. An' all men were o' my mind,—
   Ulyss. [*Aside*] Wit would be out of fashion.
   Ajax. 'A should not bear it so, 'a should eat swords
first: shall pride carry it?
   Nest. [*Aside*] An' 't would, you 'd carry half.
   Ulyss. [*Aside*] 'A would have ten shares.
   Ajax. I will knead him; I will make him supple.
   Nest. [*Aside*] He 's not yet thorough warm: force him
with praises. Pour in, pour in; his ambition is dry.
   Ulyss. [*To Agamemnon*] My lord, you feed too much
      on this dislike.
   Nest. Our noble general, do not do so.
   Dio. You must prepare to fight without Achilles.
   Ulyss. Why, 't is his naming of him does him harm.
Here is a man—But 't is before his face;
I will be silent.
   Nest.   Wherefore should you so?

He is not emulous, as Achilles is.
    Ulyss. Know the whole world, he is as valiant.
    Ajax. A whoreson dog, that shall palter thus with us!
Would he were a Trojan!
    Nest. What a vice were it in Ajax now,—
    Ulyss. If he were proud,—
    Dio.   Or covetous of praise,—
    Ulyss. Ay, or surly borne,—
    Dio.   Or strange, or self-affected!
    Ulyss. Thank the heavens, lord, thou art of sweet
            composure;
Praise him that got thee, she that gave thee suck:
Famed be thy tutor, and thy parts of nature
Thrice-famed, beyond all erudition:
But he that disciplined thine arms to fight,
Let Mars divide eternity in twain
And give him half: and, for thy vigour, let
Bull-bearing Milo his addition yield
To sinewy Ajax. I will not praise thy wisdom,
Which, like a bourn, a pale, a shore, confines
Thy spacious and dilated parts: here's Nestor,—
Instructed by the antiquary times,
He must, he is, he cannot but be wise:—
But pardon, father Nestor, were your days
As green as Ajax', and your brain so tempered,
You should not have the eminence of him,
But be as Ajax.
    Ajax.   Shall I call you father?
    Nest. Ay, my good son.
    Dio.   Be ruled by him, Lord Ajax.
    Ulyss. There is no tarrying here: the hart Achilles
Keeps thicket. Please it our great general
To call together all his state of war;
Fresh kings are come to Troy: to-morrow, then,
We must with all our main of power stand fast:
And here 's a lord,—come knights from east to west,
And cull their flower, Ajax shall cope the best.
    Agam. Go we to council. Let Achilles sleep:
Light boats sail swift, though greater hulks draw deep.
                              [Exeunt

ACT THREE

SCENE I.—Troy. A Room in PRIAM's Palace

Enter PANDARUS *and a Servant*

    Pan. Friend, you,—pray you, a word: do not you
follow the young Lord Paris?

Serv. Ay, sir, when he goes before me.

Pan. You depend upon him, I mean.

Serv. Sir, I do depend upon the lord.

Pan. You depend upon a noble gentleman; I must needs praise him.

Serv. The lord be praised!

Pan. You know me, do you not?

Serv. Faith, sir, superficially.

Pan. Friend, know me better. I am the Lord Pandarus.

Serv. I hope, I shall know your honour better.

Pan. I do desire it.

Serv. You are in the state of grace.

Pan. Grace! not so friend; honour and lordship are my titles.—[*Music within*] What music is this?

Serv. I do but partly know, sir: it is music in parts.

Pan. Know you the musicians?

Serv. Wholly, sir.

Pan. Who play they to?

Serv. To the hearers, sir.

Pan. At whose pleasure, friend?

Serv. At mine, sir, and theirs that love music.

Pan. Command, I mean, friend.

Serv. Who shall I command, sir?

Pan. Friend, we understand not one another: I am too courtly, and thou art too cunning. At whose request do these men play?

Serv. That's to 't, indeed, sir. Marry, sir, at the request of Paris, my lord, who is there in person; with him the mortal Venus, the heart-blood of beauty, love's invisible soul,—

Pan. Who, my cousin Cressida?

Serv. No, sir, Helen: could you not find out that by her attributes?

Pan. It should seem, fellow, that thou has not seen the Lady Cressida. I come to speak with Paris from the Prince Troilus: I will make a complimental assault upon him, for my business seethes.

Serv. Sodden business: there's a stewed phrase, indeed.

Enter PARIS *and* HELEN, *attended*

Pan. Fair be to you, my lord, and to all this fair company! fair desires, in all fair measure, fairly guide them!—especially to you, fair queen, fair thoughts be your fair pillow!

Helen. Dear lord, you are full of fair words.

Pan. You speak your fair pleasure, sweet queen.—Fair prince, here is good broken music.

Par. You have broke it, cousin; and, by my life, you

45

shall make it whole again; you shall piece it out with a piece of your performance.—Nell, he is full of harmony.

Pan.   Truly, lady, no.

Helen.   O, sir,—

Pan.   Rude, in sooth; in good sooth, very rude.

Par.   Well said, my lord! well, you say so in fits.

Pan.   I have business to my lord, dear queen.— My lord, will you vouchsafe me a word?

Helen.   Nay, this shall not hedge us out: we 'll hear you sing, certainly.

Pan.   Well, sweet queen, you are pleasant with me.— But, marry, thus, my lord.—My dear lord, and most esteemed friend, your brother Troilus,—

Helen.   My Lord Pandarus; honey-sweet lord,—

Pan.   Go to, sweet queen, go to:—commends himself most affectionately to you,—

Helen.   You shall not bob us out of our melody: if you do, our melancholy upon your head!

Pan.   Sweet queen, sweet queen; that's a sweet queen, i' faith,—

Helen.   And to make a sweet lady sad is a sour offence.

Pan.   Nay, that shall not serve your turn; that shall it not, in truth, la! Nay, I care not for such words; no, no.—And, my lord, he desires you, that if the king call for him at supper, you will make his excuse.

Helen.   My Lord Pandarus,—

Pan.   What says my sweet queen,—my very very sweet queen?

Par.   What exploit 's in hand? where sups he to-night?

Helen.   Nay, but, my lord,—

Pan.   What says my sweet queen?—My cousin will fall out with you.   You must not know where he sups.

Par.   I 'll lay my life, with my disposer Cressida.

Pan.   No, no; no such matter; you are wide: come, your disposer is sick.

Par.   Well, I 'll make excuse.

Pan.   Ay, good my lord.   Why should you say Cressida? no, your poor disposer 's sick.

Par.   I spy.

Pan.   You spy! what do you spy?—Come, give me an instrument.—Now, sweet queen.

Helen.   Why, this is kindly done.

Pan.   My niece is horribly in love with a thing you have, sweet queen.

Helen.   She shall have it, my lord, if it be not my Lord Paris.

Pan.   He! no, she 'll none of him; they two are twain.

Helen.   Falling in, after falling out, may make them three.

Pan. Come, come, I 'll hear no more of this.—I 'll sing
you a song now.

Helen. Ay, ay, pr'ythee now. By my troth, sweet
lord thou hast a fine forehead.

Pan. Ay, you may, you may.

Helen. Let thy song be love: this love will undo us all.
O Cupid, Cupid, Cupid!

Pan. Love! ay, that it shall, i' faith.

Par. Ay, good now, love, love, nothing but love.

Pan. In good troth, it begins so.   [*Sings*

> *Love, love, nothing but love; still more!*
> > *For, O, love's bow*
> > *Shoots buck and doe:*
> > *The shaft confounds,*
> > *Not that it wounds,*
> *But tickles still the sore.*
> *These lovers cry—Oh! oh! they die!*
> > *Yet that which seems the wound to kill*
> *Doth turn oh! oh! to ha! ha! he!*
> > *So dying love lives still!*
> *Oh! oh! a while, but ha! ha! ha!*
> *Oh! oh! groans out for ha! ha! ha!*

Heigh-ho!

Helen. In love, i' faith, to the very tip of the nose.

Par. He eats nothing but doves, love; and that breeds
hot blood, and hot blood begets hot thoughts, and hot
thoughts beget hot deeds, and hot deeds is love.

Pan. Is this the generation of love? hot blood, hot
thoughts, and hot deeds? Why, they are vipers: is love
a generation of vipers?—Sweet lord, who 's afield to-day?

Par. Hector, Deiphobus, Helenus, Antenor, and all
the gallantry of Troy: I would fain have armed to-day,
but my Nell would not have it so. How chance my brother
Troilus went not?

Helen. He hangs the lip at something:—you know all,
Lord Pandarus.

Pan. Not I, honey-sweet queen.—I long to hear how
they sped to-day.—You 'll remember your brother's excuse?

Par. To a hair.

Pan. Farewell, sweet queen.

Helen. Commend me to your niece.

Pan. I will, sweet queen.   [*Exit*
          [*A retreat sounded*

Par. They're come from field: let us to Priam's hall,
To greet the warriors. Sweet Helen, I must woo you
To help unarm our Hector: his stubborn buckles,
With these your white enchanting fingers touched,

Shall more obey than to the edge of steel
Or force of Greekish sinews; you shall do more
Than all the island kings,—disarm great Hector.
   Helen. 'T will make us proud to be his servant, Paris:
Yea, what he shall receive of us in duty
Gives us more palm in beauty than we have,
Yea, overshines ourself.
   Par. Sweet, above thought I love thee.

                                      [Exeunt

SCENE II.—The same. PANDARUS' Orchard

Enter PANDARUS *and* TROILUS' BOY, *meeting*

   Pan. How now? where 's thy master? at my cousin
Cressida's?
   Serv. No, sir: he stays for you to conduct him thither.

Enter TROILUS

   Pan. O, here he comes.—How now, how now?
   Tro. Sirrah, walk off.   *[Exit Boy*
   Pan. Have you seen my cousin?
   Tro. No, Pandarus: I stalk about her door,
Like a strange soul upon the Stygian banks
Staying for waftage. O, be thou my Charon,
And give me swift transportation to those fields
Where I may wallow in the lily-beds
Proposed for the deserver. O gentle Pandarus,
From Cupid's shoulder pluck his painted wings,
And fly with me to Cressid.
   Pan. Walk here i' the orchard. I'll bring her straight.
                                         [Exit
   Tro. I 'm giddy; expectation whirls me round.
The imaginary relish is so sweet
That it enchants my sense: what will it be,
When that the watery palate tastes indeed
Love's thrice-repuréd nectar? death, I fear me;
Swooning destruction; or some joy too fine,
Too subtle-potent, tuned too sharp in sweetness
For the capacity of my ruder powers:
I fear it much; and I do fear besides,
That I shall lose distinction in my joys;
As doth a battle, when they charge on heaps
The enemy flying.

Re-enter PANDARUS

   Pan. She 's making her ready, she'll come straight:
you must be witty now. She does so blush, and fetches

her wind so short, as if she were frayed with a sprite:
I'll fetch her. It is the prettiest villain: she fetches her
breath as short as a new-ta'en sparrow.   [*Exit*

Tro.   Even such a passion doth embrace my bosom:
My heart beats thicker than a feverous pulse;
And all my powers do their bestowing lose,
Like vassalage at unawares encountering
The eye of majesty.

Enter PANDARUS *and* CRESSIDA

Pan.   Come, come, what need you blush? shame's a
baby.—Here she is now: swear the oaths now to her, that
you have sworn to me.—What, are you gone again? you
must be watched ere you be made tame, must you? Come
your ways, come your ways; an you draw backward, we 'll
put you i' the fills.—Why do you not speak to her?—Come,
draw this curtain, and let 's see your picture.—Alas the
day, how loath you are to offend daylight! and 't were
dark, you 'd close sooner. So, so; rub on, and kiss the
mistress. How now! a kiss in fee-farm! Build there, car-
penter; the air is sweet. Nay, you shall fight your hearts
out ere I part you. The falcon has the tercel for all the
ducks i' the river: go to, go to.

Tro.   You have bereft me of all words, lady.

Pan.   Words pay no debts, give her deeds: but she 'll
bereave you of the deeds too, if she call your activity in
question. What, billing again? Here 's—'In witness
whereof the parties interchangeably'—Come in, come in:
I'll go get a fire.   [*Exit*

Cres.   Will you walk in, my lord?

Tro.   O Cressida, how often have I wished me thus!

Cres.   Wished, my lord!—The gods grant—O my lord!

Tro.   What should they grant? what makes this pretty
abruption? What too curious dreg espies my sweet lady
in the fountain of our love?

Cres.   More dregs than water, if my fears have eyes.

Tro.   Fears make devils of cherubins; they never see
truly.

Cres.   Blind fear that seeing reason leads finds safer
footing than blind reason stumbling without fear: to
fear the worst oft cures the worst.

Tro.   O, let my lady apprehend no fear: in all Cupid's
pageant there is presented no monster.

Cres.   Nor nothing monstrous neither?

Tro.   Nothing, but our undertakings, when we vow to
weep seas, live in fire, eat rocks, tame tigers; thinking it
harder for our mistress to devise imposition enough than
for us to undergo any difficulty imposed. This is the mon-

strosity in love, lady,—that the will is infinite, and the execution confined; that the desire is boundless, and the act a slave to limit.

Cres. They say, all lovers swear more performance than they are able, and yet reserve an ability that they never perform; vowing more than the perfection of ten, and discharging less than the tenth part of one. They that have the voice of lions, and the act of hares, are they not monsters?

Tro. Are there such? such are not we. Praise us as we are tasted; allow us as we prove; our head shall go bare, till merit crown it. No perfection in reversion shall have a praise in present: we will not name desert before his birth, and, being born, his addition shall be humble. Few words to fair faith: Troilus shall be such to Cressid as what envy can say worst shall be a mock for his truth; and what truth can speak truest, not truer than Troilus.

Cres. Will you walk in, my lord?

Re-enter PANDARUS

Pan. What, blushing still? have you not done talking yet?

Cres. Well, uncle, what folly I commit, I dedicate to you.

Pan. I thank you for that: if my lord get a boy of you, you'll give him me. Be true to my lord; if he flinch, chide me for it.

Tro. You know now your hostages; your uncle's word, and my firm faith.

Pan. Nay, I'll give my word for her too. Our kindred, though they be long ere they are wooed, they are constant being won: they are burs, I can tell you; they 'll stick where they are thrown.

Cres. Boldness comes to me now, and brings me heart.
Prince Troilus, I have loved you night and day,
For many weary months.

Tro. Why was my Cressid then so hard to win?

Cres. Hard to seem won; but I was won, my lord,
With the first glance that ever—pardon me—
If I confess much, you will play the tyrant.
I love you now; but not, till now, so much,
But I might master it:—in faith I lie:
My thoughts were like unbridled children, grown
Too headstrong for their mother:—see, we fools!
Why have I blabbed? who shall be true to us
When we are so unsecret to ourselves?—
But, though I loved you well, I woo'd you not;
And yet, good faith, I wished myself a man,
Or that we women had men's privilege
Of speaking first. Sweet, bid me hold my tongue;

For, in this rapture, I shall surely speak
The thing I shall repent. See, see, your silence,
Cunning in dumbness, from my weakness draws
My very soul of counsel. Stop my mouth.
    Tro. And shall, albeit sweet music issues thence.
    Pan. Pretty, i' faith.
    Cres. My lord, I do beseech you, pardon me;
'T was not my purpose thus to beg a kiss:
I am ashamed:—O heavens! what have I done?—
For this time will I take my leave, my lord.
    Tro. Your leave, sweet Cressid?
    Pan. Leave! an you take leave till to-morrow morning—
    Cres. Pray you, content you.
    Tro.   What offends you, lady?
    Cres. Sir, mine own company.
    Tro. You cannot shun yourself.
    Cres. Let me go and try.
I have a kind of self resides with you;
But an unkind self, that itself will leave,
To be another's fool.—I would be gone.
Where is my wit?—I speak I know not what.
    Tro. Well know they what they speak, that speak so
          wisely.
    Cres. Perchance, my lord, I show more craft than love,
And fell so roundly to a large confession
To angle for your thoughts: but you are wise,
Or else you love not; for to be wise and love
Exceeds man's might; that dwells with gods above.
    Tro. O, that I thought it could be in a woman,—
As, if it can, I will presume in you,—
To feed for aye her lamp and flames of love;
To keep her constancy in plight and youth,
Outliving beauty's outward, with a mind
That doth renew swifter than blood decays.
Or that persuasion could but thus convince me
That my integrity and truth to you
Might be affronted with the match and weight
Of such a winnowed purity in love;
How were I then uplifted! but, alas,
I am as true as truth's simplicity,
And simpler than the infancy of truth.
    Cres. In that I 'll war with you.
    Tro.   O virtuous fight,
When right with right wars who shall be most right!
True swains in love shall, in the world to come,
Approve their truths by Troilus: when their rhymes,
Full of protest, of oath, and big compare,
Want similes, truth tired with iteration,—
As true as steel, as plantage to the moon,

As sun to-day, as turtle to her mate,
As iron to adamant, as earth to the centre,—
Yet, after all comparisons of truth,
As truth's authentic author to be cited,
As true as Troilus shall crown up the verse,
And sanctify the numbers.
   Cres.   Prophet may you be!
If I be false, or swerve a hair from truth,
When time is old and hath forgot itself,
When waterdrops have worn the stones of Troy,
And blind oblivion swallowed cities up,
And mighty states charácterless are grated
To dusty nothing; yet let memory,
From false to false, among false maids in love,
Upbraid my falsehood! when they have said, as false
As air, as water, wind, or sandy earth,
As fox to lamb, as wolf to heifer's calf,
Pard to the hind, or stepdame to her son,—
Yea, let them say, to stick the heart of falsehood,
As false as Cressid.
   Pan.   Go to, a bargain made; seal it, seal it: I 'll be
the witness.—Here I hold your hand; here, my cousin's.
If ever you prove false one to another, since I have taken
such pains to bring you together, let all pitiful goers-
between be called to the world's end after my name, call
them all Pandars; let all constant men be Troiluses, all
false women Cressids, and all brokers between Pandars!
say, Amen.
   Tro.   Amen.
   Cres.   Amen.
   Pan.   Amen.   Whereupon I will show you a chamber
with a bed; which bed, because it shall not speak of your
pretty encounters, press it to death: away!
And Cupid grant all tongue-tied maidens here
Bed, chamber, Pandar to provide this gear!
                                   [*Exeunt*

SCENE III.—The Grecian Camp

Enter AGAMEMNON, ULYSSES, DIOMEDES, NESTOR, AJAX,
MENELAUS, *and* CALCHAS

   Cal.   Now, princes, for the service I have done you,
The advantage of the time prompts me aloud
To call for recompense. Appear it to your mind,
That, through the sight I bear in things to Jove,
I have abandoned Troy, left my possession,

Incurred a traitor's name; exposed myself,
From certain and possessed conveniences,
To doubtful fortunes; sequestering from me all
That time, acquaintance, custom and condition,
Made tame and most familiar to my nature;
And here, to do you service, am become
As new into the world, strange, unacquainted:
I do beseech you, as in way of taste,
To give me now a little benefit
Out of those many registered in promise,
Which, you say, live to come in my behalf.
  Agam. What wouldst thou of us, Trojan? make demand.
  Cal. You have a Trojan prisoner, called Antenor,
Yesterday took: Troy holds him very dear.
Oft have you—often have you thanks therefore—
Desired my Cressid in right great exchange,
Whom Troy hath still denied; but this Antenor,
I know, is such a wrest in their affairs,
That their negotiations all must slack,
Wanting his manage; and they will almost
Give us a prince of blood, a son of Priam,
In change of him: let him be sent, great princes,
And he shall buy my daughter; and her presence,
Shall quite strike off all service I have done,
In most accepted pain.
  Agam.   Let Diomedes bear him,
And bring us Cressid hither: Calchas shall have
What he requests of us.—Good Diomed,
Furnish you fairly for this interchange:
Withal, bring word, if Hector will to-morrow
Be answered in his challenge: Ajax is ready.
  Dio. This shall I undertake; and 't is a burden
Which I am proud to bear.
        [*Exeunt Diomedes and Calchas*

  Enter ACHILLES *and* PATROCLUS, *before their tent*

  Ulyss. Achilles stands i' the entrance of his tent:
Please it our general to pass strangely by him
As if he were forgot; and, princes all,
Lay negligent and loose regard upon him:
I will come last. 'Tis like, he 'll question me,
Why such unplausive eyes are bent on him;
If so, I have derision medicinable
To use between your strangeness and his pride,
Which his own will shall have desire to drink.
It may do good: pride hath no other glass
To show itself, but pride; for supple knees
Feed arrogance, and are the proud man's fees.

 Agam. We 'll execute your purpose, and put on
A form of strangeness as we pass along:—
So do each lord; and either greet him not,
Or else disdainfully, which shall shake him more
Than if not looked on. I will lead the way.
 Achil. What! comes the general to speak with me?
You know my mind: I 'll fight no more 'gainst Troy.
 Agam. What says Achilles? would he aught with us?
 Nest. Would you, my lord, aught with the general?
 Achil. No.
 Nest. Nothing, my lord.
 Agam. The better.

       [Exeunt Agamemnon and Nestor
 Achil. Good day, good day.
 Men. How do you? how do you?

            [Exit
 Achil. What! does the cuckold scorn me?
 Ajax. How now, Patroclus?
 Achil. Good morrow, Ajax.
 Ajax. Ha?
 Achil. Good morrow.
 Ajax. Ay, and good next day too.   *[Exit*
 Achil. What mean these fellows? Know they not
    Achilles?
 Patr. They pass by strangely: they were used to bend,
To send their smiles before them to Achilles:
To come as humbly as they used to creep
To holy altars.
 Achil.   What, am I poor of late?
'Tis certain, greatness, once fallen out with fortune,
Must fall out with men too: what the declined is,
He shall as soon read in the eyes of others
As feel in his own fall; for men, like butterflies,
Show not their mealy wings but to the summer,
And not a man, for being simply man,
Hath any honour, but honour for those honours
That are without him, as place, riches, favour,
Prizes of accident as oft as merit:
Which, when they fall, as being slippery standers,
The love that leaned on them as slippery too,
Doth one pluck down another, and together
Die in the fall. But 't is not so with me:
Fortune and I are friends: I do enjoy
At ample point all that I did possess,
Save these men's looks; who do, methinks, find out
Something not worth in me such rich beholding
As they have often given. Here is Ulysses:
I 'll interrupt his reading.—
How now. Ulysses?

Ulyss.   Now, great Thetis' son!
Achil.   What are you reading?
Ulyss.   A strange fellow here
Writes me: That man, how dearly ever parted,
How much in having, or without, or in,
Cannot make boast to have that which he hath,
Nor feels not what he owes, but by reflection;
As when his virtues shining upon others
Heat them, and they retort that heat again
To the first giver.
    Achil.   That is not strange, Ulysses.
The beauty that is borne here in the face
The bearer knows not, but commends itself
To others' eyes: nor doth the eye itself,
That most pure spirit of sense, behold itself,
Not going from itself; but eye to eye opposed
Salutes each other with each other's form:
For speculation turns not to itself
Till it hath travelled, and is married there
Where it may see itself.   This is not strange at all.
    Ulyss.   I do not strain at the position,
It is familiar, but at the author's drift;
Who in his circumstance expressly proves
That no man is the lord of anything,
Though in and of him there be much consisting,
Till he communicate his parts to others:
Nor doth he of himself know them for aught
Till he behold them formed in the applause
Where they're extended; who, like an arch reverberates
The voice again, or, like a gate of steel
Fronting the sun, receives and renders back
His figure and his heat.   I was much rapt in this;
And apprehended here immediately
The unknown Ajax.
Heavens, what a man is there! a very horse;
That has he knows not what.   Nature, what things there
      are,
Most abject in regard, and dear in use!
What things, again, most dear in the esteem,
And poor in worth!   Now shall we see to-morrow—
An act that very chance doth throw upon him—
Ajax renowned.   O heavens, what some men do,
While some men leave to do!
How some men creep in skittish Fortune's hall,
While others play the idiots in her eyes!
How one man eats into another's pride,
While pride is feasting in his wantonness!
To see these Grecian lords!—Why, even already
They clap the lubber Ajax on the shoulder,

As if his foot were on brave Hector's breast
And great Troy shrinking.
    Achil.   I do believe it; for they passed by me
As misers do by beggars, neither gave to me
Good word nor look.   What, are my deeds forgot?
    Ulyss.   Time hath, my lord, a wallet at his back
Wherein he puts alms for oblivion;
A great sized monster of ingratitudes:
Those scraps are good deeds past; which are devoured
As fast as they are made, forgot as soon
As done: perséverance, dear my lord,
Keeps honour bright; to have done, is to hang
Quite out of fashion, like a rusty mail
In monumental mockery.   Take the instant way;
For honour travels in a strait so narrow,
Where one but goes abreast: keep then the path;
For emulation hath a thousand sons,
That one by one pursue; if you give way,
Or, hedge aside from the direct forthright,
Like to an entered tide, they all rush by,
And leave you hindmost;
Or like gallant horse fallen in first rank,
Lie there for pavement to the abject rear,
O'er-run and trampled on: then what they do in present,
Though less than yours in past, must o'er-top yours;
For time is like a fashionable host,
That slightly shakes his parting guest by the hand,
And with his arms outstretched, as he would fly,
Grasps in the comer: Welcome ever smiles,
And Farewell goes out sighing.   O, let not virtue seek
Remuneration for the thing it was;
For beauty, wit,
High birth, vigour of bone, desert in service,
Love, friendship, charity, are subjects all
To envious and calumniating time.
One touch of nature makes the whole world kin,—
That all, with one consent, praise new-born gawds,
Though they are made and moulded of things past,
And give to dust that is a little gilt
More laud than gilt o'er dusted.
The present eye praises the present object:
Then marvel not, thou great and complete man,
That all the Greeks begin to worship Ajax;
Since things in motion sooner catch the eye
Than what not stirs.   The cry went once on thee,
And still it might, and yet it may again,
If thou wouldst not entomb thyself alive,
And case thy reputation in thy tent;
Whose glorious deeds but in these fields of late,

Made emulous missions 'mongst the gods themselves,
And drave great Mars to faction.
    Achil.   Of this my privacy
I have strong reasons.
    Ulyss.   But 'gainst your privacy
The reasons are more potent and heroical.
'Tis known, Achilles, that you are in love
With one of Priam's daughters.
    Achil. Ha! known?
    Ulyss. Is that a wonder?
The providence that's in a watchful state,
Knows almost every grain of Plutus' gold,
Finds bottom in the uncomprehensive deeps,
Keeps place with thought, and almost, like the gods,
Does thoughts unveil in their dumb cradles.
There is a mystery—with whom relation
Durst never meddle—in the soul of state,
Which hath an operation more divine
Than breath, or pen, can give expressure to.
All the commérce that you have had with Troy
As perfectly is ours as yours, my lord;
And better would it fit Achilles much
To throw down Hector, than Polyxena;
But it must grieve young Pyrrhus, now at home,
When fame shall in our islands sound her trump,
And all the Greekish girls shall tripping sing,—
'Great Hector's sister did Achilles win,
But our great Ajax bravely beat down him.'
Farewell, my lord: I as your lover speak;
The fool slides o'er the ice that you should break.   [*Exit*
    Patr. To this effect, Achilles, have I moved you.
A woman impudent and mannish grown
Is not more loathed, than an effeminate man
In time of action.   I stand condemned for this:
They think, my little stomach to the war,
And your great love to me, restrains you thus.
Sweet, rouse yourself; and the weak wanton Cupid
Shall from your neck unloose his amorous fold,
And, like a dew-drop from the lion's mane,
Be shook to air.
    Achil.   Shall Ajax fight with Hector?
    Patr. Ay, and perhaps, receive much honour by him.
    Achil. I see, my reputation is at stake;
My fame is shrewdly gored.
    Patr.   O, then beware:
Those wounds heal ill that men do give themselves:
Omission to do what is necessary
Seals a commission to a blank of danger;
And danger, like an ague, subtly taints

Even then when we sit idly in the sun.
Achil.   Go call Thersites hither, sweet Patroclus.
I 'll send the fool to Ajax, and desire him
To invite the Trojan lords, after the combat,
To see us here unarmed.   I have a woman's longing,
An appetite that I am sick withal,
To see great Hector in his weeds of peace;
To talk with him, and to behold his visage,
Even to my full of view.—A labour saved!

Enter THERSITES

Ther.   A wonder!
Achil.   What?
Ther.   Ajax goes up and down the field asking for
himself.
Achil.   How so?
Ther.   He must fight singly to-morrow with Hector; and
is so prophetically proud of an heroical cudgelling, that
he raves in saying nothing.
Achil.   How can that be?
Ther.   Why, he stalks up and down like a peacock,—a
stride, and a stand: ruminates like an hostess that hath
no arithmetic but her brain to set down her reckoning:
bites his lip with a politic regard, as who should say, there
were wit in his head, and 't would out: and so there is; but
it lies as coldly in him as fire in a flint, which will not show
without knocking.   The man 's undone for ever; for if
Hector break not his neck i' the combat, he 'll break 't
himself in vainglory.   He knows not me: I said, 'Good
morrow, Ajax;' and he replies, 'Thanks, Agamemnon.'
What think you of this man, that takes me for the general?
He 's grown a very land-fish, languageless, a monster.
A plague of opinion! a man may wear it on both sides,
like a leather jerkin.
Achil.   Thou must be my ambassador to him, Thersites.
Ther.   Who, I? why, he 'll answer nobody; he professes
not answering: speaking is for beggars; he wears his
tongue in his arms.   I will put on his presence: let Patroclus
make his demands to me, you shall see the pageant of Ajax.
Achil.   To him, Patroclus: tell him, I humbly desire
the valiant Ajax to invite the most valorous Hector to
come unarmed to my tent; and to procure safe-conduct
for his person of the magnanimous, and most illustrious,
six-or-seven-times honoured captain-general of the Grecian
army, Agamemnon.   Do this.
Patr.   Jove bless great Ajax!
Ther.   Humph?
Patr.   I come from the worthy Achilles,—

Ther. Ha?

Patr. Who most humbly desires you to invite Hector to his tent,—

Ther. Humph!

Patr. And to procure safe conduct from Agamemnon.

Ther. Agamemnon?

Patr. Ay, my lord.

Ther. Ha?

Patr. What say you to 't?

Ther. God be wi' you, with all my heart.

Patr. Your answer, sir.

Ther. If to-morrow be a fair day, by eleven o'clock it will go one way or other: howsoever, he shall pay for me ere he has me.

Patr. Your answer, sir.

Ther. Fare you well, with all my heart.

Achil. Why, but he is not in this tune, is he?

Ther. No, but he's out o' tune thus. What music will be in him when Hector has knocked out his brains, I know not; but, I am sure, none, unless the fiddler Apollo get his sinews to make catlings on.

Achil. Come, thou shalt bear a letter to him straight.

Ther. Let me bear another to his horse, for that 's the more capable creature.

Achil. My mind is troubled, like a fountain stirred;
And I myself see not the bottom of it.

                              [*Exeunt Achilles and Patroclus*

Ther. Would the fountain of your mind were clear again, that I might water an ass at it. I had rather be a tick in a sheep than such a valiant ignorance.   [*Exit*

ACT FOUR

Scene I.—Troy. A Street

Enter, at one side, ÆNEAS, and Servant, with a torch; at the other, PARIS, DEIPHOBUS, ANTENOR, DIOMEDES, and others, with torches

Paris. See ho! who is that there?

Dei.   'T is the Lord Æneas.

Æne. Is the prince there in person?—
Had I so good occasion to lie long
As you, Prince Paris, nothing but heavenly business
Should rob my bed-mate of my company.

Dio. That's my mind too.—Good morrow, Lord Æneas.

Par. A valiant Greek, Æneas; take his hand:

Witness the process of your speech, wherein
You told how Diomed, a whole week by days,
Did haunt you in the field.
    Æne.   Health to you, valiant sir,
During all question of the gentle truce;
But when I meet you armed, as black defiance
As heart can think or courage execute.
    Dio.   The one and other Diomed embraces.
Our bloods are now in calm, and, so long, health:
But when contention and occasion meet,
By Jove, I 'll play the hunter for thy life
With all my force, pursuit, and policy.
    Æne.   And thou shalt hunt a lion that will fly
With his face backward.—In human gentleness,
Welcome to Troy: now, by Anchises' life,
Welcome, indeed. By Venus' hand I swear,
No man alive can love, in such a sort,
The thing he means to kill, more excellently.
    Dio.   We sympathise.—Jove, let Æneas live,
If to my sword his fate be not the glory,
A thousand complete courses of the sun!
But, in mine emulous honour, let him die,
With every joint a wound, and that to-morrow!
    Æne.   We know each other well.
    Dio.   We do; and long to know each other worse.
    Par.   This is the most despiteful gentle greeting,
The noblest hateful love, that e'er I heard of.—
What business, lord, so early?
    Æne.   I was sent for to the king; but why, I know not.
    Par.   His purpose meets you: 't was to bring this Greek
To Calchas' house; and there to render him,
For the enfreed Antenor, the fair Cressid.
Let 's have your company; or, if you please,
Haste there before us. I constantly do think,—
Or, rather, call my thought a certain knowledge,—
My brother Troilus lodges there to-night:
Rouse him, and give him note of our approach,
With the whole quality wherefore: I fear,
We shall be much unwelcome.
    Æne.   That I assure you:
Troilus had rather Troy were borne to Greece.
Than Cressid borne from Troy.
    Par.   There is no help;
The bitter disposition of the time
Will have it so. On, lord: we 'll follow you.
    Æne.   Good morrow, all.   [*Exit*
    Par.   And tell me, noble Diomed; 'faith tell me true,
Even in the soul of sound good-fellowship,—

Who, in your thoughts, merits fair Helen most,
Myself, or Menelaus?
    Dio.   Both alike:
He merits well to have her that doth seek her,
Not making any scruple of her soilure,
With such a hell of pain and world of charge;
And you as well to keep her, that defend her,
Not palating the taste of her dishonour,
With such a costly loss of wealth and friends:
He, like a puling cuckold, would drink up
The lees and dregs of a flat taméd piece;
You, like a lecher, out of whorish loins
Are pleased to breed out your inheritors:
Both merits poised, each weighs nor less nor more;
But he as he the heavier for a whore.
    Par.   You are too bitter to your country-woman.
    Dio.   She 's bitter to her country. Hear me, Paris:—
For every false drop in her bawdy veins
A Grecian's life hath sunk; for every scruple
Of her contaminated carrion weight
A Trojan hath been slain. Since she could speak
She hath not given so many good words breath,
As, for her, Greeks and Trojans suffered death.
    Par.   Fair Diomed, you do as chapmen do,
Dispraise the thing that you desire to buy;
But we in silence hold this virtue well,—
We 'll not commend what we intend not sell.
Here lies our way.
                                         [Exeunt

Scene II.—Troy. A Court before the House of Pandarus

Enter Troilus *and* Cressida

    Tro.   Dear, trouble not yourself; the morn is cold.
    Cres.   Then, sweet my lord, I 'll call mine uncle down:
He shall unbolt the gates.
    Tro.   Trouble him not;
To bed, to bed: sleep kill those pretty eyes,
And give as soft attachment to thy senses
As infants, empty of all thought!
    Cres.   Good morrow then.
    Tro.   I pr'ythee now, to bed.
    Cres.   Are you aweary of me?
    Tro.   O Cressida! but that the busy day,
Waked by the lark, hath roused the ribald crows,
And dreaming night will hide our joys no longer,
I would not from thee.
    Cres.   Night hath been too brief.

Tro. Beshrew the witch! with venomous wights she
          stays
Tedious as hell; but flies the grasps of love
With wings more momentary-swift than thought.
You will catch cold, and curse me.
                                        Cres.   Pr'ythee, tarry.—
You men will never tarry.—
O foolish Cressid!—I might have still held off,
And then you would have tarried.—Hark! there 's one
          up.
     Pan. [*Within*] What 's all the doors open here?
     Tro. It is your uncle.
     Cres. A pestilence on him; now will he be mocking:
I shall have such a life.—

Enter PANDARUS

     Pan. How now, how now! how go maidenheads?—
Here, you maid! where's my cousin Cressid?
     Cres. Go hang yourself, you naughty mocking uncle!
You bring me to do,—and then you flout me too.
     Pan. To do what? to do what?—let her say what:—
what have I brought you to do?
     Cres. Come, come; beshrew your heart! you 'll ne'er
          be good,
Nor suffer others.
     Pan. Ha, ha! Alas, poor wretch! ah, poor capocchio!—
hast not slept to-night? would he not, a naughty man, let
it sleep? a bugbear take him!   [*Knocking*
     Cres. Did not I tell you?—would he were knocked o'
          the head!—
Who 's that at door? good uncle, go and see.—
My lord, come you again into my chamber:
You smile and mock me, as if I meant naughtily.
     Tro. Ha, ha!
     Cres. Come, you are deceived; I think of no such thing—
                                                  [*Knocking*
How earnestly they knock!—Pray you, come in:
I would not for half Troy have you seen here.
                         [*Exeunt Troilus and Cressida*
     Pan. [*Going to the door*] Who 's there? what's the
matter? will you beat down the door? How now?
what 's the matter?

Enter ÆNEAS

     Æne. Good morrow, lord, good morrow.
     Pan. Who's there? my lord Æneas! By my troth,
I knew you not; what news with you so early?
     Æne. Is not Prince Troilus here?

Pan.   Here! what should he do here?

Æne.   Come, he is here, my lord; do not deny him:
It doth import him much to speak with me.

Pan.   Is he here, say you? 't is more than I know, I'll
be sworn:—for mine own part, I came in late. What
should he do here?

Æne.   Who!—nay, then:—come, come, you 'll do him
wrong ere you are 'ware. You 'll be so true to him, to
be false to him. Do not you know of him; but yet go
fetch him hither: go.

Re-enter TROILUS

Tro.   How now? what 's the matter?

Æne.   My lord, I scarce have leisure to salute you,
My matter is so rash.   There is at hand
Paris your brother, and Deiphobus,
The Grecian Diomed, and our Antenor
Delivered to us; and for him forthwith,
Ere the first sacrifice, within this hour,
We must give up to Diomedes' hand
The Lady Cressida.

Tro.   Is it concluded so?

Æne.   By Priam, and the general state of Troy:
They are at hand, and ready to effect it.

Tro.   How my achievements mock me!
I will go meet them:—and, my Lord Æneas,
We met by chance; you did not find me here.

Æne.   Good, good, my lord; the secrets of nature
Have not more gift in taciturnity.

[Exeunt Troilus and Æneas

Pan.   Is 't possible? no sooner got but lost? The devil
take Antenor! the young prince will go mad. A plague
upon Antenor! I would, they had broke 's neck!

Re-enter CRESSIDA

Cres.   How now? what is the matter? Who was here?

Pan.   Ah! ah!

Cres.   Why sigh you so profoundly? where's my lord?
gone!
Tell me,   sweet uncle, what 's the matter?

Pan.   Would I were as deep under the earth as I am
above!

Cres.   O the gods!—what 's the matter?

Pan.   Pr'ythee, get thee in. Would thou hadst ne'er
been born! I knew thou wouldst be his death:—O
poor gentleman!—A plague upon Antenor.

Cres.   Good uncle, I beseech you, on my knees
I beseech you, what 's the matter?

Pan. Thou must be gone, wench; thou must be gone:
thou art changed for Antenor. Thou must to thy father,
and be gone from Troilus: 't will be his death; 't will be
his bane; he cannot bear it.

Cres. O you immortal gods!—I will not go.

Pan. Thou must.

Cres. I will not, uncle: I have forgot my father;
I know no touch of consanguinity;
No kin, no love, no blood, no soul so near me,
As the sweet Troilus.—O you gods divine,
Make Cressid's name the very crown of falsehood,
If ever she leave Troilus! Time, force, death,
Do to this body what extremes you can,
But the strong base and building of my love
Is as the very centre of the earth,
Drawing all things to 't.—I 'll go in, and weep,—

Pan. Do, do.

Cres.   Tear my bright hair, and scratch my praiséd
              cheeks;
Crack my clear voice with sobs, and break my heart
With sounding 'Troilus!' I 'll not go from Troy.

                                                          [*Exeunt*

SCENE III.—Before PANDARUS' HOUSE

Enter PARIS, TROILUS, ÆNEAS, DEIPHOBUS, ANTENOR,
                and DIOMEDES

Par. It is great morning, and the hour prefixed
Of her delivery to this valiant Greek
Comes fast upon us.—Good my brother Troilus,
Tell you the lady what she is to do,
And haste her to the purpose.

Tro.   Walk to her house;
I 'll bring her to the Grecian presently:
And to his hand when I deliver her,
Think it an altar, and thy brother Troilus
A priest, there offering to it his own heart.   [*Exit*

Par. I know what 't is to love;
And 'would, as I shall pity, I could help!—
Please you, walk in, my lords.   [*Exeunt*

SCENE IV.—A Room in PANDARUS' House

Enter PANDARUS *and* CRESSIDA

Pan. Be moderate, be moderate.

Cres. Why tell you me of moderation?
The grief is fine, full, perfect, that I taste,

And violenteth in a sense as strong
As that which causeth it: how can I moderate it?
If I could temporise with my affection,
Or brew it to a weak and colder palate,
The like allayment could I give my grief:
My love admits no qualifying dross;
No more my grief, in such a precious loss.

Enter TROILUS

 Pan. Here, here, here he comes.—Ah, sweet ducks!
 Cres. O Troilus! Troilus!   *[Embracing him*
 Pan. What a pair of spectacles is here! Let me
embrace too: *O heart,*—as the goodly saying is,—

—O heart, heavy heart,
Why sigh'st thou without breaking?

where he answers again,

Because thou canst not ease thy smart,
By friendship nor by speaking.

There was never a truer rhyme.   Let us cast away nothing,
for we may live to have need of such a verse: we see it,
we see it.—How now, lambs?
 Tro. Cressid, I love thee in so strained a purity,
That the blessed gods—as angry with my fancy,
More bright in zeal than the devotion which
Cold lips blow to their deities—take thee from me.
 Cres. Have the gods envy?
 Pan. Ay, ay, ay, ay; 't is too plain a case.
 Cres. And is it true, that I must go from Troy?
 Tro. A hateful truth.
 Cres.   What, and from Troilus too?
 Tro. From Troy, and Troilus.
 Cres.   Is it possible?
 Tro. And suddenly; where injury of chance
Puts back leave-taking, justles roughly by
All time of pause, rudely beguiles our lip
Of all rejoindure, forcibly prevents
Our locked embrasures, strangles our dear vows
Even in the birth of our own labouring breath.
We two, that with so many thousand sighs
Did buy each other, must poorly sell ourselves
With the rude brevity and discharge of one.
Injurious time now with a robber's haste
Crams his rich thievery up he knows not how:
As many farewells as be stars in heaven,
With distinct breath and consigned kisses to them,
He fumbles up into a loose adieu;
And scants us with a single famished kiss,
Distasted with the salt of broken tears.

65

Æne. [*Within*] My lord, is the lady ready?
Tro. Hark! you are called: some say, the Genius so
Cries 'Come!' to him that instantly must die.
Bid them have patience; she shall come anon.
Pan. Where are my tears? rain, to lay this wind, or
my heart will be blown up by the root!

[*Exit*

Cres. I must then to the Grecians?
Tro.   No remedy.
Cres. A woful Cressid 'mongst the merry Greeks!
When shall we see again?
Tro. Hear me, my love. Be thou but true of heart,—
Cres. I true! how now? what wicked deem is this?
Tro. Nay, we must use expostulation kindly,
For it is parting from us:
I speak not, 'be thou true,' as fearing thee;
For I will throw my glove to Death himself,
That there 's no maculation in thy heart;
But, 'be thou true,' say I, to fashion in
My sequent protestation; be thou true,
And I will see thee.
Cres. O, you shall be exposed, my lord, to dangers
As infinite as imminent! but I 'll be true.
Tro. And I 'll grow friend with danger. Wear this
    sleeve.
Cres. And you this glove. When shall I see you?
Tro. I will corrupt the Grecian sentinels,
To give thee nightly visitation.
But yet, be true.
Cres.   O heavens!—'be true,' again?
Tro. Hear why I speak it, love:
The Grecian youths are full of quality;
Their loving well composed with gift of nature,
Flowing and swelling o'er with arts and exercise:
How novelties may move, and parts with person
Alas, a kind of godly jealousy—
Which, I beseech you, call a virtuous sin—
Makes me afraid.
Cres.   O heavens! you love me not.
Tro. Die I a villain then!
In this I do not call your faith in question
So mainly as my merit: I cannot sing,
Nor heel the high lavolt, nor sweeten talk,
Nor play at subtle games; fair virtues all,
To which the Grecians are most prompt and pregnant:
But I can tell that in each grace of these
There lurks a still and dumb discoursive devil
That tempts most cunningly: but be not tempted.
Cres. Do you think I will?

   Tro. No.
But something may be done that we will not:
And sometimes we are devils to ourselves,
When we will tempt the frailty of our powers,
Presuming on their changeful potency.
   Æne. [*Within*] Nay, good my lord,—
   Tro.   Come, kiss; and let us part.
   Par. [*Within*] Brother Troilus!
   Tro.   Good brother, come you hither;
And bring Æneas and the Grecian with you.
   Cres. My lord, will you be true?
   Tro. Who I? alas, it is my vice, my fault:
Whiles others fish with craft for great opinion,
I with great truth catch mere simplicity;
Whilst some with cunning gild their copper crowns,
With truth and plainness I do wear mine bare.
Fear not my truth; the moral of my wit
Is—plain, and true,—there 's all the reach of it.

Enter ÆNEAS, PARIS, ANTENOR, DEIPHOBUS, *and* DIOMEDES

Welcome, Sir Diomed. Here is the lady
Which for Antenor we deliver you:
At the port, lord, I 'll give her to thy hand,
And by the way possess thee what she is.
Entreat her fair; and, by my soul, fair Greek,
If e'er thou stand at mercy of my sword,
Name Cressid, and thy life shall be as safe
As Priam is in Ilion.
   Dio.   Fair Lady Cressid,
So please you, save the thanks this prince expects:
The lustre in your eye, heaven in your cheek,
Pleads your fair usage; and to Diomed
You shall be mistress, and command him wholly.
   Tro. Grecian, thou dost not use me courteously,
To shame the seal of my petition to thee
In praising her. I tell thee, lord of Greece,
She is as far high-soaring o'er thy praises
As thou unworthy to be called her servant.
I charge thee, use her well, even for my charge;
For, by the dreadful Pluto, if thou dost not,
Though the great bulk Achilles be thy guard,
I 'll cut thy throat.
   Dio.   O, be not moved, Prince Troilus.
Let me be privileged by my place and message
To be a speaker free: when I am hence,
I 'll answer to my lust: and know you, lord,
I 'll nothing do on charge. To her own worth
She shall be prized; but that you say—'Be 't so,'

I 'll speak it in my spirit and honour,—No.
   Tro.   Come, to the port.—I 'll tell thee, Diomed,
This brave shall oft make thee to hide thy head.—
Lady, give me your hand; and, as we walk,
To our own selves bend we our needful talk.
                  [Exeunt Troilus, Cressida, and Diomedes
                             [Trumpet sounded
   Par.   Hark! Hector's trumpet.
   Æne.   How have we spent this morning!
The prince must think me tardy and remiss,
That swore to ride before him to the field.
   Par.   'T is Troilus' fault. Come, come, to field with
          him.
   Dei.   Let us make ready straight.
   Æne.   Yea, with a bridegroom's fresh alacrity,
Let us address to tend on Hector's heels.
The glory of our Troy doth this day lie
On his fair worth and single chivalry.   *[Exeunt*

SCENE V.—*The Grecian Camp.   Lists set out*

Enter AJAX, *armed;* AGAMEMNON, ACHILLES, PATROCLUS,
    MENELAUS, ULYSSES, NESTOR, *and others*

   Agam.   Here art thou in appointment fresh and fair,
Anticipating time with starting courage.
Give with thy trumpet a loud note to Troy,
Thou dreadful Ajax; that the appallèd air
May pierce the head of the great combatant,
And hale him hither.
   Ajax.   Thou, trumpet, there 's my purse.
Now crack thy lungs, and split thy brazen pipe:
Blow, villain, till thy spherèd bias cheek
Outswell the colic of puffed Aquilon.
Come, stretch thy chest, and let thy eyes spout blood:
Thou blow'st for Hector.   *[Trumpet sounds*
   Ulyss.   No trumpet answers.
   Achil.   'T is but early days.
   Agam.   Is not yond Diomed with Calchas' daughter?
   Ulyss.   'T is he, I ken the manner of his gait;
He rises on the toe: that spirit of his
In aspiration lifts him from the earth.

Enter DIOMEDES, *with* CRESSIDA

   Agam.   Is this the Lady Cressid?
   Dio.   Even she.
   Agam.   Most dearly welcome to the Greeks, sweet lady.

Nest.   Our general doth salute you with a kiss.
Ulyss.   Yet is the kindness but particular;
'T were better she were kissed in general.
Nest.   And very courtly counsel: I'll begin.—
So much for Nestor.
Achil.   I'll take that winter from your lips, fair lady:
Achilles bids you welcome.
Men.   I had good argument for kissing once.
Patr.   But that's no argument for kissing now:
For thus popped Paris in his hardiment,
And parted thus you and your argument.
Ulyss.   O deadly gall, and theme of all our scorns!
For which we lose our heads, to gild his horns.
Patr.   The first was Menelaus' kiss;—this, mine:
Patroclus kisses you.
Men.   O, this is trim.
Patr.   Paris and I kiss evermore for him.
Men.   I'll have my kiss, sir.—Lady, by your leave.
Cres.   In kissing do you render or receive?
Patr.   Both take and give.
Cres.   I'll make my match to live,
The kiss you take is better than you give;
Therefore no kiss.
Men.   I'll give you boot; I'll give you three for one.
Cres.   You 're an odd man: give even, or give none.
Men.   An odd man, lady? every man is odd.
Cres.   No, Paris is not; for, you know, 't is true,
That you are odd, and he is even with you.
Men.   You fillip me o' the head.
Cres.   No, I'll be sworn.
Ulyss.   It were no match, your nail against his horn.—
May I, sweet lady, beg a kiss of you?
Cres.   You may.
Ulyss.   I do desire it.
Cres.   Why, beg then.
Ulyss.   Why then, for Venus' sake, give me a kiss,
When Helen is a maid again, and his.
Cres.   I am your debtor; claim it when 't is due.
Ulyss.   Never 's my day, and then a kiss of you.
Dio.   Lady, a word:—I'll bring you to your father.
                 [*Diomedes leads out Cressida*
Nest.   A woman of quick sense.
Ulyss.   Fie, fie upon her!
There 's language in her eye, her cheek, her lip,
Nay, her foot speaks; her wanton spirits look out
At every point and motive of her body.
O, these encounterers, so glib of tongue,
That give accosting welcome ere it comes,
And wide unclasp the tables of their thoughts

To every ticklish reader,—set them down
For sluttish spoils of opportunity,
And daughters of the game.　　　　　　*[Trumpet within*
　All.　The Trojans' trumpet.
　Agam.　　　　　　　Yonder comes the troop.

Enter HECTOR, *armed;* ÆNEAS, TROILUS, *and other
Trojans, with Attendants*

　Æne.　Hail, all you state of Greece! what shall be done
To him that victory commands? Or do you purpose,
A victor shall be known? will you, the knights
Shall to the edge of all extremity
Pursue each other, or shall be divided
By any voice or order of the field?
Hector bade ask.
　Agam.　Which way would Hector have it?
　Æne.　He cares not; he'll obey conditions.
　Achil.　'T is done like Hector; but securely done,
A little proudly, and great deal disprising
The knight opposed.
　Æne.　　　　　　If not Achilles, sir,
What is your name?
　Achil.　　　　　　If not Achilles, nothing.
　Æne.　Therefore Achilles: but whate'er, know this:—
In the extremity of great and little,
Valour and pride excel themselves in Hector;
The one almost as infinite as all,
The other blank as nothing.　Weigh him well,
And that which looks like pride is courtesy.
This Ajax is half made of Hector's blood:
In love whereof half Hector stays at home;
Half heart, half hand, half Hector comes to seek
This blended knight, half Trojan and half Greek.
　Achil.　A maiden battle, then?　O, I perceive you.

Re-enter DIOMEDES

　Agam.　Here is Sir Diomed.—Go, gentle knight,
Stand by our Ajax: as you and Lord Æneas
Consent upon the order of their fight,
So be it; either to the uttermost,
Or else a breath: the combatants being kin,
Half stints their strife before their strokes begin.
　　　　　　　　　[Ajax and Hector enter the lists
　Ulyss.　They are opposed already.
　Agam.　What Trojan is that same that looks so heavy?
　Ulyss.　The youngest son of Priam, a true knight;
Not yet mature, yet matchless; firm of word,
Speaking in deeds, and deedless in his tongue;

Not soon provoked, nor, being provoked, soon calmed:
His heart and hand both open, and both free;
For what he has, he gives; what thinks, he shows;
Yet gives he not till judgment guide his bounty,
Nor dignifies an impure thought with breath.
Manly as Hector, but more dangerous;
For Hector, in his blaze of wrath, subscribes
To tender objects; but he, in heat of action,
Is more vindicative than jealous love.
They call him Troilus; and on him erect
A second hope, as fairly built as Hector.
Thus says Æneas; one that knows the youth,
Even to his inches, and with private soul
Did in great Ilion thus translate him to me.

                    [Alarum. Hector and Ajax fight
   Agam.   They are in action.
   Nest.   Now, Ajax, hold thine own!
   Tro.   Hector, thou sleep'st: awake thee!
   Agam.   His blows are well disposed:—there, Ajax!
   Dio.   You must no more.   *[Trumpets cease*
   Æne.   Princes, enough, so please you.
   Ajax.   I am not warm yet: let us fight again.
   Dio.   As Hector pleases.
   Hect.   Why, then will I no more.—
Thou art, great lord, my father's sister's son,
A cousin-german to great Priam's seed;
The obligation of our blood forbids
A gory emulation 'twixt us twain
Were thy commixtion Greek and Trojan so
That thou couldst say—'This hand is Grecian all,
And this is Trojan; the sinews of this leg
All Greek, and this all Troy; my mother's blood
Runs on the dexter cheek, and this sinister
Bounds-in my father's;' by Jove multipotent
Thou shouldst not bear from me a Greekish member
Wherein my sword had not impressure made
Of our rank feud.   But the just gods gainsay,
That any drop thou borrow'dst from thy mother,
My sacred aunt, should by my mortal sword
Be drained!   Let me embrace thee, Ajax.—
By him that thunders, thou hast lusty arms;
Hector would have them fall upon him thus:
Cousin, all honour to thee!
   Ajax.   I thank thee, Hector:
Thou art too gentle, and too free a man.
I came to kill thee, cousin, and bear hence
A great addition earnéd in thy death.
   Hect.   Not Neoptolemus so mirable—
On whose bright crest Fame with her loudest *Oyez*

Cries, 'This is he!'—could promise to himself
A thought of added honour torn from Hector.
    Æne.   There is expectance here from both the sides
What further you will do.
    Hect.   We 'll answer it;
The issue is embracement:—Ajax, farewell.
    Ajax.   If I might in entreaties find success,
As seld I have the chance, I would desire
My famous cousin to our Grecian tents.
    Dio.   'T is Agamemnon's wish; and great Achilles
Doth long to see unarmed the valiant Hector.
    Hect.   Æneas, call my brother Troilus to me:
And signify this loving interview
To the expecters of our Trojan part;
Desire them home.—Give me thy hand, my cousin;
I will go eat with thee, and see your knights.
    Ajax.   Great Agamemnon comes to meet us here.
    Hect.   The worthiest of them tell me name by name;
But for Achilles, mine own searching eyes
Shall find him by his large and portly size.
    Agam.   Worthy of arms! as welcome as to one
That would be rid of such an enemy;
But that's no welcome: understand more clear,
What 's past and what 's to come is strewed with husks
And formless ruin of oblivion;
But in this extant moment, faith and troth,
Strained purely from all hollow bias-drawing,
Bids thee, with most divine integrity,
From heart of very heart, great Hector, welcome.
    Hect.   I thank thee, most imperious Agamemnon.
    Agam.   [*To Troilus*] My well-famed lord of Troy, no
          less to you.
    Men.   Let me confirm my princely brother's greeting:
You brace of warlike brothers, welcome hither.
    Hect.   Who must we answer?
    Æne.   The noble Menelaus.
    Hect.   O, you, my lord? by Mars his gauntlet, thanks.
Mock not, that I affect the untraded oath;
Your *quondam* wife swears still by Venus' glove;
She's well, but bade me not commend her to you.
    Men.   Name her not now, sir; she's a deadly theme.
    Hect.   O, pardon: I offend.
    Nest.   I have, thou gallant Trojan, seen thee oft,
Labouring for destiny, make cruel way
Through ranks of Greekish youth: and I have seen thee,
As hot as Perseus, spur thy Phrygian steed,
And seen thee scorning forfeits and subduements,
When thou hast hung thy advanced sword i' the air,
Not letting it decline on the declined;

That I have said unto my standers-by,
'Lo, Jupiter is yonder, dealing life!'
And I have seen thee pause, and take thy breath,
When that a ring of Greeks have hemmed thee in,
Like an Olympian wrestling: this have I seen;
But this thy countenance, still locked in steel,
I never saw till now.   I knew thy grandsire;
And once fought with him: he was a soldier good;
But, by great Mars, the captain of us all,
Never like thee.   Let an old man embrace thee;
And, worthy warrior, welcome to our tents.
   Æne.   'T is the old Nestor.
   Hect.   Let me embrace thee, good old chronicle,
Thou hast so long walked hand in hand with time.—
Most reverend Nestor, I am glad to clasp thee.
   Nest.   I would my arms could match thee in contention,
As they contend with thee in courtesy.
   Hect.   I would they could.
   Nest.   Ha!
By this white beard, I 'd fight with thee to-morrow.
Well, welcome, welcome!   I have seen the time.—
   Ulyss.   I wonder now how yonder city stands,
When we have here her base and pillar by us.
   Hect.   I know your favour, Lord Ulysses, well.
Ah, sir, there 's many a Greek and Trojan dead,
Since first I saw yourself and Diomed
In Ilion, on your Greekish embassy.
   Ulyss.   Sir, I foretold you then what would ensue;
My prophecy 's but half his journey yet;
For yonder walls that pertly front your town,
Yond towers whose wanton tops do buss the clouds,
Must kiss their own feet.
   Hect.   I must not believe you:
There they stand yet; and modestly I think,
The fall of every Phrygian stone will cost
A drop of Grecian blood: the end crowns all
And that old common arbitrator, Time,
Will one day end it.
   Ulyss.   So to him we leave it.
Most gentle, and most valiant Hector, welcome.
After the general, I beseech you next
To feast with me, and see me at my tent.
   Achil.   I shall forestall thee, Lord Ulysses, thou!—
Now, Hector, I have fed mine eyes on thee:
I have with exact view perused thee, Hector,
And quoted joint by joint.
   Hect.   Is this Achilles?
   Achil.   I am Achilles.
   Hect.   Stand fair, I pray thee: let me look on thee.

Achil.   Behold thy fill.
Hect.   Nay, I have done already.
Achil.   Thou art too brief; I will the second time,
As I would buy thee, view thee limb by limb.
Hect.   O, like a book of sport thou 'lt read me o'er;
But there 's more in me than thou understand'st.
Why dost thou so oppress me with thine eye?
Achil.   Tell me, you heavens, in which part of his body
Shall I destroy him, whether there, or there, or there?
That I may give the local wound a name,
And make distinct the very breach, whereout
Hector's great spirit flew.   Answer me, heavens!
Hect.   It would discredit the blessed gods, proud man,
To answer such a question.   Stand again:
Think'st thou to catch my life so pleasantly,
As to prenominate in nice conjecture,
Where thou wilt hit me dead?
Achil.   I tell thee, yea.
Hect.   Wert thou the oracle to tell me so,
I 'd not believe thee.   Henceforth guard thee well,
For I 'll not kill thee there, nor there, nor there;
But, by the forge that stithied Mars his helm,
I 'll kill thee everywhere, yea, o'er and o'er.—
You, wisest Grecians, pardon me this brag:
His insolence draws folly from my lips;
But I 'll endeavour deeds to match these words,
Or may I never—
Ajax.   Do not chafe thee, cousin;—
And you, Achilles, let these threats alone,
Till accident or purpose bring you to 't;
You may have every day enough of Hector,
If you have stomach.   The general state, I fear,
Can scarce entreat you to be odd with him.
Hect.   I pray you, let us see you in the field;
We have had pelting wars since you refused
The Grecians' cause.
Achil.   Dost thou entreat me, Hector?
To-morrow do I meet thee, fell as death;
To-night, all friends.
Hect.   Thy hand upon that match.
Agam.   First, all you peers of Greece, go to my tent;
There in the full convive we: afterwards,
As Hector's leisure and your bounties shall
Concur together, severally entreat him.—
Beat loud the tabourines, let the trumpets blow,
That this great soldier may his welcome know.
                    [*Exeunt all but Troilus and Ulysses*

Tro.   My Lord Ulysses, tell me, I beseech you,
In what place of the field doth Calchas keep?

                    74

Ulyss. At Menelaus' tent, most princely Troilus:
There Diomed doth feast with him to-night;
Who neither looks on heaven, nor on earth,
But gives all gaze and bent of amorous view
On the fair Cressid.
    Tro. Shall I, sweet lord, be bound to you so much,
After we part from Agamemnon's tent,
To bring me thither?
    Ulyss.   You shall command me, sir.
As gentle tell me, of what honour was
This Cressida in Troy? Had she no lover there,
That wails her absence?
    Tro. O, sir, to such as boasting show their scars,
A mock is due. Will you walk on, my lord?
She was beloved, she loved; she is, and doth:
But, still, sweet love is food for fortune's tooth.   [*Exeunt*

ACT FIVE

Scene I.—The Grecian Camp. Before Achilles' Tent

Enter Achilles *and* Patroclus

Achil. I 'll heat his blood with Greekish wine to-night,
Which with my scimitar I 'll cool to-morrow.—
Patroclus, let us feast him to the height.
    Patr. Here comes Thersites.

Enter Thersites

Achil.   How now, thou core of envy!
Thou crusty batch of nature, what 's the news?
    Ther. Why, thou picture of what thou seemest, and
idol of idiot worshippers, here 's a letter for thee.
    Achil. From whence, fragment?
    Ther. Why, thou full dish of fool, from Troy.
    Patr. Who keeps the tent now?
    Ther. The surgeon's box, or the patient's wound.
    Patr. Well said, Adversity! and what need these
tricks?
    Ther. Pr'ythee, be silent, boy; I profit not by thy talk;
thou art thought to be Achilles' male varlet.
    Patr. Male varlet, you rogue! what 's that?
    Ther. Why, his masculine whore. Now the rotten
diseases of the south, the guts-griping, ruptures, catarrhs,
loads o' gravel i' the back, lethargies, cold palsies, raw eyes,
dirt-rotten livers, wheezing lungs, bladders full of impos-

thume, sciaticas, lime-kilns i' the palm, incurable bone-ache,
and the rivelled fee-simple of the tetter, take and take
again such preposterous discoveries!

Patr. Why, thou damnable box of envy, thou, what
meanest thou to curse thus?

Ther. Do I curse thee?

Patr. Why, no, you ruinous butt; you whoreson
indistinguishable cur, no.

Ther. No! why art thou then exasperate, thou idle
immaterial skein of sleave silk, thou green sarcenet flap
for a sore eye, thou tassel of a prodigal's purse, thou?
Ah, how the poor world is pestered with such water-flies,
diminutives of nature!

Patr. Out, gall!

Ther. Finch-egg!

Achil. My sweet Patroclus, I am thwarted quite
From my great purpose in to-morrow's battle.
Here is a letter from Queen Hecuba;
A token from her daughter, my fair love;
Both taxing me, and gaging me to keep
An oath that I have sworn.   I will not break it:
Fall, Greeks; fail, fame; honour, or go, or stay;
My major vow lies here, this I'll obey.—
Come, come, Thersites, help to trim my tent;
This night in banqueting must all be spent.—
Away, Patroclus.

[Exeunt Achilles and Patroclus

Ther. With too much blood, and too little brain, these
two may run mad; but if with too much brain and too
little blood they do, I'll be a curer of madmen.   Here's
Agamemnon,—an honest fellow enough, and one that
loves quails, but he has not so much brain as ear-wax:
and the goodly transformation of Jupiter there, his brother,
the bull, the primitive statue, and oblique memorial of
cuckolds; a thrifty shoeing-horn in a chain, hanging at
his brother's leg,—to what form, but that he is, should
wit larded with malice, and malice forced with wit, turn
him to?   To an ass were nothing; he is both ass and ox;
to an ox were nothing: he is both ox and ass.   To be a dog,
a mule, a cat, a fitchew, a toad, a lizard, an owl, a puttock,
or a herring without a roe, I would not care; but to be
Menelaus,—I would conspire against destiny.   Ask me
not what I would be, if I were not Thersites, for I care not
to be the louse of a lazar, so I were not Menelaus—Heyday!
spirits and fires!

Enter HECTOR, TROILUS, AJAX, AGAMEMNON, ULYSSES,
NESTOR, MENELAUS, *and* DIOMEDES, *with lights*

Agam. We go wrong; we go wrong.

   Ajax. No, yonder 't is;
There, where we see the lights.
   Hect.   I trouble you.
   Ajax. No, not a whit.
   Ulyss.   Here comes himself to guide you.

Re-enter ACHILLES

   Achil. Welcome, brave Hector: welcome, princes all.
   Agam. So now, fair prince of Troy, I bid good night.
Ajax commands the guard to tend on you.
   Hect. Thanks and good night to the Greeks' general.
   Men. Good night, my lord.
   Hect. Good night, sweet Lord Menelaus.
   Ther. Sweet draught: sweet, quoth 'a! sweet sink,
sweet sewer.
   Achil. Good night, and welcome, both at once to those
That go or tarry.
   Agam. Good night.
                 [*Exeunt Agamemnon and Menelaus*
   Achil. Old Nestor tarries; and you too, Diomed,
Keep Hector company an hour or two.
   Dio. I cannot, lord; I have important business,
The tide whereof is now.—Good night, great Hector.
   Hect. Give me your hand.
   Ulyss. [*Aside to Troilus*] Follow his torch, he goes to
                Calchas' tent:
I 'll keep you company.
   Tro. Sweet sir, you honour me.
   Hect.   And so, good night.
      [*Exit Diomedes; Ulysses and Troilus following*
   Achil. Come, come; enter my tent.
      [*Exeunt Achilles, Hector, Ajax, and Nestor*
   Ther. That same Diomed's a false-hearted rogue,
a most unjust knave: I will no more trust him when he
leers, than I will a serpent when he hisses. He will spend
his mouth and promise, like Brabbler the hound; but
when he performs, astronomers foretell it: it is prodigious,
there will come some change: the sun borrows of the moon,
when Diomed keeps his word. I will rather leave to see
Hector, than not to dog him: they say he keeps a Trojan
drab, and uses the traitor Calchas' tent. I'll after.—
Nothing but lechery; all incontinent varlets!   [*Exit*

SCENE II.—*The Same. Before* CALCHAS' *Tent*

Enter DIOMEDES

   Dio. What, are you up here, ho! speak.
   Cal. [*Within*] Who calls?

Dio. Diomed.—Calchas, I think.—Where's your daughter?

Cal. [*Within*] She comes to you.

Enter TROILUS *and* ULYSSES, *at a distance; after them,*
       THERSITES

Ulyss. Stand where the torch may not discover us.

Enter CRESSIDA

Tro. Cressid comes forth to him!
Dio.   How now, my charge?
Cres. Now, my sweet guardian.—Hark! a word with
 you.   [*Whispers*
Tro. Yea, so familiar!
Ulyss. She will sing any man at first sight.
Ther. And any man may sing her, if he can take her
cliff; she 's noted.
Dio. Will you remember?
Cres. Remember? Yes.
Dio. Nay, but do then;
And let your mind be coupled with your words.
Tro. What should she remember?
Ulyss. List!
Cres. Sweet honey Greek, tempt me no more to folly.
Ther. Roguery!
Dio. Nay, then,—
Cres. I 'll tell you what,—
Dio. Pho, pho! come, tell a pin: you are forsworn.
Cres. In faith, I cannot. What would you have me
do?
Ther. A juggling trick,—to be secretly open.
Dio. What did you swear you would bestow on me?
Cres. I pry'thee, do not hold me to mine oath;
Bid me do anything but that, sweet Greek.
Dio. Good night.
Tro.   Hold, patience!
Ulyss.   How now, Trojan?
Cres.   Diomed,—
Dio. No, no; good night: I 'll be your fool no more.
Tro. Thy better must.
Cres.   Hark, one word in your ear.
Tro. O plague and madness!
Ulyss. You are moved, prince: let us depart, I pray you,
Lest your displeasure should enlarge itself
To wrathful terms: this place is dangerous;
The time right deadly: I beseech you, go.
Tro. Behold, I pray you!
Ulyss.   Nay, good my lord, go off:

You flow to great distraction; come, my lord.
    Tro.   I pray thee, stay.
    Ulyss.   You have not patience; come.
    Tro.   I pray you, stay. By hell, and all hell's torments,
I will not speak a word!—
    Dio.   And so, good night.
    Cres.   Nay, but you part in anger.—
    Tro.   Doth that grieve thee?
O withered truth!
    Ulyss.   Why, how now, lord?
    Tro.   By Jove,
I will be patient.—
    Cres.   Guardian!—why, Greek!
    Dio.   Pho, pho! adieu; you palter.
    Cres.   In faith, I do not: come hither once again.—
    Ulyss.   You shake, my lord, at something: will you go?
You will break out.
    Tro.   She strokes his cheek!
    Ulyss.   Come, come.
    Tro.   Nay, stay; by Jove, I will not speak a word:
There is between my will and all offences
A guard of patience:—stay a little while.
    Ther.   How the devil Luxury, with his fat rump and
potato-finger, tickles these together! Fry, lechery, fry!—
    Dio.   But will you then?
    Cres.   In faith, I will, la; never trust me else.
    Dio.   Give me some token for the surety of it.
    Cres.   I 'll fetch you one.—   *[Exit*
    Ulyss.   You have sworn patience.
    Tro.   Fear me not, sweet lord;
I will not be myself, nor have cognition
Of what I feel: I am all patience.

Re-enter CRESSIDA

    Ther.   Now the pledge; now, now, now!
    Cres.   Here, Diomed, keep this sleeve.—
    Tro.   O beauty, where is thy faith?
    Ulyss.   My lord,—
    Tro.   I will be patient; outwardly, I will.—
    Cres.   You look upon that sleeve: behold it well.—
He loved me—O false wench!—Give 't me again.
    Dio.   Whose was 't?
    Cres.   It is no matter, now I have 't again.
I will not meet with you to-morrow night:
I pr'ythee, Diomed, visit me no more.
    Ther.   Now she sharpens:—well said, whetstone!—
    Dio.   I shall have it.
    Cres.   What, this?

Dio.   Ay, that.
Cres.   O, all you gods!—O pretty, pretty pledge!
Thy master now lies thinking in his bed
Of thee, and me; and signs, and takes my glove,
And gives memorial dainty kisses to it,
As I kiss thee.—Nay, do not snatch it from me;
He that takes that doth take my heart withal.
Dio.   I had your heart before; this follows it.—
Tro.   I did swear patience.—
Cres.   You shall not have it, Diomed; 'faith, you shall
      not;
I 'll give you something else.
Dio.   I will have this.   Whose was it?
Cres.   'T is no matter.
Dio.   Come, tell me whose it was.
Cres.   'T was one's that loved me better than you will.
But, now you have it, take it.
Dio.   Whose was it?
Cres.   By all Diana's waiting-women, yond,
And by herself, I will not tell you whose.
Dio.   To-morrow will I wear it on my helm,
And grieve his spirit that dares not challenge it.—
Tro.   Wert thou the devil, and wor'st it on thy horn,
It should be challenged.—
Cres.   Well, well, 't is done, 't is past;—and yet it is
      not:
I will not keep my word.
Dio.   Why then, farewell;
Thou never shalt mock Diomed again.
Cres.   You shall not go.—One cannot speak a word,
But it straight starts you.
Dio.   I do not like this fooling.—
Ther.   Nor I, by Pluto: but that that likes not me,
Pleases me best.
Dio.   What, shall I come? the hour?
Cres.   Ay, come:—O Jove!—do come:—I shall be
      plagued.
Dio.   Farewell till then.
Cres.   Good night: I pr'ythee, come.—
                                                    [*Exit Diomedes*
Troilus, farewell! one eye yet looks on thee,
But with my heart the other eye doth see.
Ah, poor our sex! this fault in us I find,
The error of our eye directs our mind:
What error leads, must err.   O, then conclude,
Minds swayed by eyes are full of turpitude.   [*Exit*
Ther.   A proof of strength she could not publish more,
Unless she said, "My mind is now turned whore."
Ulyss.   All 's done, my lord.

Tro.   It is.
Ulyss.   Why stay we then?
Tro.   To make a recordation to my soul
Of every syllable that here was spoke.
But if I tell how these two did co-act,
Shall I not lie in publishing a truth?
Sith yet there is a credence in my heart,
An esperance so obstinately strong,
That doth invert the attest of eyes and ears,
As if those organs had deceptious functions,
Created only to calumniate.
Was Cressid here?
    Ulyss.   I cannot conjure, Trojan.
    Tro.   She was not, sure.
    Ulyss.   Most sure she was.
    Tro.   Why, my negation hath no taste of madness.
    Ulyss.   Nor mine, my lord: Cressid was here but now.
    Tro.   Let it not be believed for womanhood!
Think, we had mothers; do not give advantage
To stubborn critics,—apt, without a theme,
For depravation,—to square the general sex
By Cressid's rule: rather think this not Cressid.
    Ulyss.   What hath she done, prince, that can soil our
        mothers?
    Tro.   Nothing at all, unless that this were she.
    Ther.   Will he swagger himself out on 's own eyes?
    Tro.   This she? no, this is Diomed's Cressida.
If beauty have a soul, this is not she:
If souls guide vows, if vows be sanctimonies,
If sanctimony be the gods' delight,
If there be rule in unity itself,
This is not she.   O madness of discourse,
That cause sets up with and against thyself!
Bi-fold authority! where reason can revolt
Without perdition, and loss assume all reason
Without revolt: this is, and is not, Cressid!
Within my soul there doth conduce a fight
Of this strange nature, that a thing inseparate
Divides more wider than the sky and earth;
And yet the spacious breadth of this division
Admits no orifice for a point as subtle
As Ariachne's broken woof, to enter.
Instance, O instance; strong as Pluto's gates;
Cressid is mine, tied with the bonds of heaven:
Instance, O instance! strong as heaven itself;
The bonds of heaven are slipped, dissolved, and loosed;
And with another knot, five-finger-tied,
The fractions of her faith, orts of her love,
The fragments, scraps, the bits, and greasy reliques

Of her o'er-eaten faith, are bound to Diomed.
    Ulyss. May worthy Troilus be half attached
With that which here his passion doth express?
    Tro. Ay, Greek; and that shall be divulgéd well
In characters as red as Mars his heart
Inflamed with Venus: never did young man fancy
With so eternal and so fixed a soul.
Hark, Greek;—as much as I do Cressid love,
So much by weight hate I her Diomed;
That sleeve is mine that he 'll bear in his helm:
Were it a casque composed by Vulcan's skill,
My sword should bite it. Not the dreadful spout
Which shipmen do the hurricano call,
Constringed in mass by the almighty sun,
Shall dizzy with more clamour Neptune's ear
In his descent, than shall my prompted sword
Falling on Diomed.
    Ther. He 'll tickle it for his concupy.
    Tro. O Cressid! O false Cressid! false, false, false!
Let all untruths stand by thy stainéd name,
And they 'll seem glorious.
    Ulyss.   O, contain yourself;
Your passion draws ears hither.

Enter ÆNEAS

    Æne. I have been seeking you this hour, my lord.
Hector by this is arming him in Troy;
Ajax, your guard, stays to conduct you home.
    Tro. Have with you, prince.—My courteous lord,
        adieu.—
Farewell, revolted fair!—and, Diomed,
Stand fast, and wear a castle on thy head!
    Ulyss. I 'll bring you to the gates.
    Tro. Accept distracted thanks.
                      [Exeunt Troilus, Æneas, and Ulysses
    Ther. *[Coming forward]* Would I could meet that rogue
Diomed! I would croak like a raven; I would bode, I
would bode. Patroclus will give me anything for the
intelligence of this whore: the parrot will not do more
for an almond, than he for a commodious drab. Lechery,
lechery; still, wars and lechery: nothing else holds fashion.
A burning devil take them!   *[Exit*

SCENE III.—Troy. Before PRIAM's Palace

Enter HECTOR and ANDROMACHE

    And. When was my lord so much ungently tempered,
To stop his ears against admonishment?

Unarm, unarm, and do not fight to-day.
   Hect.   You train me to offend you; get you gone:
By all the everlasting gods I 'll go.
   And.   My dreams will, sure, prove ominous to the day.
   Hect.   No more, I say.

Enter CASSANDRA

   Cas.   Where is my brother Hector?
   And.   Here, sister, armed and bloody in intent.
Consort with me in loud and dear petition;
Pursue we him on knees; for I have dreamed
Of bloody turbulence, and this whole night
Hath nothing been but shapes and forms of slaughter.
   Cas.   O, 'tis true.
   Hect.   Ho! bid my trumpet sound!
   Cas.   No notes of sally for the heavens, sweet brother.
   Hect.   Be gone, I say; the gods have heard me swear.
   Cas.   The gods are deaf to hot and peevish vows:
They are polluted offerings, more abhorred
Than spotted livers in the sacrifice.
   And.   O, be persuaded: do not count it holy
To hurt by being just: it is as lawful,
For we would give much, to use violent thefts,
And rob in the behalf of charity.
   Cas.   It is the purpose that makes strong the vow;
But vows to every purpose must not hold:
Unarm, sweet Hector.
   Hect.   Hold you still, I say;
Mine honour keeps the weather of my fate:
Life every man holds dear; but the brave man
Holds honour far more precious-dear than life.—

Enter TROILUS

How now, young man! mean'st thou to fight to-day?
   And.   Cassandra, call my father to persuade.
                                 [Exit Cassandra
   Hect.   No, 'faith, young Troilus; doff thy harness, youth;
I am to-day i' the vein of chivalry.
Let grow thy sinews till their knots be strong,
And tempt not yet the brushes of the war.
Unarm thee, go; and doubt thou not, brave boy,
I 'll stand to-day for thee, and me, and Troy.
   Tro.   Brother, you have a vice of mercy in you,
Which better fits a lion than a man.
   Hect.   What vice is that, good Troilus? chide me for it.
   Tro.   When many times the captive Grecian falls,
Even in the fan and wind of your fair sword,
You bid them rise and live.

Hect.   O, 'tis fair play.
Tro.   Fool's play, by heaven, Hector.
Hect.   How now? how now?
Tro.   For the love of all the gods
Let 's leave the hermit pity with our mothers,
And when we have our armours buckled on,
The venomed vengeance ride upon our swords:
Spur them to ruthful work, rein them from ruth.
Hect.   Fie, savage, fie!
Tro.   O Hector, then 'tis wars.
Hect.   Troilus, I would not have you fight to-day.
Tro.   Who should withhold me?
Not fate, obedience, nor the hand of Mars
Beckoning with fiery truncheon my retire;
Not Priamus and Hecuba on knees,
Their eyes o'ergallèd with recourse of tears;
Nor you, my brother, with your true sword drawn,
Opposed to hinder me, should stop my way,
But by my ruin.

Re-enter CASSANDRA *with* PRIAM

Cas.   Lay hold upon him, Priam, hold him fast:
He is thy crutch; now, if thou lose thy stay,
Thou on him leaning, and all Troy on thee,
Fall all together.
Pri.   Come, Hector, come; go back:
Thy wife hath dreamed; thy mother hath had visions;
Cassandra doth foresee; and I myself
Am like a prophet suddenly enrapt,
To tell thee that this day is ominous:
Therefore, come back.
Hect.   Æneas is afield;
And I do stand engaged to many Greeks,
Even in the faith of valour, to appear
This morning to them.
Pri.   Ay, but thou shalt not go.
Hect.   I must not break my faith.
You know me dutiful; therefore, dear sir,
Let me not shame respect, but give me leave
To take that course by your consent and voice,
Which you do here forbid me, royal Priam.
Cas.   O Priam! yield not to him.
And.   Do not, dear father.
Hect.   Andromache, I am offended with you:
Upon the love you bear me, get you in.
                                [*Exit Andromache*
Tro.   This foolish, dreaming, superstitious girl
Makes all these bodements.

Cas.   O farewell, dear Hector!
Look, how thou diest! look, how thy eye turns pale!
Look, how thy wounds do bleed at many vents!
Hark, how Troy roars! how Hecuba cries out!
How poor Andromache shrills her dolour forth!
Behold, distraction, frenzy, and amazement,
Like witless anticks, one another meet,
And all cry—'Hector!' 'Hector 's dead!' O Hector!
   Tro.   Away! away!
   Cas.   Farewell.—Yet, soft!—Hector, I take my leave:
Thou dost thyself and all our Troy deceive.   [*Exit*
   Hect.   You are amazed, my liege, at her exclaim.
Go in and cheer the town: we'll forth and fight,
Do deeds worth praise, and tell you them at night.
   Pri.   Farewell: the gods with safety stand about thee!
             [*Exeunt severally Priam and Hector*
                               [*Alarums*
   Tro.   They are at it; hark!—Proud Diomed, believe,
I come to lose my arm, or win my sleeve.   [*Going*

Enter PANDARUS

   Pan.   Do you, hear, my lord? do you hear?
   Tro.   What now?
   Pan.   Here 's a letter come from yond poor girl.
   Tro.   Let me read.
   Pan.   A whoreson tisick, a whoreson rascally tisick so
troubles me, and the foolish fortune of this girl; and what
one thing, what another, that I shall leave you one o' these
days: and I have a rheum in mine eyes too; and such an
ache in my bones, that, unless a man were cursed, I cannot
tell what to think on 't.—What says she there?
   Tro.   Words, words, mere words; no matter from the
         heart;   [*Tearing the letter*
The effect doth operate another way.—
Go, wind to wind, there turn and change together.—
My love with words and errors still she feeds,
But edifies another with her deeds.

                               [*Exeunt severally*

SCENE IV.—Between Troy and the Grecian Camp

Alarums: Excursions. Enter THERSITES

   Ther.   Now they are clapper-clawing one another:
I 'll go look on. That dissembling abominable varlet,
Diomed, has got that same scurvy doting foolish young
knave's sleeve of Troy there in his helm: I would fain see
them meet; that that same young Trojan ass, that loves the

whore there, might send that Greekish whoremasterly villain, with the sleeve, back to the dissembling luxurious drab of a sleeveless errand. O' the other side, the policy of those crafty swearing rascals,—that stale old mouse-eaten dry cheese, Nestor, and that same dog-fox, Ulysses,—is not proved worth a blackberry:—they set me up, in policy, that mongrel cur, Ajax, against that dog of as bad a kind, Achilles; and now is the cur Ajax prouder than the cur Achilles, and will not arm to-day: whereupon the Grecians begin to proclaim barbarism, and policy grows into an ill opinion. Soft! here comes sleeve, and t' other.

Enter DIOMEDES, TROILUS *following*

Tro. Fly not; for shouldst thou take the river Styx, I would swim after.
Dio.   Thou dost miscall retire:
I do not fly, but advantageous care
Withdrew me from the odds of multitude.
Have at thee!
Ther. Hold thy whore, Grecian!—now for thy whore, Trojan!—now the sleeve! now the sleeve!
                    [*Exeunt Troilus and Diomedes, fighting*

Enter HECTOR

Hect. What art thou, Greek? art thou for Hector's match?
Art thou of blood and honour?
Ther. No, no;—I am a rascal; a scurvy railing knave; a very filthy rogue.
Hect. I do believe thee:—live.   [*Exit*
Ther. God-a-mercy, that thou wilt believe me; but a plague break thy neck for frighting me! What's become of the wenching rogues? I think they have swallowed one another: I would laugh at that miracle;—yet, in a sort, lechery eats itself. I'll seek them.

                    [*Exit*

SCENE V.—The Same

Enter DIOMEDES *and a Servant*

Dio. Go, go, my servant, take thou Troilus' horse;
Present the fair steed to my Lady Cressid.
Fellow, commend my service to her beauty:
Tell her, I have chastised the amorous Trojan,
And am her knight by proof.
Serv.   I go, my lord.   [*Exit*

Enter AGAMEMNON

Agam.   Renew, renew! The fierce Polydamas
Hath beat down Menon: bastard Margarelon
Hath Doreus prisoner,
And stands colossus-wise, waving his beam,
Upon the pashéd corses of the kings
Epistrophus and Cedius: Polixenes is slain:
Amphimachus, and Thoas, deadly hurt;
Patroclus ta'en, or slain; and Palamedes
Sore hurt and bruised; the dreadful Sagittary
Appals our numbers. Haste we, Diomed,
To reinforcement, or we perish all.

Enter NESTOR

Nest.   Go, bear Patroclus' body to Achilles;
And bid the snail-paced Ajax arm for shame.—
There is a thousand Hectors in the field:
Now here he fights on Galathe his horse,
And there lacks work; anon, he 's there afoot,
And there they fly, or die, like scaléd sculls
Before the belching whale; then is he yonder,
And there the strawy Greeks, ripe for his edge,
Fall down before him, like the mower's swath;
Here, there, and everywhere, he leaves, and takes;
Dexterity so obeying appetite
That what he will he does; and does so much,
That proof is called impossibility.

Enter ULYSSES

Ulyss.   O, courage, courage, princes! great Achilles
Is arming, weeping, cursing, vowing vengeance:
Patroclus' wounds have rousèd his drowsy blood,
Together with his mangled Myrmidons,
That noseless, handless, hacked and chipped, come to him,
Crying on Hector. Ajax hath lost a friend,
And foams at mouth, and he is armed, and at it,
Roaring for Troilus; who hath done to-day
Mad and fantastic execution,
Engaging and redeeming of himself,
With such a careless force, and forceless care,
As if that luck, in very spite of cunning,
Bade him win all.

Enter AJAX

Ajax.   Troilus! thou coward Troilus!   [*Exit*
Dio.   Ay, there, there.
Nest.   So, so, we draw together.

Enter ACHILLES

Achil.   Where is this Hector?
Come, come, thou boy-queller, show thy face;
Know what it is to meet Achilles angry.
Hector! where 's Hector? I will none but Hector.

                                       [*Exeunt*

SCENE VI.—Another Part of the Field

Enter AJAX

Ajax.   Troilus, thou coward Troilus, show thy head!

Enter DIOMEDES

Dio.   Troilus, I say! where 's Troilus?
Ajax.   What wouldst thou?
Dio.   I would correct him.
Ajax.   Were I the general, thou shouldst have my office
Ere that correction.—Troilus, I say! what, Troilus!

Enter TROILUS

Tro.   O traitor Diomed!—turn thy false face, thou
        traitor.
And pay the life thou ow'st me for my horse!
Dio.   Ha! art thou there?
Ajax.   I'll fight with him alone; stand, Diomed.
Dio.   He is my prize; I will not look upon.
Tro.   Come both, you cogging Greeks; have at you
        both.   [*Exeunt, fighting*

Enter HECTOR

Hect.   Yea, Troilus? O, well fought, my youngest
        brother!

Enter ACHILLES

Achil.   Now do I see thee. Ha!—Have at thee, Hector.
Hect.   Pause, if thou wilt.
Achil.   I do disdain thy courtesy, proud Trojan.
Be happy that my arms are out of use:
My rest and negligence befriend thee now,
But thou anon shalt hear of me again;
Till when, go seek thy fortune.   [*Exit*
Hect.   Fare thee well.—
I would have been much more a fresher man,
Had I expected thee.

Re-enter TROILUS

                        How now, my brother?
  Tro. Ajax hath ta'en Æneas: shall it be?
No, by the flame of yonder glorious heaven,
He shall not carry him: I 'll be ta'en too,
Or bring him off:—Fate, hear me what I say!
I reck not though I end my life to-day.   [*Exit*

Enter one in sumptuous armour

  Hect. Stand, stand, thou Greek: thou art a goodly
            mark.—
No? wilt thou not?—I like thy armour well;
I 'll frush it, and unlock the rivets all,
But I 'll be master of it.—Wilt thou not, beast, abide?
Why then, fly on, I 'll hunt thee for thy hide.   [*Exeunt*

SCENE VII.—*Another Part of the Plain*

Enter ACHILLES, *with Myrmidons*

  Achil. Come here about me, you my Myrmidons;
Mark what I say.   Attend me where I wheel:
Strike not a stroke, but keep yourselves in breath;
And when I have the bloody Hector found,
Empale him with your weapons round about,
In fellest manner execute your aims.
Follow me, sirs, and my proceedings eye:—
It is decreed, Hector the great must die.   [*Exeunt*

Enter MENELAUS *and* PARIS, *fighting: then,* THERSITES

  Ther. The cuckold and the cuckold-maker are at it.
Now, bull! now, dog! 'Loo, Paris, 'loo! now, my double-
henned sparrow! 'loo, Paris, 'loo! The bull has the game:
—'ware horns, ho!   [*Exeunt Paris and Menelaus*

Enter MARGARELON

  Mar.   Turn, slave, and fight.
  Ther. What art thou?
  Mar.   A bastard son of Priam's.
  Ther. I am a bastard too.   I love bastards; I am a
bastard begot, bastard instructed, bastard in mind, bastard
in valour, in everything illegitimate.   One bear will not
bite another, and wherefore should one bastard?   Take
heed, the quarrel 's most ominous to us: if the son of a
whore fight for a whore, he tempts judgment.   Farewell,
bastard.
  Mar.   The devil take thee, coward!   [*Exeunt*

SCENE VIII.—Another Part of the Plain

Enter HECTOR

Hect.   Most putrefiéd core, so fair without,
Thy goodly armour thus hath cost thy life.
Now is my day's work done; I'll take good breath:
Rest, sword; thou hast thy fill of blood and death!
                    [*Puts off his helmet, and lays his sword aside*

Enter ACHILLES *and* MYRMIDONS

Achil.   Look, Hector, how the sun begins to set;
How ugly night comes breathing at his heels:
Even with the vail and darkening of the sun,
To close the day up, Hector's life is done.
Hect.   I am unarmed: forego this vantage, Greek.
Achil.   Strike, fellows, strike: this is the man I seek.
                                        [*Hector falls*
So, Ilion, fall thou next! now, Troy, sink down!
Here lies thy heart, thy sinews, and thy bone.
On, Myrmidons; and cry you all amain,
"Achilles hath the mighty Hector slain."
                                [*A retreat sounded*
Hark! a retreat upon our Grecian part.
Myr.   The Trojan trumpets sound the like, my lord.
Achil.   The dragon wing of night o'erspreads the earth,
And, stickler-like, the armies separates.
My half-supped sword, that frankly would have fed,
Pleased with this dainty bit, thus goes to bed.—
                                [*Sheathes his sword*
Come, tie his body to my horse's tail;
Along the field I will the Trojan trail.   [*Exeunt*

SCENE IX.—The Same

Enter AGAMEMNON, AJAX, MENELAUS, NESTOR, DIOMEDES,
and others, marching. Shouts within

Agam.   Hark! hark! what shout is that?
Nest.   Peace, drums!
[*Within*]   Achilles! Achilles! Hector's slain! Achilles!
Dio.   The bruit is, Hector's slain, and by Achilles.
Ajax.   If it be so, yet bragless let it be:
Great Hector was a man as good as he.
Agam.   March patiently along.—Let one be sent
To pray Achilles see us at our tent.—

If in his death the gods have us befriended,
Great Troy is ours, and our sharp wars are ended.

[Exeunt marching

SCENE X.—Another part of the Field

Enter ÆNEAS and Trojan forces

Æne. Stand, ho! yet are we masters of the field.
Never go home: here starve we out the night.

Enter TROILUS

Tro. Hector is slain.
All.   Hector?—The gods forbid!
Tro.   He 's dead: and at the murderer's horse's tail,
In beastly sort, dragged through the shameful field.—
Frown on, you heavens, effect your rage with speed!
Sit, gods, upon your thrones, and smite at Troy!
I say, at once let your brief plagues be mercy,
And linger not our sure destructions on!
Æne.   My lord, you do discomfort all the host.
Tro.   You understand me not, that tell me so.
I do not speak of flight, of fear of death;
But dare all imminence that gods and men
Address their dangers in.   Hector is gone!
Who shall tell Priam so, or Hecuba?
Let him that will a screech-owl aye be called
Go in to Troy, and say there—Hector's dead:
There is a word will Priam turn to stone,
Make wells and Niobes of the maids and wives,
Cold statues of the youth; and, in a word,
Scare Troy out of itself.   But, march, away:
Hector is dead; there is no more to say.
Stay yet.—You vile abominable tents,
Thus proudly pight upon our Phrygian plains,
Let Titan rise as early as he dare,
I 'll through and through you?—And thou, great-sized
                coward,
No space of earth shall sunder our two hates:
I 'll haunt thee like a wicked conscience still,
That mouldeth goblins swift as frenzy thoughts.—
Strike a free march to Troy!—with comfort go:
Hope of revenge shall hide our inward woe.

[Exeunt Æneas and Trojan forces

As TROILUS *is going out, enter, from the other side,*
                PANDARUS
Pan.   But hear you, hear you!

Tro.   Hence, broker-lackey! ignomy and shame
Pursue thy life, and live aye with thy name!   [*Exit*
   Pan.   A goodly medicine for mine aching bones.—O,
world! world! world! thus is the poor agent despised.
O traitors and bawds, how earnestly are you set a-work,
and how ill requited! why should our endeavour be so
desired, and the performance so loathed? what verse for
it? what instance for it?—Let me see.—

> *Full merrily the humble-bee doth sing,*
> *Till he hath lost his honey and his sting;*
> *And being once subdued in armed tail,*
> *Sweet honey and sweet notes together fail.—*

Good traders in the flesh, set this in your painted cloths.
As many as be here of pander's hall,
Your eyes, half out, weep out at Pandar's fall;
Or, if you cannot weep, yet give some groans,
Though not for me, yet for your aching bones.
Brethren, and sisters, of the hold-door trade,
Some two months hence my will shall here be made:
It should be now, but that my fear is this.—
Some galled goose of Winchester would hiss.
Till then I 'll sweat, and seek about for eases;
And at that time bequeath you my diseases.   [*Exit*

TWELFTH-NIGHT
OR
WHAT YOU WILL

DRAMATIS PERSONÆ

ORSINO, *Duke Illyria*
SEBASTIAN, *brother to Viola*
ANTONIO, *a sea captain, friend to Sebastian*
A *Sea Captain, friend to Viola*
VALENTINE
CURIO } *gentlemen attending on the Duke*
SIR TOBY BELCH, *uncle to Olivia*
SIR ANDREW AGUE-CHEEK
MALVOLIO, *steward to Olivia*
FABIAN
FESTE, *a Clown* } *servants to Olivia*

OLIVIA, *a rich Countess*
VIOLA, *sister to Sebastian*
MARIA, *Olivia's woman*

Lords, a Priest, Sailors, Officers, Musicians, and Attendants.

SCENE.—*A City in Illyria; and the sea-coast near it*

94

TWELFTH-NIGHT

OR, WHAT YOU WILL

ACT ONE

Scene I.—A Room in the Duke's Palace

Enter Duke, Curio, *Lords; Musicians attending*

Duke. If music be the food of love, play on;
Give me excess of it, that, surfeiting,
The appetite may sicken, and so die.—
That strain again!—it had a dying fall:
O, it came o'er my ear like the sweet sound
That breathes upon a bank of violets,
Stealing and giving odour!—Enough; no more:
'T is not so sweet now as it was before.
O spirit of love, how quick and fresh art thou,
That, notwithstanding thy capacity
Receiveth as the sea, naught enters there,
Of what validity and pitch soe'er,
But falls into abatement and low price
Even in a minute! so full of shapes is fancy,
That it alone is high-fantastical.
 Cur. Will you go hunt, my lord?
 Duke.   What, Curio?
 Cur.   The hart.
 Duke. Why, so I do, the noblest that I have.
O, when mine eyes did see Olivia first,
Methought she purged the air of pestilence!
That instant was I turned into a hart.
And my desires, like fell and cruel hounds,
E'er since pursue me.—

Enter Valentine

         How now? what news from her?
 Val. So please my lord, I might not be admitted,
But from her handmaid do return this answer:
The element itself, till seven years hence,
Shall not behold her face at ample view;
But, like a cloistress, she will veiléd walk.

And water once a day her chamber round
With eye-offending brine: all this to season
A brother's dead love, which she would keep fresh
And lasting in her sad remembrance.
    Duke. O, she that hath a heart of that fine frame
To pay this debt of love but to a brother,
How will she love, when the rich golden shaft
Hath killed the flock of all affections else
That live in her; when liver, brain, and heart,
These sovereign thrones, are all supplied and filled—
Her sweet perfections—with one self king!—
Away before me to sweet beds of flowers:
Love-thoughts lie rich when canopied with bowers.
                                                 [Exeunt

Scene II.—The Sea-coast

Enter Viola, Captain *and Sailors*

    Vio. What country, friends, is this?
    Cap.   Illyria, lady.
    Vio. And what should I do in Illyria?
My brother he is in Elysium.
Perchance, he is not drowned:—what think you, sailors?
    Cap. It is perchance that you yourself were saved.
    Vio. O my poor brother! and so, perchance, may he be.
    Cap. True, madam: and, to comfort you with chance,
Assure yourself, after your ship did split,
When you, and this poor number saved with you,
Hung on our driving boat, I saw your brother,
Most provident in peril, bind himself—
Courage and hope both teaching him the practice—
To a strong mast that lived upon the sea;
Where, like Arion on the dolphin's back,
I saw him hold acquaintance with the waves
So long as I could see.
    Vio.   For saying so, there 's gold.
Mine own escape unfoldeth to my hope—
Whereto thy speech serves for authority—
The like of him. Know'st thou this country?
    Cap. Ay, madam, well; for I was bred and born
Not three hours' travel from this very place.
    Vio. Who governs here?
    Cap. A noble duke, in nature as in name.
    Vio. What is his name?
    Cap.   Orsino.
    Vio. Orsino! I have heard my father name him:
He was a bachelor then.
    Cap. And so is now, or was so very late;

For but a month ago I went from hence,
And then 't was fresh in murmur—as, you know,
What great ones do, the less will prattle of—
That he did seek the love of fair Olivia.
   Vio.   What 's she?
   Cap.   A virtuous maid, the daughter of a count
That died some twelvemonth since, then leaving her
In the protection of his son, her brother,
Who shortly also died; for whose dear loss,
They say, she hath abjured the company
And sight of men.
   Vio.   O, that I served that lady,
And might not be delivered to the world,
Till I had made mine own occasion mellow,
What my estate is.
   Cap.   That were hard to compass;
Because she will admit no kind of suit,
No, not the duke's.
   Vio.   There is a fair behaviour in thee, captain;
And though that nature with a beauteous wall
Doth oft close-in pollution, yet of thee
I will believe, thou hast a mind that suits
With this thy fair and outward character.
I prithee,—and I 'll pay thee bounteously,—
Conceal me what I am; and be my aid
For such disguise as haply shall become
The form of my intent.   I 'll serve this duke:
Thou shalt present me as an eunuch to him:
It may be worth thy pains; for I can sing,
And speak to him in many sorts of music,
That will allow me very worth his service.
What else may hap, to time I will commit;
Only shape thou thy silence to my wit.
   Cap.   Be you his eunuch, and your mute I 'll be.
When my tongue blabs, then let mine eyes not see.
   Vio.   I thank thee. Lead me on.   *[Exeunt*

SCENE III.—A Room in OLIVIA'S House

Enter SIR TOBY BELCH *and* MARIA

   Sir To.   What a plague means my niece, to take the
death of her brother thus? I am sure care 's an enemy
to life.
   Mar.   By my troth, Sir Toby, you must come in earlier
o' nights: your cousin, my lady, takes great exceptions
to your ill hours.
   Sir To.   Why, let her except before excepted.

Mar. Ay, but you must confine yourself within the modest limits of order.

Sir To. Confine? I 'll confine myself no finer than I am. These clothes are good enough to drink in; and so be these boots too,—an they be not, let them hang themselves in their own straps.

Mar. That quaffing and drinking will undo you: I heard my lady talk of it yesterday; and of a foolish knight that you brought in one night here to be her wooer.

Sir To. Who? Sir Andrew Ague-cheek?

Mar. Ay, he.

Sir To. He 's as tall a man as any 's in Illyria.

Mar. What 's that to the purpose?

Sir To. Why, he has three thousand ducats a year.

Mar. Ay, but he'll have but a year in all these ducats; he 's a very fool, and a prodigal.

Sir To. Fie, that you 'll say so! he plays o' the viol-de-gamboys, and speaks three or four languages word for word without book, and hath all the good gifts of nature.

Mar. He hath, indeed,—almost natural; for, besides that he 's a fool, he 's a great quarreller; and, but that he hath the gift of a coward to allay the gust he hath in quarrelling, 't is thought among the prudent he would quickly have the gift of a grave.

Sir To. By this hand, they are scoundrels and substractors that say so of him. Who are they?

Mar. They that add, moreover, he 's drunk nightly in your company.

Sir To. With drinking healths to my niece. I 'll drink to her as long as there is a passage in my throat, and drink in Illyria. He 's a coward and a coystrel that will not drink to my niece till his brains turn o' the toe like a parish-top. What, wench! *Castiliano vulgo;* for here comes Sir Andrew Ague-face.

Enter SIR ANDREW AGUE-CHEEK

Sir And. Sir Toby Belch, how now, Sir Toby Belch?

Sir To. Sweet Sir Andrew!

Sir And. Bless you, fair shrew.

Mar. And you too, sir.

Sir To. Accost, Sir Andrew, accost.

Sir And. What 's that?

Sir To. My niece's chambermaid.

Sir And. Good Mistress Accost, I desire better acquaintance.

Mar. My name is Mary, sir.

Sir And. Good Mistress Mary Accost,—

Sir To. You mistake, knight; "accost" is front her, board her, woo her, assail her.

Sir And. By my troth, I would not undertake her in this company. Is that the meaning of "accost"?

Mar. Fare you well, gentlemen.

Sir To. An thou let her part so, Sir Andrew, would thou mightest never draw sword again!

Sir And. An you part so, mistress, I would I might never draw sword again. Fair lady, do you think you have fools in hand?

Mar. Sir, I have not you by the hand.

Sir And. Marry, but you shall have: and here's my hand.

Mar. Now, sir, thought is free. I pray you, bring your hand to the buttery-bar, and let it drink.

Sir And. Wherefore, sweet-heart? what 's your metaphor?

Mar. It 's dry, sir.

Sir And. Why, I think so: I am not such an ass, but I can keep my hand dry. But what's your jest?

Mar. A dry jest, sir.

Sir And. Are you full of them?

Mar. Ay, sir; I have them at my fingers' ends: marry, now I let go your hand, I am barren.   [*Exit Maria*

Sir To. O knight, thou lack'st a cup of canary. When did I see thee so put down?

Sir And. Never in your life, I think; unless you saw canary put me down. Methinks sometimes I have no more wit than a Christian, or an ordinary man has: but I am a great eater of beef, and I believe that does harm to my wit.

Sir To. No question.

Sir And. An I thought that, I 'd forswear it.—I 'll ride home to-morrow, Sir Toby.

Sir To. *Pourquoi*, my dear knight?

Sir And. What is *pourquoi*? do or not do? I would I had bestowed that time in the tongues that I have in fencing, dancing, and bear-baiting. O, had I but followed the arts!

Sir To. Then hadst thou had an excellent head of hair.

Sir And. Why, would that have mended my hair?

Sir To. Past question; for thou seest it will not curl by nature.

Sir And. But it becomes me well enough, does 't not?

Sir To. Excellent; it hangs like flax on a distaff, and I hope to see a housewife take thee between her legs and spin it off.

Sir And. 'Faith, I 'll home to-morrow Sir Toby: your niece will not be seen; or if she be, it 's four to one she 'll none of me. The count himself, here hard by, woos her.

Sir To. She 'll none o' the count; she 'll not match above her degree, neither in estate, years, nor wit; I have heard her swear it. Tut, there 's life in 't, man.

Sir And. I'll stay a month longer. I am a fellow o' the strangest mind i' the world: I delight in masques and revels sometimes altogether.

Sir To. Art thou good at these kick-shaws, knight?

Sir And. As any man in Illyria, whatsoever he be under the degree of my betters: and yet I will not compare with an old man.

Sir To. What is thy excellence in a galliard, knight?

Sir And. 'Faith, I can cut a caper.

Sir To. And I can cut the mutton to 't.

Sir And. And I think I have the back-trick simply as strong as any man in Illyria.

Sir To. Wherefore are these things hid? wherefore have these gifts a curtain before them? are they like to take dust, like Mistress Mall's picture? why dost thou not go to church in a galliard, and come home in a coranto? My very walk should be a jig: I would not so much as make water but in a sink-a-pace. What dost thou mean? is it a world to hide virtues in? I did think, by the excellent constitution of thy leg, it was formed under the star of a galliard.

Sir And. Ay, 't is strong, and does indifferent well in a flame-coloured stock. Shall we set about some revels?

Sir To. What shall we do else? were we not born under Taurus?

Sir And. Taurus? that 's sides and heart.

Sir To. No, sir, it is legs and thighs. Let me see thee caper. [*Sir Andrew dances*] Ha! higher: ha, ha!— excellent!   [*Exeunt*

SCENE IV.—A Room in the DUKE'S Palace

Enter VALENTINE, *and* VIOLA *in man's attire*

Val. If the duke continue these favours towards you, Cesario, you are like to be much advanced: he hath known you but three days, and already you are no stranger.

Vio. You either fear his humour or my negligence, that you call in question the continuance of his love. Is he inconstant, sir, in his favours?

Val. No, believe me.

Vio. I thank you. Here comes the count.

Enter DUKE, CURIO, *and Attendants*

Duke. Who saw Cesario, ho?

Vio. On your attendance, my lord; here.

Duke.   Stand you awhile aloof.—Cesario,
Thou know'st no less but all; I have unclasped
To thee the book even of my secret soul:
Therefore, good youth, address thy gait unto her;
Be not denied access, stand at her doors,
And tell them, there thy fixéd foot shall grow
Till thou have audience.
Vio.   Sure, my noble lord,
If she be so abandoned to her sorrow
As it is spoke, she never will admit me.
Duke.   Be clamorous, and leap all civil bounds
Rather than make unprofited return.
Vio.   Say, I do speak with her, my lord, what then?
Duke.   O, then unfold the passion of my love.
Surprise her with discourse of my dear faith:
It shall become thee well to act my woes;
She will attend it better in thy youth
Than in a nuncio of more grave aspect.
Vio.   I think not so, my lord.
Duke.   Dear lad, believe it;
For they shall yet belie thy happy years
That say thou art a man: Diana's lip
Is not more smooth and rubious; thy small pipe
Is as the maiden's organ, shrill in sound,
And all is semblative a woman's part.
I know, thy constellation is right apt
For this affair:—some four, or five, attend him;
All, if you will; for I myself am best
When least in company.—Prosper well in this,
And thou shalt live as freely as thy lord,
To call his fortunes thine.
Vio.   I 'll do my best
To woo your lady:—[*aside*] yet, a barful strife!
Whoe'er I woo, myself would be his wife.   [*Exeunt*

SCENE V.—A Room in OLIVIA'S House

Enter MARIA *and Clown*

Mar.   Nay, either tell me where thou hast been, or I
will not open my lips so wide as a bristle may enter, in way
of thy excuse.   My lady will hang thee for thy absence.
Clo.   Let her hang me: he that is well hanged in this
world needs to fear no colours.
Mar.   Make that good.
Clo.   He shall see none to fear.
Mar.   A good lenten answer.   I can tell thee where
that saying was born, of—I fear no colours.

Clo. Where, good Mistress Mary?

Mar. In the wars; and that may you be bold to say in your foolery.

Clo. Well, God give them wisdom that have it; and those that are fools, let them use their talents.

Mar. Yet you will be hanged for being so long absent; or, to be turned away,—is not that as good as a hanging to you?

Clo. Many a good hanging prevents a bad marriage; and, for turning away, let summer bear it out.

Mar. You are resolute, then?

Clo. Not so, neither; but I am resolved on two points.

Mar. That if one break the other will hold; or, if both break, your gaskins fall.

Clo. Apt, in good faith; very apt. Well, go thy way: if Sir Toby would leave drinking, thou wert as witty a piece of Eve's flesh as any in Illyria.

Mar. Peace, you rogue, no more o' that. Here comes my lady: make your excuse wisely, you were best. [*Exit*

Clo. Wit, an 't be thy will, put me into good fooling! Those wits that think they have thee, do very oft prove fools; and I, that am sure I lack thee, may pass for a wise man: for what says Quinapalus? Better a witty fool than a foolish wit.

Enter OLIVIA *and* MALVOLIO

God bless thee, lady!

Oli. Take the fool away.

Clo. Do you not hear, fellows? Take away the lady.

Oli. Go to, you 're a dry fool; I 'll no more of you: besides, you grow dishonest.

Clo. Two faults, madonna, that drink and good counsel will amend: for give the dry fool drink, then is the fool not dry; bid the dishonest man mend himself: if he mend, he is no longer dishonest; if he cannot, let the botcher mend him: anything that 's mended is but patched: virtue that transgresses is but patched with sin; and sin that amends is but patched with virtue. If that this simple syllogism will serve, so; if it will not, what remedy? As there is no true cuckold but calamity, so beauty 's a flower.—The lady bade take away the fool; therefore, I say again, take her away.

Oli. Sir, I bade them take away you.

Clo. Misprision in the highest degree!—Lady, *cucullus non facit monachum;* that 's as much to say as, I wear not motley in my brain. Good madonna, give me leave to prove you a fool.

Oli. Can you do it?

Clo. Dexteriously, good madonna.

Oli. Make your proof.

Clo. I must catechise you for it, madonna. Good my mouse of virtue, answer me.

Oli. Well, sir, for want of other idleness, I'll bide your proof.

Clo. Good madonna, why mourn'st thou?

Oli. Good fool, for my brother's death.

Clo. I think his soul is in hell, madonna.

Oli. I know his soul is in heaven, fool.

Clo. The more fool, madonna, to mourn for your brother's soul being in heaven.—Take away the fool, gentlemen.

Oli. What think you of this fool, Malvolio? doth he not mend?

Mal. Yes, and shall do, till the pangs of death shake him: infirmity, that decays the wise, doth ever make the better fool.

Clo. God send you, sir, a speedy infirmity, for the better increasing your folly; Sir Toby will be sworn that I am no fox; but he will not pass his word for twopence that you are no fool.

Oli. How say you to that, Malvolio?

Mal. I marvel your ladyship takes delight in such a barren rascal: I saw him put down the other day with an ordinary fool that has no more brain than a stone. Look you now, he's out of his guard already; unless you laugh and minister occasion to him, he is gagged. I protest, I take these wise men that crow so at these set kind of fools, no better than the fools' zanies.

Oli. O, you are sick of self-love, Malvolio, and taste with a distempered appetite. To be generous, guiltless, and of free disposition, is to take those things for bird-bolts that you deem cannon-bullets. There is no slander in an allowed fool, though he do nothing but rail; nor no railing in a known discreet man, though he do nothing but reprove.

Clo. Now, Mercury endue thee with leasing, for thou speakest well of fools.

Re-enter MARIA

Mar. Madam, there is at the gate a young gentleman much desires to speak with you.

Oli. From the Count Orsino, is it?

Mar. I know not, madam: 't is a fair young man, and well attended.

Oli. Who of my people hold him in delay?

Mar. Sir Toby, madam, your kinsman.

Oli. Fetch him off, I pray you; he speaks nothing

103

but madman: fie on him! [*Exit Maria*] Go you, Malvolio:
if it be a suit from the count, I am sick, or not at home;
what you will, to dismiss it. [*Exit Malvolio*]—Now
you see, sir, how your fooling grows old, and people dis-
like it.

Clo. Thou hast spoke for us, madonna, as if thy eldest
son should be a fool,—whose skull Jove cram with brains!
for here comes one of thy kin has a most weak *pia mater*.

Enter SIR TOBY BELCH

Oli. By mine honour, half drunk.—What is he at the
gate, cousin?

Sir To. A gentleman.

Oli. A gentleman! what gentleman?

Sir To. 'T is a gentleman here—a plague o' these
pickle-herring!—How now, sot?

Clo. Good Sir Toby!—

Oli. Cousin, cousin, how have you come so early by
this lethargy?

Sir To. Lechery! I defy lechery. There 's one at the
gate.

Oli. Ay, marry; what is he?

Sir To. Let him be the devil, and he will, I care not:
give me faith, say I. Well, it 's all one. [*Exit*

Oli. What 's a drunken man like, fool?

Clo. Like a drowned man, a fool, and a madman: one
draught above heat makes him a fool; the second mads
him; and a third drowns him.

Oli. Go thou and seek the crowner, and let him sit o'
my coz; for he 's in the third degree of drink,—he 's
drowned: go, look after him.

Clo. He is but mad yet, madonna; and the fool shall
look to the madman. [*Exit*

Re-enter MALVOLIO

Mal. Madam, yond young fellow swears he will speak
with you. I told him you were sick; he takes on him to
understand so much, and therefore comes to speak with
you: I told him you were asleep; he seems to have a
foreknowledge of that too, and therefore comes to speak
with you. What is to be said to him, lady? he 's fortified
against any denial.

Oli. Tell him, he shall not speak with me.

Mal. 'Has been told so; and he says, he 'll stand at
your door like a sheriff's post, and be the supporter to a
bench, but he 'll speak with you.

Oli. What kind o' man is he?

Mal. Why, of man kind.

Oli.   What manner of man?
Mal.   Of very ill manner; he 'll speak with you, will you or no.
Oli.   Of what personage and years is he?
Mal.   Not yet old enough for a man, nor young enough for a boy; as a squash is before 't is a peascod, or a codling when 't is almost an apple: 't is with him e'en standing water, between boy and man.   He is very well-favoured, and he speaks very shrewishly; one would think his mother's milk were scarce out of him.
Oli.   Let him approach: call in my gentlewoman.
Mal.   Gentlewoman, my lady calls.   [*Exit*

Re-enter MARIA

Oli.   Give me my veil: come, throw it o'er my face.
We'll once more hear Orsino's embassy.

Enter VIOLA

Vio.   The honourable lady of the house, which is she?
Oli.   Speak to me; I shall answer for her.   Your will?
Vio.   Most radiant, exquisite, and unmatchable beauty,
—I pray you, tell me, if this be the lady of the house, for I never saw her: I would be loath to cast away my speech; for, besides that it is excellently well penned, I have taken great pains to con it.   Good beauties, let me sustain no scorn; I am very comptible even to the least sinister usage.
Oli.   Whence came you, sir?
Vio.   I can say little more than I have studied, and that question 's out of my part.   Good gentle one, give me modest assurance if you be the lady of the house, that I may proceed in my speech.
Oli.   Are you a comedian?
Vio.   No, my profound heart; and yet, by the very fangs of malice I swear I am not that I play.   Are you the lady of the house?
Oli.   If I do not usurp myself, I am.
Vio.   Most certain, if you are she, you do usurp yourself; for what is yours to bestow is not yours to reserve. But this is from my commission: I will on with my speech in your praise, and then show you the heart of my message.
Oli.   Come to what is important in 't: I forgive you the praise.
Vio.   Alas! I took great pains to study it, and 't is poetical.
Oli.   It is the more like to be feigned: I pray you, keep it in.   I heard you were saucy at my gates, and allowed your approach rather to wonder at you than to hear you. If you be not mad, be gone; if you have reason, be brief:

't is not that time of moon with me to make one in so skipping a dialogue.

Mar. Will you hoist sail, sir? here lies your way.

Vio. No, good swabber; I am to hull here a little longer.—Some mollification for your giant, sweet lady.

Oli. Tell me your mind.

Vio. I am a messenger.

Oli. Sure, you have some hideous matter to deliver, when the courtesy of it is so fearful. Speak your office.

Vio. It alone concerns your ear. I bring no overture of war, no taxation of homage: I hold the olive in my hand; my words are as full of peace as matter.

Oli. Yet you began rudely. What are you? what would you?

Vio. The rudeness that hath appeared in me, have I learned from my entertainment. What I am, and what I would, are as secret as maidenhead: to your ears, divinity; to any other's profanation.

Oli. Give us the place alone: we will hear this divinity. [*Exit Maria*] Now, sir, what is your text?

Vio. Most sweet lady,—

Oli. A comfortable doctrine, and much may be said of it. Where lies your text?

Vio. In Orsino's bosom.

Oli. In his bosom! In what chapter of his bosom?

Vio. To answer by the method, in the first of his heart.

Oli. O, I have read it: it is heresy. Have you no more to say?

Vio. Good madam, let me see your face.

Oli. Have you any commission from your lord to negotiate with my face? You are now out of your text: but we will draw the curtain, and show you the picture. Look you, sir; such a one I was this present: is 't not well done? [*Unveiling*

Vio. Excellently done, if God did all.

Oli. 'T is in grain, sir; 't will endure wind and weather.

Vio. 'T is beauty truly blent, whose red and white
Nature's own sweet and cunning hand laid on.
Lady, you are the cruell'st she alive,
If you will lead these graces to the grave
And leave the world no copy.

Oli. O, sir, I will not be so hard-hearted; I will give out divers schedules of my beauty: it shall be inventoried, and every particle and utensil labelled to my will:—as, item, two lips indifferent red; item, two grey eyes with lids to them; item, one neck, one chin, and so forth. Were you sent hither to praise me?

Vio. I see you, what you are,—you are too proud;
But, if you were the devil, you are fair.

My lord and master loves you: O, such love
Could be but recompensed, though you were crowned
The nonpareil of beauty!
    Oli.   How does he love me?
    Vio. With adorations, with fertile tears,
With groans that thunder love, with sighs of fire.
    Oli.   Your lord does know my mind; I cannot love him:
Yet I suppose him virtuous, know him noble:
Of great estate, of fresh and stainless youth;
In voices well divulged, free, learned, and valiant;
And in dimension and the shape of nature,
A gracious person: but yet I cannot love him;
He might have took his answer long ago.
    Vio. If I did love you in my master's flame,
With such a suffering, such a deadly life,
In your denial I would find no sense:
I would not understand it.
    Oli.   Why, what would you?
    Vio. Make me a willow cabin at your gate,
And call upon my soul within the house;
Write loyal cantons of contemnéd love,
And sing them loud even in the dead of night;
Holla your name to the reverberate hills,
And make the babbling gossip of the air
Cry out, "Olivia!" O, you should not rest
Between the elements of air and earth,
But you should pity me.
    Oli. You might do much. What is your parentage?
    Vio. Above my fortunes, yet my state is well:
I am a gentleman.
    Oli.   Get you to your lord:
I cannot love him: let him send no more;—
Unless, perchance, you come to me again,
To tell me how he takes it. Fare you well:
I thank you for your pains: spend this for me.
    Vio. I am no fee'd post, lady; keep your purse:
My master, not myself, lacks recompense.
Love make his heart of flint that you shall love;
And let your fervour, like my master's, be
Placed in contempt! Farewell, fair cruelty.   *[Exit*
    Oli. "What is your parentage?"
"Above my fortunes, yet my state is well:
I am a gentleman."—I 'll be sworn thou art;
Thy tongue, thy face, thy limbs, actions, and spirit,
Do give thee five-fold blazon:—not too fast;—soft! soft!
Unless the master were the man.—How now!
Even so quickly may one catch the plague?
Methinks, I feel this youth's perfections
With an invisible and subtle stealth

To creep in at mine eyes.—Well, let it be.—
What, ho! Malvolio.

Re-enter MALVOLIO

Mal.   Here, madam, at your service.
  Oli.   Run after that same peevish messenger,
The county's man: he left this ring behind him,
Would I or not: tell him, I 'll none of it.
Desire him not to flatter with his lord,
Nor hold him up with hopes; I am not for him:
If that the youth will come this way to-morrow,
I 'll give him reasons for 't. Hie thee, Malvolio.
  Mal. Madam, I will.   [*Exit*
  Oli.   I do I know not what, and fear to find
Mine eye too great a flatterer for my mind.
Fate, show thy force: ourselves we do not owe;
What is decreed must be,—and be this so!   [*Exit*

ACT TWO

SCENE I.—The Sea-coast

Enter ANTONIO *and* SEBASTIAN

  Ant. Will you stay no longer? nor will you not that I
go with you?
  Seb. By your patience, no. My stars shine darkly
over me: the malignancy of my fate might, perhaps, distemper yours; therefore, I shall crave of you your leave,
that I may bear my evils alone. It were a bad recompense
for your love, to lay any of them on you.
  Ant. Let me yet know of you whither you are bound.
  Seb. No, sooth, sir. My determinate voyage is mere
extravagancy. But I perceive in you so excellent a touch
of modesty, that you will not extort from me what I am
willing to keep in; therefore, it charges me in manners the
rather to express myself. You must know of me then,
Antonio, my name is Sebastian, which I called Roderigo.
My father was that Sebastian of Messaline, whom I know
you have heard of. He left behind him myself and a sister,
both born in an hour: if the heavens had been pleased,
would we had so ended! but you, sir, altered that; for
some hour before you took me from the breach of the sea
was my sister drowned.
  Ant. Alas the day!
  Seb. A lady, sir, though it was said she much resembled
me, was yet of many accounted beautiful: but, though

I could not, with such estimable wonder, overfar believe that, yet thus far I will boldly publish her,—she bore a mind that envy could not but call fair. She is drowned already, sir, with salt water, though I seem to drown her remembrance again with more.

Ant. Pardon me, sir, your bad entertainment.

Seb. O good Antonio, forgive me your trouble.

Ant. If you will not murder me for my love, let me be your servant.

Seb. If you will not undo what you have done, that is, kill him whom you have recovered, desire it not. Fare ye well at once: my bosom is full of kindness; and I am yet so near the manners of my mother, that, upon the least occasion more, mine eyes will tell tales of me. I am bound to the Count Orsino's court: farewell.   [*Exit*

Ant. The gentleness of all the gods go with thee!
I have many enemies in Orsino's court,
Else would I very shortly see thee there;
But, come what may, I do adore thee so,
That danger shall seem sport, and I will go.   [*Exit*

SCENE II.—A Street

Enter VIOLA; MALVOLIO *following*

Mal. Were not you even now with the Countess Olivia?

Vio. Even now, sir; on a moderate pace I have since arrived but hither.

Mal. She returns this ring to you, sir: you might have saved me my pains, to have taken it away yourself. She adds, moreover, that you should put your lord into a desperate assurance she will none of him. And one thing more, that you be never so hardy to come again in his affairs, unless it be to report your lord's taking of this. Receive it so.

Vio. She took the ring of me;—I 'll none of it.

Mal. Come, sir; you peevishly threw it to her; and her will is, it should be so returned: if it be worth stooping for there it lies in your eye; if not, be it his that finds it.   [*Exit*

Vio. I left no ring with her: what means this lady?
Fortune forbid my outside have not charmed her!
She made good view of me; indeed, so much,
That, as methought, her eyes had lost her tongue,
For she did speak in starts distractedly.
She loves me, sure: the cunning of her passion
Invites me in this churlish messenger.
None of my lord's ring! why, he sent her none.
I am the man:—If it be so,—as 't is,—

Poor lady, she were better love her dream.
Disguise, I see, thou art a wickedness,
Wherein the pregnant enemy does much.
How easy is it for the proper-false
In women's waxen hearts to set their forms!
Alas, our frailty is the cause, not we,
For such as we are made of, such we be.—
How will this fadge? My master loves her dearly;
And I, poor monster, fond as much on him
As she, mistaken, seems to dote on me.
What will become of this? As I am man,
My state is desperate for my master's love;
As I am woman,—now alas the day!—
What thriftless sighs shall poor Olivia breathe!
O Time, thou must untangle this, not I;
It is too hard a knot for me to untie.   [*Exit*

Scene III.—A Room in Olivia's House

Enter Sir Toby Belch *and* Sir Andrew Ague-cheek

Sir To. Approach, Sir Andrew: not to be a-bed after midnight is to be up betimes; and *diluculo surgere,* thou knowest,—
Sir And. Nay, by my troth, I know not: but I know, to be up late, is to be up late.
Sir To. A false conclusion: I hate it as an unfilled can. To be up after midnight, and to go to bed then, is early: so that, to go to bed after midnight, is to go to bed betimes. Does not our life consist of the four elements?
Sir And. Faith, so they say; but I think, it rather consists of eating and drinking.
Sir To. Thou 'rt a scholar: let us therefore eat and drink.—Maria, I say!—a stoop of wine!
Sir And. Here comes the fool, i' faith.

Enter Clown

Clo. How now, my hearts! Did you never see the picture of We Three?
Sir To. Welcome, ass. Now let 's have a catch.
Sir And. By my troth, the fool has an excellent breast. I had rather than forty shillings I had such a leg, and so sweet a breath to sing, as the fool has. In sooth, thou wast in very gracious fooling last night when thou spokest of Pigrogromitus, of the Vapians passing the equinoctial of Queubus: 't was very good, i' faith. I sent thee sixpence for thy leman: hadst it?

Clo. I did impeticos thy gratillity; for Malvolio's nose is no whipstock; my lady has a white hand, and the Myrmidons are no bottle-ale houses.

Sir And. Excellent! Why, this is the best fooling, when all is done. Now, a song.

Sir To. Come on; there is sixpence for you: let 's have a song.

Sir And. There's a testril of me too: if one knight give a——

Clo. Would you have a love-song, or a song of good life?

Sir To. A love-song, a love-song.

Sir And. Ay, ay; I care not for good life.

Song

Clo.   *O mistress mine ! where are you roaming ?*
          O, stay and hear : your true love 's coming,
              That can sing both high and low ;
          Trip no farther, pretty sweeting ;
          Journeys end in lovers' meeting,
              Every wise man's son doth know.

Sir And. Excellent good, i' faith.

Sir To. Good, good.

Clo.   *What is love ? 't is not hereafter ;*
          Present mirth hath present laughter ;
              What 's to come is still unsure ;
          In delay there lies no plenty ;
          Then come kiss me, sweet-and-twenty,
              Youth's a stuff will not endure.

Sir And. A mellifluous voice, as I am true knight.

Sir To. A contagious breath.

Sir And. Very sweet and contagious, i' faith.

Sir To. To hear by the nose, it is dulcet in contagion. But shall we make the welkin dance indeed? Shall we rouse the night-owl in a catch that will draw three souls out of one weaver? shall we do that?

Sir And. An you love me, let 's do 't: I am dog at a catch.

Clo. By 'r lady, sir, and some dogs will catch well.

Sir And. Most certain. Let our catch be, *Thou knave.*

Clo. *Hold thy peace, thou knave,* knight? I shall be constrained in 't to call thee knave, knight.

Sir And. 'T is not the first time I have constrained one to call me knave. Begin, fool: it begins, *Hold thy peace.*

Clo. I shall never begin, if I hold my peace.

Sir And. Good, i' faith. Come, begin.

                                            [*They sing the catch*

111

Enter MARIA

Mar. What a caterwauling do you keep here! If my lady have not called up her steward Malvolio and bid him turn you out of doors, never trust me.

Sir To. My lady 's a Cataian; we are politicians; Malvolio 's a Peg-a-Ramsey, and *Three merry men be we.* Am not I consanguineous? am I not of her blood? Tilly-vally, lady! [*Sings*] *There dwelt a man in Babylon, lady, lady!*

Clo. Beshrew me, the knight 's in admirable fooling.

Sir And. Ay, he does well enough, if he be disposed, and so do I too: he does it with a better grace, but I do it more natural.

Sir To. [*Sings*] *O, the twelfth day of December,*—

Mar. For the love o' God, peace!

Enter MALVOLIO

Mal. My masters, are you mad? or what are you? Have you no wit, manners, nor honesty, but to gabble like tinkers at this time of night? Do ye make an ale-house of my lady 's house, that ye squeak out your coziers' catches without any mitigation or remorse of voice? Is there no respect of place, persons, nor time, in you?

Sir To. We did keep time, sir, in our catches. Snick-up!

Mal. Sir Toby, I must be round with you. My lady bade me tell you, that, though she harbours you as her kinsman, she's nothing allied to your disorders. If you can separate yourself and your misdemeanours, you are welcome to the house; if not, an it would please you to take leave of her, she is very willing to bid you farewell.

Sir To. Farewell, dear heart, since I must needs be gone.

Mar. Nay, good Sir Toby.

Clo. His eyes do show, his days are almost done.

Mal. Is 't even so?

Sir. To. But I will never die.

Clo. Sir Toby, there you lie.

Mal. This is much credit to you.

Sir To. Shall I bid him go?

Clo. What an if you do?

Sir To. Shall I bid him go, and spare not?

Clo. O, no, no, no, no, you dare not.

Sir To. Out o' time!—Sir, ye lie. Art any more than a steward? Dost thou think, because thou art virtuous, there shall be no more cakes and ale?

Clo. Yes, by Saint Anne; and ginger shall be hot i' the mouth too.

Sir To. Thou 'rt i' the right.—Go, sir, rub your chain with crumbs.—A stoop of wine, Maria!

Mal. Mistress Mary, if you prized my lady's favour at anything more than contempt, you would not give means for this uncivil rule: she shall know of it, by this hand.   [*Exit*

Mar. Go shake your ears.

Sir And. 'T were as good a deed as to drink when a man 's a-hungry, to challenge him the field, and then to break promise with him, and make a fool of him.

Sir To. Do 't, knight: I 'll write thee a challenge; or I 'll deliver thy indignation to him by word of mouth.

Mar. Sweet Sir Toby, be patient for to-night. Since the youth of the count's was to-day with my lady, she is much out of quiet. For Monsieur Malvolio, let me alone with him: if I do not gull him into a nay-word, and make him a common recreation do not think I have wit enough to lie straight in my bed; I know, I can do it.

Sir To. Possess us, possess us; tell us something of him.

Mar. Marry, sir, sometimes he is a kind of puritan.

Sir And. O, if I thought that, I 'd beat him like a dog.

Sir To. What, for being a puritan! thy exquisite reason, dear knight?

Sir And. I have no exquisite reason for 't, but I have reason good enough.

Mar. The devil a puritan that he is, or anything constantly, but a time-pleaser; an affectioned ass, that cons state without book, and utters it by great swaths: the best persuaded of himself, so crammed, as he thinks, with excellences, that it is his ground of faith that all that look on him love him: and on that vice in him will my revenge find notable cause to work.

Sir To. What wilt thou do?

Mar. I will drop in his way some obscure epistles of love; wherein, by the colour of his beard, the shape of his leg, the manner of his gait, the expressure of his eye, forehead, and complexion, he shall find himself most feelingly personated: I can write very like my lady, your niece; on a forgotten matter we can hardly make distinction of our hands.

Sir To. Excellent! I smell a device.

Sir And. I have 't in my nose too.

Sir To. He shall think, by the letters that thou wilt drop, that they come from my niece, and that she 's in love with him?

Mar. My purpose is, indeed, a horse of that colour.

Sir And. And your horse, now, would make him an ass.

Mar. Ass, I doubt not.

Sir And. O! 'twill be admirable.

Mar. Sport royal, I warrant you: I know, my physic will work with him.   I will plant you two and let the fool make a third, where he shall find the letter: observe his construction of it.   For this night, to bed, and dream on the event.   Farewell.

Sir To. Good night, Penthesilea.   *[Exit Maria*

Sir And. Before me, she 's a good wench.

Sir To. She 's a beagle, true-bred, and one that adores me: what o' that?

Sir And. I was adored once too.

Sir To. Let 's to bed, knight.—Thou hadst need send for more money.

Sir And. If I cannot recover your niece, I am a foul way out.

Sir To. Send for money, knight: if thou hast her not i' the end, call me cut.

Sir And. If I do not, never trust me, take it how you will.

Sir To. Come, come; I 'll go burn some sack; 't is too late to go to bed now: come, knight; come, knight.

                                                           [Exeunt

Scene IV.—A Room in the Duke's Palace

Enter Duke, Viola, Curio, *and others*

Duke. Give me some music:—now, good morrow, friends:—

Now, good Cesario, but that piece of song,
That old and antique song we heard last night;
Methought it did relieve my passion much,
More than light airs and recollected terms
Of these most brisk and giddy-pacéd times:
Come, but one verse.

Cur. He is not here, so please your lordship, that should sing it.

Duke. Who was it?

Cur. Feste, the jester, my lord; a fool, that the lady Olivia's father took much delight in.   He is about the house.

Duke. Seek him out, and play the tune the while.

                                    [Exit Curio.—Music plays

Come hither, boy: if ever thou shalt love,
In the sweet pangs of it remember me;
For such as I am all true lovers are,—
Unstaid and skittish in all motions else,
Save in the constant image of the creature
That is beloved.—How dost thou like this tune?

Vio. It gives a very echo to the seat
Where love is throned.

Thou dost speak masterly.
My life upon 't, young though thou art, thine eye
Hath stayed upon some favour that it loves;
Hath it not, boy?
Vio.   A little, by your favour.
Duke. What kind of woman is 't?
Vio.   Of your complexion.
Duke. She is not worth thee then. What years, i'
    faith?
Vio. About your years, my lord.
Duke. Too old, by Heaven: let still the woman take
An elder than herself; so wears she to him,
So sways she level in her husband's heart:
For, boy, however we do praise ourselves,
Our fancies are more giddy and unfirm,
More longing, wavering, sooner lost and worn,
Than women's are.
Vio.   I think it well, my lord.
Duke. Then, let thy love be younger than thyself,
Or thy affection cannot hold the bent;
For women are as roses, whose fair flower,
Being once displayed, doth fall that very hour.
Vio. And so they are: alas, that they are so,—
To die, even when they to perfection grow!

Re-enter CURIO *and* Clown

Duke. O fellow, come, the song we had last night,—
Mark it, Cesario; it is old, and plain:
The spinsters and the knitters in the sun,
And the free maids that weave their thread with bones,
Do use to chant it: it is silly sooth,
And dallies with the innocence of love
Like the old age.
Clo. Are you ready, sir?
Duke. Ay; prithee, sing   [*Music*

SONG

Clo.   *Come away, come away, death,*
    And in sad cypress let me be laid;
        Fly away, fly away, breath;
    I am slain by a fair cruel maid.
    My shroud of white, stuck all with yew,
            O, prepare it:
    My part of death, no one so true
            Did share it.

    Not a flower, not a flower sweet,
    On my black coffin let there be strown:

Not a friend, not a friend greet
My poor corse, where my bones shall be thrown:
A thousand thousand sighs to save,
Lay me, O, where
Sad true lover never find my grave,
To weep there.

Duke. There 's for thy pains.
Clo. No pains, sir; I take pleasure in singing, sir.
Duke. I 'll pay thy pleasure then.
Clo. Truly, sir, and pleasure will be paid, one time or another.
Duke. Give me now leave to leave thee.
Clo. Now, the melancholy god protect thee; and the tailor make thy doublet of changeable taffeta, for thy mind is a very opal!—I would have men of such constancy put to sea, that their business might be everything, and their intent everywhere; for that 's it, that always makes a good voyage of nothing.—Farewell.   [*Exit*
Duke. Let all the rest give place.—
                              [*Exeunt Curio and Attendants*
Get thee to yond same sovereign cruelty:
Tell her, my love, more noble than the world,
Prizes not quantity of dirty lands;
The parts that Fortune hath bestowed upon her,
Tell her I hold as giddily as Fortune;
But 't is that miracle and queen of gems
That nature pranks her in attracts my soul.
   Vio. But if she cannot love you, sir?
   Duke. I cannot be so answered.
   Vio.   Sooth, but you must
Say, that some lady, as perhaps there is,
Hath for your love as great a pang of heart
As you have for Olivia: you cannot love her;
You tell her so; must she not then be answered?
   Duke. There is no woman's sides
Can bide the beating of so strong a passion
As love doth give my heart; no woman's heart
So big to hold so much: they lack retention.
Alas, their love may be called appetite,—
No motion of the liver, but the palate,—
That suffer surfeit, cloyment, and revolt;
But mine is all as hungry as the sea,
And can digest as much.   Make no compare
Between that love a woman can bear me,
And that I owe Olivia.
   Vio.   Ay, but I know—
   Duke. What dost thou know?
   Vio. Too well what love women to men may owe

In faith, they are as true of heart as we.
My father had a daughter loved a man,
As it might be, perhaps, were I a woman,
I should your lordship.
    Duke.   And what 's her history?
    Vio. A blank, my lord. She never told her love,
But let concealment, like a worm i' the bud,
Feed on her damask cheek: she pined in thought;
And, with a green and yellow melancholy,
She sat like Patience on a monument,
Smiling at grief. Was not this love indeed?
We men may say more, swear more, but, indeed,
Our shows are more than will, for still we prove
Much in our vows, but little in our love.
    Duke. But died thy sister of her love, my boy?
    Vio. I am all the daughters of my father's house,
And all the brothers too;—and yet I know not.—
Sir, shall I to this lady?
    Duke.   Ay, that 's the theme.
To her in haste: give her this jewel; say,
My love can give no place, bide no denay.

                              [Exeunt

SCENE V.—OLIVIA's Garden

Enter SIR TOBY BELCH, SIR ANDREW, *and* FABIAN

    Sir To. Come thy ways, Signior Fabian.
    Fab. Nay, I 'll come: if I lose a scruple of this sport,
let me be boiled to death with melancholy.
    Sir To. Wouldst thou not be glad to have the niggardly,
rascally sheep-biter come by some notable shame?
    Fab. I would exult, man: you know, he brought me
out o' favour with my lady about a bear-baiting here.
    Sir To. To anger him, we 'll have the bear again; and
we will fool him black and blue;—shall we not, Sir Andrew?
    Sir And. An we do not, it is pity of our lives.
    Sir To. Here comes the little villain.—

Enter MARIA

How now, my nettle of India?
    Mar. Get ye all three into the box tree: Malvolio 's
coming down this walk: he has been yonder i' the sun
practising behaviour to his own shadow this half-hour.
Observe him, for the love of mockery; for, I know, this
letter will make a contemplative idiot of him. Close, in

the name of jesting! [*The men hide themselves*] Lie thou
there [*throws down a letter*]; for here comes the trout that
must be caught with tickling.   [*Exit*

Enter MALVOLIO

Mal. 'T is but fortune; all is fortune. Maria once
told me she did affect me: and I have heard herself come
thus near, that, should she fancy, it should be one of my
complexion. Besides, she uses me with a more exalted
respect than any one else that follows her. What should I
think on 't?—

Sir To. Here 's an overweening rogue!

Fab. O, peace. Contemplation makes a rare turkey-
cock of him: how he jets under his advanced plumes!

Sir And. 'Slight, I could so beat the rogue!

Sir To. Peace, I say.—

Mal. To be Count Malvolio,—

Sir To. Ah, rogue!

Sir And. Pistol him, pistol him.

Sir To. Peace, peace!—

Mal. There is example for 't; the lady of the Strachy
married the yeoman of the wardrobe.—

Sir And. Fie on him, Jezebel!

Fab. O, peace! now he 's deeply in; look how imagination blows him.—

Mal. Having been three months married to her, sitting
in my state,—

Sir To. O, for a stone bow, to hit him in the eye!—

Mal. Calling my officers about me, in my branched
velvet gown; having come from a day-bed, where I have
left Olivia sleeping,—

Sir To. Fire and brimstone!

Fab. O, peace, peace!—

Mal. And then to have the humour of state; and after
a demure travel of regard,—telling them I know my place,
as I would they should do theirs—to ask for my kinsman
Toby.

Sir To. Bolts and shackles!

Fab. O, peace, peace, peace! now, now.—

Mal. Seven of my people, with an obedient start,
make out for him. I frown the while; and, perchance,
wind up my watch, or play with some rich jewel. Toby
approaches; court'sies there to me.—

Sir To. Shall this fellow live?

Fab. Though our silence be drawn from us by th' ears,
yet peace!—

Mal. I extend my hand to him thus, quenching my
familiar smile with an austere regard of control,—

Sir To. And does not Toby take you a blow o' the lips then?

Mal. Saying, "Cousin Toby, my fortunes having cast me on your niece, give me this prerogative of speech,"—

Sir. To. What, what?—

Mal. "You must amend your drunkenness."—

Sir To. Out, scab!

Fab. Nay, patience, or we break the sinews of our plot.—

Mal. "Besides, you waste the treasure of your time with a foolish knight,"—

Sir And. That's me, I warrant you.—

Mal. "One Sir Andrew,"—

Sir And. I knew 't was I; for many do call me fool.—

Mal. [*Seeing the letter*] What employment have we here?

Fab. Now is the woodcock near the gin.

Sir To. O, peace! and the spirit of humours intimate reading aloud to him!

Mal. [*Taking up the letter*] By my life, this is my lady's hand! these be her very *C's*, her *U's* and her *T's*; and thus makes she her great *P's.* It is, in contempt of question, her hand.

Sir And. Her *C's*, her *U's*, and her *T's*; why that?

Mal. [*Reads*] *To the unknown beloved, this, and my good wishes:* her very phrases!—By your leave, wax.—Soft!— and the impressure her Lucrece, with which she uses to seal: 't is my lady. To whom should this be?—

Fab. This wins him, liver and all.—

Mal. [*Reads*] *Jove knows, I love;*
            But who?
        Lips, do not move:
        No man must know.

No man must know. What follows? the number 's altered! *No man must know:* if this should be thee,—Malvolio?

Sir To. Marry, hang thee, brock!

Mal. [*Reads*] *I may command, where I adore;*
            But silence, like a Lucrece knife,
        With bloodless stroke my heart doth gore:
        M, O, A, I, doth sway my life.—

Fab. A fustian riddle.

Sir To. Excellent wench, say I.—

Mal. *M, O, A, I, doth sway my life.*
Nay, but first, let me see,—let me see.—

Fab. What a dish of poison has she dressed him!

Sir To. And with what wing the staniel checks at it!—

Mal. *I may command, where I adore.* Why, she may command me: I serve her: she is my lady. Why, this is evident to any formal capacity. There is no obstruction in this;—and the end,—what should that alphabetical

position portend? If I could make that resemble something in me,—Softly!—*M, O, A, I,*—

Sir To. O! ay! make up that. He is now at a cold
scent.

Fab. Sowter will cry upon 't, for all this, though it be
as rank as a fox.

Mal. *M,*—Malvolio:—*M,* why, that begins my name.

Fab. Did not I say, he would work it out? the cur
is excellent at faults.—

Mal. *M,*—but then there is no consonancy in the
sequel; that suffers under probation: *A* should follow,
but *O* does.—

Fab. And *O* shall end, I hope.

Sir To. Ay, or I'll cudgel him, and make him cry *O!*—

Mal. And then *I* comes behind.—

Fab. Ay, an you had an eye behind you, you might
see more detraction at your heels than fortunes before you.

Mal. *M, O, A, I:*—this simulation is not as the former:
—and yet, to crush this a little, it would bow to me, for
every one of these letters are in my name. Soft! here
follows prose.—[*Reads*] *If this fall into thy hand, revolve.
In my stars I am above thee, but be not afraid of greatness:
some are born great, some achieve greatness, and some have
greatness thrust upon them. Thy Fates open their hands;
let thy blood and spirit embrace themt and, to inure thyself
to what thou art like to be, cast thy humble slough, and appear
fresh. Be opposite with a kinsman, surly with servants; let
thy tongue tang arguments of state; put thyself into the trick of
singularity: she thus advises thee that sighs for thee. Remember who commended thy yellow stockings, and wished to
see thee ever cross-gartered; I say, remember. Go to, thou
art made if thou desirest to be so; if not, let me see thee a
steward still, the fellow of servants, and not worthy to touch
Fortune's fingers. Farewell. She that would alter services
with thee.*   The Fortunate-Unhappy.
Daylight and champain discover not more: this is open.
I will be proud, I will read politic authors, I will baffle
Sir Toby, I will wash off gross acquaintance, I will be point-
de-vise the very man. I do not now fool myself, to let
imagination jade me; for every reason excites to this, that
my lady loves me. She did commend my yellow stockings
of late; she did praise my leg being cross-gartered; and
in this she manifests herself to my love. and, with a kind
of injunction, drives me to these habits of her liking.
I thank my stars, I am happy. I will be strange, stout,
in yellow stockings, and cross-gartered, even with the
swiftness of putting on. Jove and my stars be praised!—
Here is yet a postscript. [*Reads*] *Thou canst not choose
but know who I am. If thou entertainest my love, let it*

appear in thy smiling: thy smiles become thee well; therefore in my presence still smile, dear my sweet, I prithee.—Jove, I thank thee.—I will smile; I will do everything that thou wilt have me.   *[Exit*

Fab. I will not give my part of this sport for a pension of thousands to be paid from the Sophy.

Sir To. I could marry this wench for this device,—

Sir And. So could I too.

Sir To. And ask no other dowry with her, but such another jest.

Sir And. Nor I neither.

Fab. Here comes my noble gull-catcher.

Re-enter MARIA

Sir To. Wilt thou set thy foot o' my neck?

Sir And. Or o' mine either?

Sir To. Shall I play my freedom at tray-trip, and become thy bond-slave?

Sir And. I' faith, or I either?

Sir To. Why, thou hast put him in such a dream, that when the image of it leaves him he must run mad.

Mar. Nay, but say true; does it work upon him?

Sir To. Like aqua-vitæ with a midwife.

Mar. If you will, then, see the fruits of the sport, mark his first approach before my lady: he will come to her in yellow stockings, and 't is a colour she abhors; and cross-gartered, a fashion she detests; and he will smile upon her, which will now be so unsuitable to her disposition, being addicted to a melancholy as she is, that it cannot but turn him into a notable contempt. If you will see it, follow me,

Sir To. To the gates of Tartar, thou most excellent devil of wit!

Sir And. I 'll make one too.   *[Exeunt*

ACT THREE

Scene I.—Olivia's Garden

Enter VIOLA, *and* Clown *with a tabor*

Vio. Save thee, friend, and thy music! dost thou live by thy tabor?

Clo. No, sir, I live by the church.

Vio. Art thou a churchman?

Clo. No such matter, sir: I do live by the church, for I do live at my house, and my house doth stand by the church.

Vio. So thou may'st say, the king lies by a beggar, if a beggar dwell near him; or, the church stands by thy tabor, if thy tabor stand by the church.

Clo. You have said, sir.—To see this age!—A sentence is but a cheveril glove to a good wit: how quickly the wrong side may be turned outward!

Vio. Nay, that's certain: they, that dally nicely with words, may quickly make them wanton.

Clo. I would therefore, my sister had had no name, sir.

Vio. Why, man?

Clo. Why, sir, her name 's a word; and to dally with that word might make my sister wanton. But, indeed, words are very rascals, since bonds disgraced them.

Vio. Thy reason, man?

Clo. Troth, sir, I can yield you none without words; and words are grown so false, I am loth to prove reason with them.

Vio. I warrant thou art a merry fellow, and carest for nothing.

Clo. Not so, sir, I do care for something; but in my conscience, sir, I do not care for you: if that be to care for nothing, sir, I would it would make you invisible.

Vio. Art not thou the Lady Olivia's fool?

Clo. No, indeed, sir; the Lady Olivia has no folly: she will keep no fool, sir, till she be married; and fools are like husbands as pilchards are to herrings,—the husband's the bigger: I am, indeed, not her fool, but her corrupter of words.

Vio. I saw thee late at the Count Orsino's.

Clo. Foolery, sir, does walk about the orb; like the sun: it shines everywhere. I would be sorry, sir, but the fool should be as oft with your master as with my mistress: I think I saw your wisdom there.

Vio. Nay, an thou pass upon me, I 'll no more with thee. Hold, there 's expenses for thee.

[*Gives a piece of money*

Clo. Now, Jove, in his next commodity of hair, send thee a beard!

Vio. By my troth, I'll tell thee,—I am almost sick for one; though I would not have it grow on my chin. Is thy lady within?

Clo. Would not a pair of these have bred, sir?

Vio. Yes, being kept together, and put to use.

Clo. I would play Lord Pandarus of Phrygia, sir, to bring a Cressida to this Troilus.

Vio. I understand you, sir [*gives another piece of money*], 't is well begged.

Clo. The matter, I hope, is not great, sir, begging but a beggar: Cressida was a beggar. My lady is within, sir.

I will construe to them whence you come: who you are,
and what you would, are out of my welkin,—I might say,
element, but the word is overworn.   [*Exit*
    Vio. This fellow 's wise enough to play the fool,
And to do that well craves a kind of wit:
He must observe their mood on whom he jests,
The quality of persons, and the time,
And, like the haggard, check at every feather
That comes before his eye.   This is a practice
As full of labour as a wise man's art:
For folly that he wisely shows, is fit;
But wise men folly-fallen, quite taint their wit.

Enter SIR TOBY BELCH *and* SIR ANDREW

    Sir To. 'Save you, gentleman.
    Vio. And you, sir.
    Sir And.   Dieu vous garde, monsieur.
    Vio.   Et vous aussi; votre serviteur.
    Sir And. I hope, sir, you are; and I am yours.
    Sir To. Will you encounter the house? my niece is
desirous you should enter, if your trade be to her.
    Vio. I am bound to your niece, sir: I mean, she is the
list of my voyage.
    Sir To. Taste your legs, sir; put them to motion.
    Vio. My legs do better understand me, sir, than I
understand what you mean by bidding me taste my legs.
    Sir To. I mean, to go, sir, to enter.
    Vio. I will answer you with gait and entrance:—but
we are prevented.

Enter OLIVIA *and* MARIA

Most excellent-accomplished lady, the heavens rain odours
on you!
    Sir And. That youth 's a rare courtier. 'Rain odours!'
—well.
    Vio. My matter hath no voice, lady, but to your own
most pregnant and vouchsafed ear.
    Sir And. 'Odours,' 'pregnant,' and 'vouchsafed:'—I'll
get 'em all three all ready.
    Oli. Let the garden door be shut, and leave me to my
hearing. [*Exeunt Sir Toby, Sir Andrew, and Maria*]
Give me your hand, sir.
    Vio. My duty, madam, and most humble service.
    Oli. What is your name?
    Vio. Cesario is your servant's name, fair princess.
    Oli. My servant, sir? 'T was never merry world,
Since lowly feigning was called compliment.
You're servant to the Count Orsino, youth.

Vio. And he is yours, and his must needs be yours:
Your servant's servant is your servant, madam.
  Oli. For him, I think not on him: for his thoughts,
Would they were blanks, rather than filled with me!
  Vio. Madam, I come to whet your gentle thoughts
On his behalf:—
  Oli.   O, by your leave, I pray you,—
I bade you never speak again of him:
But, would you undertake another suit,
I had rather hear you to solicit that
Than music from the spheres.
  Vio.   Dear lady,—
  Oli. Give me leave, beseech you. I did send
After the last enchantment you did here,
A ring in chase of you: so did I abuse
Myself, my servant, and, I fear me, you.
Under your hard construction must I sit,
To force that on you, in a shameful cunning,
Which you knew none of yours: what might you think?
Have you not set mine honour at the stake,
And baited it with all the unmuzzled thoughts
That tyrannous heart can think? To one of your receiving
Enough is shown; a cyprus, not a bosom,
Hides my heart. So, let me hear you speak.
  Vio. I pity you.
  Oli.   That 's a degree to love.
  Vio. No, not a grise; for 't is a vulgar proof,
That very oft we pity enemies.
  Oli. Why then, methinks, 't is time to smile again.
O world, how apt the poor are to be proud!
If one should be a prey, how much the better
To fall before the lion than the wolf! [*Clock strikes*
The clock upbraids me with the waste of time.—
Be not afraid, good youth, I will not have you;
And yet, when wit and youth is come to harvest,
Your wife is like to reap a proper man:
There lies your way, due west.
  Vio.   Then westward-ho—
Grace, and good disposition tend your ladyship!
You 'll nothing, madam, to my lord by me?
  Oli. Stay:
I prithee, tell me what thou think'st of me.
  Vio. That you do think you are not what you are.
  Oli. If I think so, I think the same of you.
  Vio. Then think you right: I am not what I am.
  Oli. I would you were as I would have you be!
  Vio. Would it be better, madam, than I am,
I wish it might; for now I am your fool.
  Oli. O, what a deal of scorn looks beautiful

In the contempt and anger of his lip!
A murderous guilt shows not itself more soon
Than love that would seem hid, love's night is noon.
Cesario, by the roses of the spring,
By maidhood, honour, truth, and everything,
I love thee so, that, maugre all thy pride,
Nor wit nor reason can my passion hide.
Do not extort thy reasons from this clause,
But that I woo, thou therefore hast no cause;
But rather, reason thus with reason fetter,—
Love sought is good, but given unsought is better.
    Vio. By innocence I swear, and by my youth,
I have one heart, one bosom, and one truth,—
And that no woman has; nor never none
Shall mistress be of it, save I alone.
And so adieu, good madam: never more
Will I my master's tears to you deplore.
    Oli. Yet come again; for thou perhaps may'st move
That heart which now abhors, to like his love.

                                        [Exeunt

SCENE II.—A Room in OLIVIA'S House

Enter SIR TOBY BELCH, SIR ANDREW *and* FABIAN

    Sir And. No, faith, I 'll not stay a jot longer.
    Sir To. Thy reason, dear venom; give thy reason.
    Fab. You must needs yield your reason, Sir Andrew.
    Sir And. Marry, I saw your niece do more favours
to the count's serving-man than ever she bestowed upon
me; I saw 't i' the orchard.
    Sir To. Did she see thee the while, old boy? tell me
that.
    Sir And. As plain as I see you now.
    Fab. This was a great argument of love in her toward
you.
    Sir And. 'Slight! will you make an ass o' me?
    Fab. I will prove it legitimate, sir, upon the oaths of
judgment and reason.
    Sir To. And they have been grand-jurymen since before
Noah was a sailor.
    Fab. She did show favour to the youth in your sight
only to exasperate you, to awake your dormouse valour,
to put fire in your heart, and brimstone in your liver. You
should then have accosted her, and with some excellent
jests, fire-new from the mint, you should have banged the
youth into dumbness. This was looked for at your hand,

and this was balked: the double gilt of this opportunity you let time wash off, and you are now sailed into the north of my lady's opinion; where you will hang like an icicle on a Dutchman's beard, unless you do redeem it by some laudable attempt either of valour or policy.

Sir And. An 't be any way, it must be with valour; for policy I hate: I had as lief be a Brownist as a politician.

Sir T. Why then, build me thy fortunes upon the basis of valour. Challenge me the count's youth to fight with him; hurt him in eleven places: my niece shall take note of it; and assure thyself, there is no love-broker in the world can more prevail in man's commendation with woman than report of valour.

Fab. There is no way but this, Sir Andrew.

Sir And. Will either of you bear me a challenge to him?

Sir To. Go, write it in a martial hand; be curst and brief; it is no matter how witty, so it be eloquent and full of invention: taunt him with the license of ink: if thou Thou'st him some thrice, it shall not be amiss; and as many Lies as will lie in thy sheet of paper, although the sheet were big enough for the bed of Ware in England, set 'em down: go, about it. Let there be gall enough in thy ink; though thou write with a goose-pen, no matter: about it.

Sir And. Where shall I find you?

Sir To. We 'll call thee at thy *cubiculo.* Go.

                 [*Exit Sir Andrew*

Fab. This is a dear manakin to you, Sir Toby.

Sir To. I have been dear to him, lad,—some two thousand strong, or so.

Fab. We shall have a rare letter from him: but you 'll not deliver 't?

Sir To. Never trust me then; and by all means stir on the youth to an answer. I think oxen and wainropes cannot hale them together. For Andrew, if he were opened and you find so much blood in his liver as will clog the foot of a flea, I 'll eat the rest of the anatomy.

Fab. And his opposite, the youth, bears in his visage no great presage of cruelty.

Sir To. Look, where the youngest wren of nine comes.

Enter MARIA

Mar. If you desire the spleen, and will laugh yourselves into stitches, follow me. Yond gull Malvolio is turned heathen, a very renegado; for there is no Christian, that means to be saved by believing rightly, can ever believe such impossible passages of grossness. He 's in yellow stockings.

Sir To. And cross-gartered?

Mar. Most villainously; like a pedant that keeps a school i' the church.—I have dogged him like his murderer. He does obey every point of the letter that I dropped to betray him: he does smile his face into more lines than are in the new map, with the augmentation of the Indies. You have not seen such a thing as 't is; I can hardly forbear hurling things at him. I know, my lady will strike him: if she do, he 'll smile, and take 't for a great favour.

Sir To. Come, bring us, bring us where he is. [*Exeunt*

SCENE III.—A Street

Enter SEBASTIAN *and* ANTONIO

Seb. I would not, by my will, have troubled you;
But, since you make your pleasure of your pains,
I will no further chide you.

Ant. I could not stay behind you; my desire,
More sharp than filéd steel, did spur me forth;
And not all love to see you,—though so much
As might have drawn one to a longer voyage,—
But jealousy what might befall your travel.
Being skilless in these parts, which to a stranger,
Unguided, and unfriended, often prove
Rough and unhospitable: my willing love,
The rather by these arguments of fear,
Set forth in your pursuit.

Seb.   My kind Antonio,
I can no other answer make, but thanks,
And thanks, and ever thanks; and oft good turns
Are shuffled off with such uncurrent pay;
But, were my worth, as is my conscience, firm,
You should find better dealing. What 's to do?
Shall we go see the reliques of this town?

Ant. To-morrow, sir: best first go see your lodging.

Seb. I am not weary, and 't is long to-night
I pray you, let us satisfy our eyes
With the memorials and things of fame
That do renown this city.

Ant.   Would, you'd pardon me:
I do not without danger walk these streets.
Once, in a sea-fight 'gainst the count his galleys,
I did some service; of such note, indeed,
That, were I ta'en here, it would scarce be answered.

Seb. Belike, you slew great number of his people,

Ant. The offence is not of such a bloody nature,
Albeit the quality of the time and quarrel
Might well have given us bloody argument.

It might have since been answered in repaying
What we took from them; which, for traffic's sake,
Most of our city did: only myself stood out;
For which, if I be lapséd in this place,
I shall pay dear.
  Seb.   Do not then walk too open.
  Ant. It doth not fit me. Hold, sir, here 's my purse.
In the south suburbs, at the Elephant,
Is best to lodge: I will bespeak our diet,
Whiles you beguile the time and feed your knowledge
With viewing of the town: there shall you have me.
  Seb. Why I your purse?
  Ant. Haply your eye shall light upon some toy
You have desire to purchase; and your store,
I think, is not for idle markets, sir.
  Seb. I 'll be your purse-bearer, and leave you for
An hour.
  Ant. To the Elephant.—
  Seb.   I do remember.
                 [*Exeunt*

SCENE IV.—OLIVIA's Garden

Enter OLIVIA *and* MARIA

  Oli. I have sent after him: he says, he 'll come;—
How shall I feast him? what bestow of him?
For youth is bought more oft than begged or borrowed.
I speak too loud.—
Where is Malvolio?—he is sad and civil,
And suits well for a servant with my fortunes:—
Where is Malvolio?
  Mar. He 's coming, madam: but in very strange
     manner. He is sure possessed, madam.
  Oli. Why, what's the matter? does he rave?
  Mar. No, madam, he does nothing but smile: your
ladyship were best to have some guard about you, if he
come; for sure the man is tainted in his wits.
  Oli. Go call him hither.—I 'm as mad as he,
If sad and merry madness equal be.—

Re-enter MARIA *with* MALVOLIO

How now, Malvolio?
  Mal. Sweet lady, ho, ho.
  Oli. Smil'st thou?
I sent for thee upon a sad occasion.

Mal. Sad, lady! I could be sad: this does make some obstruction in the blood, this cross-gartering; but what of that? if it please the eye of one, it is with me as the very true sonnet is, "Please one, and please all."

Oli. Why, how dost thou, man? what is the matter with thee?

Mal. Not black in my mind, though yellow in my legs. It did come to his hands, and commands shall be executed: I think we do know the sweet Roman hand.

Oli. Wilt thou go to bed, Malvolio?

Mal. To bed! ay, sweetheart; and I 'll come to thee.

Oli. God comfort thee! why dost thou smile so, and kiss thy hand so oft?

Mar. How do you, Malvolio?

Mal. At your request? Yes; nightingales answer daws.

Mar. Why appear you with this ridiculous boldness before my lady?

Mal. "Be not afraid of greatness:"—'t was well writ.

Oli. What meanest thou by that, Malvolio?

Mal. "Some are born great,"—

Oli. Ha?

Mal. "Some achieve greatness"—

Oli. What sayest thou?

Mal. "And some have greatness thrust upon them."

Oli. Heaven restore thee!

Mal. "Remember, who commended thy yellow stockings."—

Oli. My yellow stockings?

Mal. "And wished to see thee cross-gartered."

Oli. Cross-gartered?

Mal. "Go to, thou art made, if thou desirest to be so:"—

Oli. Am I made?

Mal. "If not, let me see thee a servant still."

Oli. Why, this is very midsummer madness.

Enter Servant

Serv. Madam, the young gentleman of the Count Orsino's is returned. I could hardly entreat him back: he attends your ladyship's pleasure.

Oli. I 'll come to him. [*Exit Servant*] Good Maria, let this fellow be looked to. Where's my cousin Toby? Let some of my people have a special care of him: I would not have him miscarry for the half of my dowry.

[*Exeunt Olivia and Maria*

Mal. Oh, ho! do you come near me now? no worse man than Sir Toby to look to me? This occurs directly with the letter: she sends him on purpose, that I may appear stubborn to him; for she incites me to that in the letter. "Cast thy humble slough," says she;—"be opposite with a kinsman, surly with servants,—let thy tongue tang with arguments of state, put thyself into the trick of singularity;"—and consequently sets down the manner how; as, a sad face, a reverend carriage, a slow tongue, in the habit of some sir of note, and so forth. I have limed her; but it is Jove's doing, and Jove make me thankful! And when she went away now, "Let this fellow be looked to:" fellow! not Malvolio, nor after my degree, but fellow. Why, everything adheres together, that no drachm of a scruple, no scruple of a scruple, no obstacle, no incredulous or unsafe circumstance——What can be said? Nothing that can be, can come between me and the full prospect of my hopes. Well, Jove, not I, is the doer of this, and he is to be thanked.

Re-enter MARIA, *with* SIR TOBY *and* FABIAN

Sir To. Which way is he, in the name of sanctity? If all the devils in hell be drawn in little, and Legion himself possessed him, yet I 'll speak to him.

Fab. Here he is, here he is.—How is 't with you, sir? how is 't with you, man?

Mal. Go off; I discard you: let me enjoy my private; go off.

Mar. Lo, how hollow the fiend speaks within him! did not I tell you?—Sir Toby, my lady prays you to have a care of him.

Mal. Ah, ha! does she so?

Sir To. Go to, go to; peace! peace! we must deal gently with him; let me alone.—How do you, Malvolio? how is 't with you? What, man! defy the devil: consider, he 's an enemy to mankind.

Mal. Do you know what you say?

Mar. La you, an you speak ill of the devil, how he takes it at heart! Pray God, he be not bewitched!

Fab. Carry his water to the wise woman.

Mar. Marry, and it shall be done to-morrow morning, if I live. My lady would not lose him for more than I 'll say.

Mal. How now, mistress?

Mar. O Lord!

Sir To. Prithee, hold thy peace: this is not the way. Do you not see you move him? let me alone with him.

Fab. No way but gentleness; gently, gently: the fiend is rough, and will not be roughly used.

Sir To. Why, how now, my bawcock! how dost thou, chuck?

Mal. Sir!

Sir To. Ay, Biddy, come with me. What, man! 't is not for gravity to play at cherry-pit with Satan: hang him, foul collier!

Mar. Get him to say his prayers; good Sir Toby, get him to pray.

Mal. My prayers, minx!

Mar. No, I warrant you; he will not hear of godliness.

Mal. Go, hang yourselves all! you are idle shallow things: I am not of your element: you shall know more hereafter.   [*Exit*

Sir To. Is 't possible?

Fab. If this were played upon a stage now, I could condemn it as an improbable fiction.

Sir To. His very genius hath taken the infection of the device, man.

Mar. Nay, pursue him now, lest the device take air, and taint.

Fab. Why, we shall make him mad, indeed.

Mar. The house will be the quieter.

Sir To. Come, we'll have him in a dark room and bound. My niece is already in the belief that he 's mad: we may carry it thus, for our pleasure and his penance, till our very pastime, tired out of breath, prompt us to have mercy on him; at which time we will bring the device to the bar, and crown thee for a finder of madmen.—But see, but see.

Fab. More matter for a May morning.

Enter SIR ANDREW

Sir And. Here 's the challenge; read it: I warrant, there 's vinegar and pepper in 't.

Fab. Is 't so saucy?

Sir And. Ay, is 't, I warrant him: do but read.

Sir To. Give me. [*Reads*] *Youth, whatsoever thou art, thou art but a scurvy fellow.*

Fab. Good, and valiant.

Sir To. [*reads*] *Wonder not, nor admire not in thy mind, why I call thee so, for I will show thee no reason for 't.*

Fab. A good note, that keeps you from the blow of the law.

Sir To. [*reads*] *Thou comest to the Lady Olivia; and in my sight she uses thee kindly: but thou liest in thy throat; that is not the matter I challenge thee for.*

Fab. Very brief, and to exceeding good sense—less.

Sir To. [*reads*] *I will waylay thee going home; where, if it be thy chance to kill me,—*

Fab. Good.

131

Sir To. [reads] *Thou killest me like a rogue and a villain.*

Fab. Still you keep o' the windy side of the law: good.

Sir To. [reads] *Fare thee well; and God have mercy upon one of our souls! He may have mercy upon mine, but my hope is better; and so look to thyself. Thy friend, as thou usest him, and thy sworn enemy,* ANDREW AGUE-CHEEK.—If this letter move him not, his legs cannot: I'll give't him.

Mar. You may have very fit occasion for 't: he is now in some commerce with my lady, and will by-and-by depart.

Sir To. Go, Sir Andrew; scout me for him at the corner of the orchard, like a bum-bailie. So soon as ever thou seest him, draw, and, as thou drawest, swear horrible; for it comes to pass oft, that a terrible oath, with a swaggering accent, sharply twanged off, gives manhood more approbation than ever proof itself would have earned him. Away!

Sir And. Nay, let me alone for swearing.   [*Exit*

Sir To. Now will not I deliver his letter: for the behaviour of the young gentleman gives him out to be of good capacity and breeding: his employment between his lord and my niece confirms no less: therefore this letter, being so excellently ignorant, will breed no terror in the youth,—he will find it comes from a clodpole. But, sir, I will deliver his challenge by word of mouth; set upon Ague-cheek a notable report of valour; and drive the gentleman—as, I know, his youth will aptly receive it—into a most hideous opinion of his rage, skill, fury, and impetuosity. This will so fright them both, that they will kill one another by the look, like cockatrices.

Fab. Here he comes with your niece: give them way, till he take leave, and presently after him.

Sir To. I will meditate the while upon some horrid message for a challenge.

[*Exeunt Sir Toby, Fabian, and Maria*

Re-enter OLIVIA, *with* VIOLA

Oli. I have said too much unto a heart of stone,
And laid mine honour too unchary out:
There 's something in me that reproves my fault,
But such a headstrong potent fault it is
That it but mocks reproof.

Vio.   With the same 'haviour that your passion bears,
Goes on my master's grief.

Oli. Here, wear this jewel for me,—'t is my picture.
Refuse it not; it hath no tongue to vex you:
And, I beseech you, come again to-morrow.

132

What shall you ask of me that I 'll deny,
That honour, saved, may upon asking give.
    Vio.   Nothing but this,—your true love for my master.
    Oli.   How with mine honour may I give him that
Which I have given to you?
    Vio.   I will acquit you.
    Oli.   Well, come again to-morrow: fare thee well:
A fiend like thee might bear my soul to hell.   [*Exit*

Re-enter SIR TOBY *and* FABIAN

    Sir To.   Gentlemen, God save thee!
    Vio.   And you, sir.
    Sir To.   That defence thou hast, betake thee to 't: of
what nature the wrongs are thou hast done him, I know
not; but thy intercepter, full of despite, bloody as the
hunter, attends thee at the orchard end: dismount thy
tuck, be yare in thy preparation; for thy assailant is quick,
skilful, and deadly.
    Vio.   You mistake, sir; I am sure, no man hath any
quarrel to me: my remembrance is very free and clear
from any image of offence done to any man.
    Sir To.   You 'll find it otherwise, I assure you: therefore,
if you hold your life at any price, betake you to your guard;
for your opposite hath in him what youth, strength, skill,
and wrath can furnish man withal.
    Vio.   I pray you, sir, what is he?
    Sir To.   He is knight, dubbed with unhatched rapier,
and on carpet consideration; but he is a devil in private
brawl; souls and bodies hath he divorced three; and his
incensement at this moment is so implacable, that satisfaction can be none but by pangs of death and sepulchre:
hob, nob, is his word: give 't or take 't.
    Vio.   I will return again into the house, and desire some
conduct of the lady.   I am no fighter.   I have heard of
some kind of men, that put quarrels purposely on others,
to taste their valour: belike, this is a man of that quirk.
    Sir To.   Sir, no; his indignation derives itself out of a
very competent injury: therefore, get you on, and give
him his desire.   Back you shall not to the house, unless
you undertake that with me which with as much safety
you might answer him: therefore, on, or strip your sword
stark naked; for meddle you must, that 's certain, or forswear to wear iron about you.
    Vio.   This is as uncivil, as strange.   I beseech you, do
me this courteous office, as to know of the knight what
my offence to him is: it is something of my negligence,
nothing of my purpose.
    Sir To.   I will do so.—Signior Fabian, stay you by this
gentleman till my return.   [*Exit*

Vio. Pray you, sir, do you know of this matter?

Fab. I know the knight is incensed against you, even to a mortal arbitrement; but nothing of the circumstance more.

Vio. I beseech you, what manner of man is he?

Fab. Nothing of that wonderful promise, to read him by his form, as you are like to find him in the proof of his valour. He is, indeed, sir, the most skilful, bloody, and fatal opposite that you could possibly have found in any part of Illyria. Will you walk towards him? I will make your peace with him, if I can.

Vio. I shall be much bound to you for 't: I am one that had rather go with sir priest, than sir knight: I care not who knows so much of my mettle. [*Exeunt*

Re-enter SIR TOBY, *with* SIR ANDREW

Sir To. Why, man, he 's a very devil; I have not seen such a firago. I had a pass with him, rapier, scabbard, and all, and he gives me the stuck-in with such a mortal motion, that it is inevitable; and on the answer, he pays you as surely as your feet hit the ground they step on: they say, he has been fencer to the Sophy.

Sir And. Pox on 't, I 'll not meddle with him.

Sir To. Ay, but he will not now be pacified: Fabian can scarce hold him yonder.

Sir And. Plague on 't; an I thought he had been valiant and so cunning in fence, I 'd have seen him damned ere I 'd have challenged him. Let him let the matter slip, and I 'll give him my horse, grey Capulet.

Sir To. I 'll make the motion: stand here, make a good show on 't: this shall end without the perdition of souls.—[*Aside*] Marry, I 'll ride your horse as well as I ride you.

Re-enter FABIAN *and* VIOLA

[*To Fabian*] I have his horse to take up the quarrel. I have persuaded him the youth 's a devil.

Fab. [*To Sir Toby*] He is as horribly conceited of him; and pants and looks pale, as if a bear were at his heels.

Sir To. [*To Viola*] There 's no remedy, sir: he will fight with you for oath's sake: marry, he hath better bethought him of his quarrel, and he finds that now scarce to be worth talking of: therefore draw for the supportance of his vow: he protests he will not hurt you.

Vio. [*Aside*] Pray God defend me! A little thing would make me tell them how much I lack of a man.

Fab. Give ground, if you see him furious.

Sir To. Come, Sir Andrew, there's no remedy: the

gentleman will, for his honour's sake, have one bout with you; he cannot by the duello avoid it: but he has promised me, as he is a gentleman and a soldier, he will not hurt you. Come on; to 't.

Sir And. Pray God, he keep his oath.   [*Draws*

Vio. I do assure you, 't is against my will.

[*Draws*

Enter ANTONIO

Ant. Put up your sword.—If this young gentleman Have done offence, I take the fault on me: If you offend him, I for him defy you.   [*Drawing*

Sir To. You, sir? why, what are you?

Ant. One, sir, that for his love dares yet do more Than you have heard him brag to you he will.

Sir To. Nay, if you be an undertaker, I am for you.

[*Draws*

Fab. O good Sir Toby, hold! here come the officers.

Sir To. I'll be with you anon.

Vio. Pray, sir, put your sword up, if you please.

Sir And. Marry, will I, sir:—and, for that I promised you, I'll be as good as my word: he will bear you easily, and reins well.

Enter two Officers

First Off. This is the man; do thy office.

Second Off. Antonio, I arrest thee at the suit Of Count Orsino.

Ant.   You do mistake me, sir.

First Off. No, sir, no jot; I know your favour well, Though now you have no sea-cap on your head.— Take him away: he knows I know him well.

Ant. I must obey.—[*To Viola*] This comes with seeking you: But there's no remedy: I shall answer it. What will you do, now my necessity Makes me to ask you for my purse?   It grieves me Much more for what I cannot do for you Than what befalls myself.   You stand amazed; But be of comfort.

Second Off. Come, sir, away.

Ant. I must entreat of you some of that money.

Vio. What money, sir? For the fair kindness you have showed me here, And, part, being prompted by your present trouble, Out of my lean and low ability, I'll lend you something.   My having is not much. I'll make division of my present with you: Hold, there is half my coffer.

135

Ant.   Will you deny me now?
Is 't possible, that my deserts to you
Can lack persuasion? Do not tempt my misery,
Lest that it make me so unsound a man
As to upbraid you with those kindnesses
That I have done for you.
    Vio.   I know of none;
Nor know I you by voice or any feature.
I hate ingratitude more in a man
Than lying, vainness, babbling drunkenness,
Or any taint of vice whose strong corruption
Inhabits our frail blood.
    Ant.   O heavens themselves!
    Second Off. Come, sir, I pray you, go.
    Ant. Let me speak a little. This youth that you see
                here
I snatched one half out of the jaws of death;
Relieved him with such sanctity of love,—
And to his image, which methought did promise
Most venerable worth, did I devotion.
    First Off. What 's that to us? The time goes by:
                away!
    Ant. But O how vile an idol proves this god!—
Thou hast, Sebastian, done good feature shame.—
In nature there 's no blemish but the mind;
None can be called deformed but the unkind:
Virtue is beauty; but the beauteous-evil
Are empty trunks, o'erflourished by the devil.
    First Off. The man grows mad: away with him!
Come, come, sir.
    Ant. Lead me on.
                            [*Exeunt Officers with Antonio*
    Vio. Methinks, his words do from such passion fly
That he believes himself: so do not I.
Prove true, imagination! O, prove true,
That I, dear brother, be now ta'en for you!
    Sir To. Come hither, knight; come hither, Fabian:
we'll whisper o'er a couplet or two of most sage saws.
    Vio. He named Sebastian: I my brother know
Yet living in my glass; even such, and so,
In favour was my brother; and he went
Still in this fashion, colour, ornament,—
For him I imitate. O, if it prove,
Tempests are kind, and salt waves fresh in love!   [*Exit*
    Sir To. A very dishonest paltry boy, and more a coward
than a hare. His dishonesty appears in leaving his friend
here in necessity, and denying him; and for his cowardship,
ask Fabian.
    Fab. A coward, a most devout coward, religious in it.

Sir And. 'Slid, I'll after him again, and beat him.

Sir To. Do; cuff him soundly, but never draw thy sword.

Sir And. An I do not,—   [*Exit*

Fab. Come, let's see the event.

Sir To. I dare lay any money 't will be nothing yet.

[*Exeunt*

ACT FOUR

Scene I.—The Street before Olivia's House

Enter Sebastian *and* Clown

Clo. Will you make me believe that I am not sent for you?

Seb. Go to, go to; thou art a foolish fellow: let me be clear of thee.

Clo. Well held out; i' faith! No, I do not know you; for I am not sent to you by my lady to bid you come speak with her; nor your name is not Master Cesario; for this is not my nose neither.—Nothing that is so is so.

Seb. I prithee, vent thy folly somewhere else:
Thou know'st not me.

Clo. Vent my folly! He has heard that word of some great man, and now applies it to a fool: vent my folly! I am afraid this great lubber, the world, will prove a cockney. I prithee now, ungird thy strangeness, and tell me what I shall vent to my lady: shall I vent to her that thou art coming?

Seb. I prithee, foolish Greek, depart from me.
There 's money for thee: if you tarry longer,
I shall give worse payment.

Clo. By my troth, thou hast an open hand.—These wise men that give fools money, get themselves a good report after fourteen years' purchase.

Enter Sir Andrew

Sir And. Now, sir, have I met you again? there's for you.   [*Striking Sebastian*

Seb. Why, there 's for thee, and there, and there.
Are all the people mad?   [*Beating Sir Andrew*

Enter Sir Toby *and* Fabian

Sir To. Hold, sir, or I 'll throw your dagger o'er the house.

Clo. This will I tell my lady straight. I would not be. in some of your coats for twopence.   [*Exit*

Sir To. Come on, sir; hold.

Sir And. Nay, let him alone; I'll go another way to work with him; I'll have an action of battery against him, if there be any law in Illyria: though I struck him first, yet it's no matter for that.

Seb. Let go thy hand.

Sir To. Come, sir, I will not let you go. Come, my young soldier, put up your iron: you are well fleshed; come on.

Seb. I will be free from thee. [*Disengages himself*] What wouldst thou now?
If thou dar'st tempt me further, draw thy sword.

Sir To. What, what? Nay, then I must have an ounce or two of this malapert blood from you.   [*Draws*

Enter OLIVIA

Oli. Hold, Toby; on thy life I charge thee, hold!

Sir To. Madam!

Oli. Will it be ever thus? Ungracious wretch,
Fit for the mountains and the barbarous caves,
Where manners ne'er were preached. Out of my sight!—
Be not offended, dear Cesario.—
Rudesby, be gone!
                    [*Exeunt Sir Toby, Sir Andrew, and Fabian*
                         I prithee, gentle friend,
Let thy fair wisdom, not thy passion, sway
In this uncivil and unjust extent
Against thy peace. Go with me to my house;
And hear thou there how many fruitless pranks
This ruffian hath botched up, that thou thereby
May'st smile at this. Thou shalt not choose but go:
Do not deny. Beshrew his soul for me,
He started one poor heart of mine in thee.

Seb. What relish is in this? how runs the stream?
Or I am mad, or else this is a dream.
Let fancy still my sense in Lethe steep;
If it be thus to dream, still let me sleep.

Oli. Nay; come, I prithee. Would thou 'dst be ruled by me!

Seb. Madam, I will.

Oli.   O! say so, and so be.   [*Exeunt*

SCENE II.—A Room in OLIVIA'S House

Enter MARIA and Clown

Mar. Nay, I prithee, put on this gown and this beard: make him believe thou art Sir Topas the curate: do it quickly; I'll call Sir Toby the whilst.   [*Exit*

Clo. Well, I'll put it on, and I will dissemble myself in 't: and I would I were the first that ever dissembled in such a gown. I am not tall enough to become the function well; nor lean enough to be thought a good student: but to be said an honest man and a good housekeeper, goes as fairly as to say a careful man and a great scholar. The competitors enter.

Enter SIR TOBY *and* MARIA

Sir To. Jove bless thee, master parson.

Clo. *Bonos dies*, Sir Toby: for as the old hermit of Prague, that never saw pen and ink, very wittily said to a niece of King Gorboduc, 'That, that is, is;' so I, being master parson, am master parson, for what is that, but that? and is, but is?

Sir To. To him, Sir Topas.

Clo. What, ho, I say,—peace in this prison.

Sir To. The knave counterfeits well; a good knave.

Mal. [*within*] Who calls there?

Clo. Sir Topas the curate, who comes to visit Malvolio the lunatic.

Mal. Sir Topas, Sir Topas, good Sir Topas, go to my lady.

Clo. Out, hyperbolical fiend! how vexest thou this man! Talkest thou nothing but of ladies?

Sir To. Well said, master parson.

Mal. Sir Topas, never was man thus wronged. Good Sir Topas, do not think I am mad: they have laid me here in hideous darkness.

Clo. Fie, thou dishonest Satan!—I call thee by the most modest terms; for I am one of those gentle ones that will use the devil himself with courtesy:—sayest thou, that house is dark?

Mal. As hell, Sir Topas.

Clo. Why, it hath bay-windows transparent as barricadoes, and the clear-stories towards the south-north are as lustrous as ebony; and yet complainest thou of obstruction?

Mal. I am not mad, Sir Topas: I say to you, this house is dark.

Clo. Madman, thou errest: I say, there is no darkness but ignorance; in which thou art more puzzled than the Egyptians in their fog.

Mal. I say, this house is as dark as ignorance, though ignorance were as dark as hell; and I say, there was never man thus abused. I am no more mad than you are: make the trial of it in any constant question.

Clo. What is the opinion of Pythagoras concerning wild-fowl?

Mal.   That the soul of our grandam might haply inhabit a bird.

Clo.   What thinkest thou of his opinion?

Mal.   I think nobly of the soul, and no way approve his opinion.

Clo.   Fare thee well. Remain thou still in darkness. Thou shalt hold the opinion of Pythagoras ere I will allow of thy wits; and fear to kill a woodcock lest thou dispossess the soul of thy grandam. Fare thee well.

Mal.   Sir Topas, Sir Topas!—

Sir To.   My most exquisite Sir Topas!

Clo.   Nay, I am for all waters.

Mar.   Thou mightest have done this without thy beard and gown: he sees thee not.

Sir To.   To him in thine own voice, and bring me word how thou findest him: I would we were well rid of this knavery. If he may be conveniently delivered, I would he were: for I am now so far in offence with my niece, that I cannot pursue with any safety this sport to the upshot. Come by-and-by to my chamber.

[*Exeunt Sir Toby and Maria*

Clo.   [*Singing*]   *Hey Robin, jolly Robin,*
          Tell me how thy lady does.

Mal.   Fool,—

Clo.   *My lady is unkind, perdy.*

Mal.   Fool,—

Clo.   *Alas, why is she so?*

Mal.   Fool, I say,—

Clo.   *She loves another.*—Who calls, ha?

Mal.   Good fool, as ever thou wilt deserve well at my hand, help me to a candle, and pen, ink, and paper: as I am a gentleman, I will live to be thankful to thee for 't.

Clo.   Master Malvolio!

Mal.   Ay, good fool.

Clo.   Alas, sir, how fell you besides your five wits?

Mal.   Fool, there was never man so notoriously abused: I am as well in my wits, fool, as thou art.

Clo.   But as well? then you are mad indeed, if you be no better in your wits than a fool.

Mal.   They have here propertied me; keep me in darkness, send ministers to me, asses! and do all they can to face me out of my wits.

Clo.   Advise you what you say: the minister is here.—Malvolio, Malvolio, thy wits the heavens restore! endeavour thyself to sleep, and leave thy vain bibble babble.

Mal.   Sir Topas,—

Clo.   Maintain no words with him, good fellow.—Who, I, sir? not I, sir. God b' wi' you, good Sir Topas.—Marry, Amen.—I will, sir, I will.

Mal. Fool, fool, fool, I say,—
Clo. Alas, sir, be patient. What say you, sir? **I** am
shent for speaking to you.
Mal. Good fool, help me to some light and some paper:
I tell thee, I am as well in my wits as any man in Illyria.
Clo. Well-a-day, that you were, sir!
Mal. By this hand, I am. Good fool, some ink, paper,
and light, and convey what I will set down to my lady:
it shall advantage thee more than ever the bearing of
letter did.
Clo. I will help you to 't. But tell me true, are you
not mad indeed? or do you but counterfeit?
Mal. Believe me, I am not; I tell thee true.
Clo. Nay, I 'll ne'er believe a madman till **I** see his
brains. I will fetch you light, and paper, and ink.
Mal. Fool, I 'll requite it in the highest degree: I
prithee, be gone.
Clo. [*Singing*] *I am gone, sir,*
                    And anon, sir,
              I'll be with you again,
                    In a trice,
                    Like to the old Vice,
              Your need to sustain;

              Who with dagger of lath,
              In his rage and his wrath,
                    Cries, Ah, ha! to the devil;
              Like a mad lad,
              Pare thy nails, dad,
                    Adieu, goodman drivel.   [*Exit*

SCENE III.—OLIVIA'S Garden

Enter SEBASTIAN

Seb. This is the air; that is the glorious sun;
This pearl she gave me, I do feel 't and see 't;
And though 't is wonder that enwraps me thus,
Yet 't is not madness. Where 's Antonio, then?
I could not find him at the Elephant;
Yet there he was, and there I found this credit,
That he did range the town to seek me out.
His counsel now might do me golden service;
For though my soul disputes well with my sense
That this may be some error, but no madness,
Yet doth this accident and flood of fortune
So far exceed all instance, all discourse,
That I am ready to distrust mine eyes,
And wrangle with my reason that persuades me

To any other trust but that I'm mad,—
Or else the lady's mad: yet, if 't were so,
She could not sway her house, command her followers,
Take and give back affairs and their despatch
With such a smooth, discreet, and stable bearing,
As, I perceive, she does: there's something in 't,
That is deceivable.   But here the lady comes.

Enter OLIVIA *and a Priest*

    Oli.   Blame not this haste of mine.   If you mean well,
Now go with me and with this holy man
Into the chantry by; there, before him,
And underneath that consecrated roof,
Plight me the full assurance of your faith;
That my most jealous and too doubtful soul
May live at peace.   He shall conceal it,
Whiles you are willing it shall come to note,
What time we will our celebration keep
According to my birth.—What do you say?
    Seb.   I 'll follow this good man, and go with you,
And, having sworn truth, ever will be true.
    Oli.   Then lead the way, good father; and heavens so
        shine,
That they may fairly note this act of mine!   [*Exeunt*

ACT FIVE

SCENE I.—The Street before OLIVIA'S House

Enter Clown *and* FABIAN

    Fab.   Now, as thou lov'st me, let me see his letter.
    Clo.   Good Master Fabian, grant me another request.
    Fab.   Anything.
    Clo.   Do not desire to see this letter.
    Fab.   This is, to give a dog, and in recompense desire
my dog again.

Enter DUKE, VIOLA, *and Attendants*

    Duke.   Belong you to the Lady Olivia, friends?
    Clo.   Ay, sir; we are some of her trappings.
    Duke.   I know thee well: how dost thou, my good
fellow
    Clo.   Truly, sir, the better for my foes, and the worse
for my friends.
    Duke.   Just the contrary; the better for thy friends.
    Clo.   No, sir, the worse.

Duke. How can that be?

Clo. Marry, sir, they praise me, and make an ass of me; now, my foes tell me plainly I am an ass: so that by my foes, sir, I profit in the knowledge of myself, and by my friends I am abused: so that, conclusions to be as kisses, if your four negatives make your two affirmatives, why, then, the worse for my friends, and the better for my foes.

Duke. Why, this is excellent.

Clo. By my troth, sir, no; though it please you to be one of my friends.

Duke. Thou shalt not be the worse for me; there's gold.   [*Gives money*

Clo. But that it would be double-dealing, sir, I would you could make it another.

Duke. O, you give me ill counsel.

Clo. Put your grace in your pocket, sir, for this once; and let your flesh and blood obey it.

Duke. Well, I will be so much a sinner to be a double-dealer: there's another.   [*Gives money*

Clo. *Primo, secundo, tertio,* is a good play; and the old saying is, the third pays for all: the *triplex,* sir, is a good tripping measure; or the bells of Saint Bennet, sir, may put you in mind,—one, two, three.

Duke. You can fool no more money out of me at this throw: if you will let your lady know I am here to speak with her, and bring her along with you, it may awake my bounty further.

Clo. Marry, sir, lullaby to your bounty, till I come again. I go, sir; but I would not have you to think, that my desire of having is the sin of covetousness: but, as you say, sir, let your bounty take a nap, I will awake it anon.
                                                                [*Exit*

Vio. Here comes the man, sir, that did rescue me.

Enter ANTONIO *and Officers*

Duke. That face of his I do remember well;
Yet when I saw it last, it was besmeared,
As black as Vulcan, in the smoke of war.
A bawbling vessel was he captain of,
For shallow draught and bulk unprizable,
With which such scathful grapple did he make
With the most noble bottom of our fleet,
That very envy, and the tongue of loss
Cried fame and honour on him.—What's the matter?

First Off. Orsino, this is that Antonio
That took the Phœnix and her fraught from Candy;
And this is he that did the Tiger board,

When your young nephew Titus lost his leg.
Here in the streets, desperate of shame and state,
In private brabble did we apprehend him.
   Vio. He did me kindness, sir; drew on my side;
But, in conclusion, put strange speech upon me;
I know not what 't was, but distraction.
   Duke. Notable pirate, thou salt-water thief,
What foolish boldness brought thee to their mercies
Whom thou, in terms so bloody and so dear,
Hast made thine enemies?
   Ant.   Orsino, noble sir,
Be pleased that I shake off these names you give me:
Antonio never yet was thief or pirate,
Though, I confess, on base and ground enough,
Orsino's enemy. A witchcraft drew me hither:
That most ingrateful boy there, by your side,
From the rude sea's enraged and foamy mouth
Did I redeem; a wrack past hope he was:
His life I gave him, and did thereto add
My love, without retention or restraint,
All his in dedication; for his sake
Did I expose myself, pure for his love
Into the danger of this adverse town;
Drew to defend him, when he was beset:
Where, being apprehended, his false cunning—
Not meaning to partake with me in danger—
Taught him to face me out of his acquaintance,
And grew a twenty-years-removéd thing
While one would wink; denied me mine own purse,
Which I had recommended to his use
Not half an hour before.
   Vio.   How can this be?
   Duke. When came he to this town?
   Ant. To-day, my lord; and for three months before—
No interim, not a minute's vacancy—
Both day and night did we keep company.
   Duke. Here comes the countess: now heaven walks on
          earth!—
But for thee, fellow,—fellow, thy words are madness:
Three months this youth hath tended upon me,
But more of that anon.—Take him aside.

Enter OLIVIA *and Attendants*

   Oli. What would my lord, but that he may not have,
Wherein Olivia may seem serviceable?—
Cesario, you do not keep promise with me.
   Vio. Madam?
   Duke. Gracious Olivia,—

Oli.   What do you say, Cesario?—Good my lord,—
Vio.   My lord would speak: my duty hushes me.
Oli.   If it be aught to the old tune, my lord,
It is as fat and fulsome to mine ear
As howling after music.
    Duke.   Still so cruel?
Oli.   Still so constant, lord.
Duke.   What, to perverseness? you uncivil lady,
To whose ingrate and inauspicious altars
My soul the faithfull'st offerings hath breathed out
That e'er devotion tendered!   What shall I do?
Oli.   Even what it please my lord, that shall become him.
Duke.   Why should I not, had I the heart to do it,
Like to the Egyptian thief at point of death,
Kill what I love? a savage jealousy,
That sometime savours nobly.—But hear me this:
Since you to non-regardance cast my faith,
And that I partly know the instrument
That screws me from my true place in your favour,
Live you, the marble-breasted tyrant, still;
But this your minion, whom, I know, you love,
And whom, by Heaven I swear, I tender dearly,
Him will I tear out of that cruel eye
Where he sits crownéd in his master's spite.—
Come, boy, with me: my thoughts are ripe in mischief:
I'll sacrifice the lamb that I do love,
To spite a raven's heart within a dove.   [*Going*
Vio.   And I, most jocund, apt, and willingly,
To do you rest, a thousand deaths would die.
                          [*Following*

Oli.   Where goes Cesario?
Vio.   After him I love
More than I love these eyes, more than my life,
More, by all mores, than e'er I shall love wife.
If I do feign, you witnesses above
Punish my life for tainting of my love!
Oli.   Ay me, detested! how am I beguiled!
Vio.   Who does beguile you? who does do you wrong?
Oli.   Hast thou forgot thyself?   Is it so long?
Call forth the holy father!
                    [*Exit an Attendant*
Duke.   [*To Viola*]   Come away.
Oli.   Whither, my lord?—Cesario, husband, stay.
Duke.   Husband?
Oli.   Ay, husband: can he that deny?
Duke.   Her husband, sirrah?
Vio.   No, my lord, not I.
Oli.   Alas! it is the baseness of thy fear
That makes thee strangle thy propriety.

Fear not, Cesario, take thy fortunes up;
Be that thou know'st thou art, and then thou art
As great as that thou fear'st.—

Re-enter Attendant with the Priest

O, welcome, father!
Father, I charge thee, by thy reverence,
Here to unfold—though lately we intended
To keep in darkness what occasion now
Reveals before 't is ripe—what thou dost know
Hath newly passed between this youth and me.
  Priest.   A contract and eternal bond of love,
Confirmed by mutual joinder of your hands,
Attested by the holy close of lips,
Strengthened by interchangement of your rings:
And all the ceremony of this compáct
Sealed in my function, by my testimony:
Since when, my watch hath told me, toward my grave
I have travelled but two hours.
  Duke.   O thou dissembling cub! what wilt thou be,
When time hath sowed a grizzle on thy case?
Or will not else thy craft so quickly grow,
That thine own trip shall be thine overthrow?
Farewell, and take her; but direct thy feet,
Where thou and I henceforth may never meet.
  Vio.   My lord, I do protest—
  Oli.   O, do not swear!
Hold little faith, though thou hast too much fear.

Enter SIR ANDREW, with his head bleeding

  Sir And.   For the love of God, a surgeon! send one
presently to Sir Toby.
  Oli.   What's the matter?
  Sir And.   He has broke my head across, and has given
Sir Toby a bloody coxcomb too. For the love of God,
your help!   I had rather than forty pound I were at home.
  Oli.   Who has done this, Sir Andrew?
  Sir And.   The count's gentleman, one Cesario; we took
him for a coward, but he's the very devil incardinate.
  Duke.   My gentleman, Cesario?
  Sir And.   Od's lifelings! here he is.—You broke my
head for nothing! and that that I did, I was set on to do 't
by Sir Toby.
  Vio.   Why do you speak to me?   I never hurt you:
You drew your sword upon me without cause;
But I bespake you fair, and hurt you not.
  Sir And.   If a bloody coxcomb be a hurt, you have
hurt me: I think you set nothing by a bloody coxcomb.

146

Here comes Sir Toby halting,—you shall hear more; but
if he had not been in drink, he would have tickled you
othergates than he did.

Enter SIR TOBY *and* Clown

Duke. How now, gentleman? how is 't with you?
Sir To. That 's all one: he has hurt me, and there's
the end on 't.—Sot, didst see Dick surgeon, sot?
Clo. O, he's drunk, Sir Toby, an hour agone: his eyes
were set at eight i' the morning.
Sir To. Then he's a rogue, and a passy-measures pavin.
I hate a drunken rogue.
Oli. Away with him! Who hath made this havoc with
them?
Sir And. I 'll help you, Sir Toby, because we 'll be
dressed together.
Sir To. Will you help,—an ass-head and a coxcomb,
and a knave, a thin-faced knave, a gull!
Oli. Get him to bed! and let his heart be looked to.
     [*Exeunt* Clown, Fabian, Sir Toby, *and* Sir Andrew

Enter SEBASTIAN

Seb. I am sorry, madam, I have hurt your kinsman;
But had it been the brother of my blood,
I must have done no less, with wit and safety.
You throw a strange regard upon me, and by that
I do perceive it hath offended you:
Pardon me, sweet one, even for the vows
We made each other but so late ago.
Duke. One face, one voice, one habit, and two persons;
A natural pérspective, that is, and is not!
Seb. Antonio, O my dear Antonio!
How have the hours racked and tortured me,
Since I have lost thee!
Ant. Sebastian are you?
Seb.   Fear'st thou that, Antonio!
Ant. How have you made division of yourself?—
An apple cleft in two is not more twin
Than these two creatures. Which is Sebastian?
Oli. Most wonderful!
Seb. Do I stand there? I never had a brother;
Nor can there be that deity in my nature,
Of here and everywhere. I had a sister
Whom the blind waves and surges have devoured.
[*To Viola*] Of charity, what kin are you to me?
What countryman? what name? what parentage?
Vio. Of Messaline: Sebastian was my father;
Such a Sebastian was my brother too,

147

So went he suited to his watery tomb.
If spirits can assume both form and suit,
You come to fright us.
  Seb.   A spirit I am indeed;
But am in that dimension grossly clad
Which from the womb I did participate.
Were you a woman, as the rest goes even,
I should my tears let fall upon your cheek
And say—Thrice welcome, drownéd Viola!
  Vio. My father had a mole upon his brow,—
  Seb. And so had mine.
  Vio. And died that day, when Viola from her birth
Had numbered thirteen years.
  Seb. O, that recórd is lively in my soul.
He finishéd, indeed, his mortal act
That day that made my sister thirteen years.
  Vio. If nothing lets to make us happy both,
But this my masculine usurped attire,
Do not embrace me, till each circumstance
Of place, time, fortune, do cohere, and jump,
That I am Viola: which to confirm,
I'll bring you a captain in this town,
Where lie my maid's weeds, by whose gentle help
I was preserved to serve this noble count.
All the occurrence of my fortune since
Hath been between this lady and this lord.
  Seb. [*To Olivia*] So comes it, lady, you have been
   mistook;
But nature to her bias drew in that.
You would have been contracted to a maid,
Nor are you therein, by my life, deceived.
You are betrothed both to a maid and man.
  Duke. Be not amazed; right noble is his blood.—
If this be so, as yet the glass seems true,
I shall have share in this most happy wrack.
[*To Viola*] Boy, thou hast said to me a thousand times
Thou never shouldst love woman like to me.
  Vio. And all those sayings will I overswear,
And all those swearings keep as true in soul
As doth that orbéd continent, the fire
That severs day from night.
  Duke.   Give me thy hand;
And let me see thee in thy woman's weeds.
  Vio. The captain, that did bring me first on shore
Hath my maid's garments: he, upon some action,
Is now in durance, at Malvolio's suit,
A gentleman and follower of my lady's.
  Oli. He shall enlarge him:—fetch Malvolio hither:—
And yet, alas, now I remember me,

They say, poor gentleman, he 's much distract.
A most extracting frenzy of mine own
From my remembrance clearly banished his.—

Re-enter Clown, *with a letter, and* FABIAN

How does he, sirrah?
   Clo. Truly, madam, he holds Beelzebub at the stave's
end as well as a man in his case may do: 'has here writ a
letter to you: I should have given 't you to-day morning,—
but as a madman's epistles are no gospels, so it skills not
much when they are delivered.
   Oli. Open it, and read it.
   Clo. Look then to be well edified, when the fool delivers
the madman.—[*Reads*] *By the Lord, madam,*—
   Oli. How now! Art thou mad?
   Clo. No, madam, I do but read madness: and your
ladyship will have it as it ought to be, you must allow *vox.*
   Oli. Prithee, read i' thy right wits.
   Clo. So I do, madonna; but to read his right wits,
is to read thus: therefore perpend, my princess, and give
ear.
   Oli. [*To Fabian*] Read it you, sirrah.
   Fab. [*Reads*] *By the Lord, madam, you wrong me, and the
world shall know it : though you have put me into darkness,
and given your drunken cousin rule over me, yet have I the
benefit of my senses as well as your ladyship. I have your
own letter that induced me to the semblance I put on ; with the
which I doubt not but to think myself much right, or you much
shame. Think of me as you please. I leave my duty a
little unthought of, and speak of my injury*
              THE MADLY-USED MALVOLIO
   Oli. Did he write this?
   Clo. Ay, madam.
   Duke. This savours not much of distraction.
   Oli. See him delivered, Fabian: bring him hither.
                          [*Exit Fabian*
My lord, so please you, these things further thought on,
To think me as well a sister as a wife,
One day shall crown the alliance on 't, so please you,
Here at my house, and at my proper cost.
   Duke. Madam, I am most apt to embrace your offer.—
[*To Viola*] Your master quits you; and, for your service
          done him,
So much against the mettle of your sex,
So far beneath your soft and tender breeding.
And since you called me master for so long,
Here is my hand: you shall from this time be
Your master's mistress.
   Oli.   A sister!—you are she

Re-enter FABIAN, *with* MALVOLIO

Duke. Is this the madman?
Oli.   Ay, my lord—this same.
How now, Malvolio?
Mal.   Madam, you have done me wrong,
Notorious wrong.
Oli.   Have I, Malvolio? no.
Mal. Lady, you have. Pray you, peruse that letter.
You must not now deny it is your hand:
Write from it, if you can, in hand or phrase;
Or say, 't is not your seal, nor your invention:
You can say none of this: well, grant it then,
And tell me, in the modesty of honour,
Why you have given me such clear lights of favour,
Bade me come smiling and cross-gartered to you,
To put on yellow stockings, and to frown
Upon Sir Toby, and the lighter people;
And, acting this in an obedient hope,
Why have you suffered me to be imprisoned,
Kept in a dark house, visited by the priest,
And made the most notorious geck and gull
That e'er invention played on? tell me why.
Oli. Alas, Malvolio, this is not my writing,
Though, I confess, much like the character:
But, out of question, 't is Maria's hand.
And now I do bethink me, it was she
First told me thou wast mad; thou cam'st in smiling,
And in such forms which here were presupposed
Upon thee in the letter. Prithee, be content;
This practice hath most shrewdly passed upon thee;
But when we know the grounds and authors of it,
Thou shalt be both the plaintiff and the judge
Of thine own cause.
Fab.   Good madam, hear me speak;
And let no quarrel nor no brawl to come
Taint the condition at this present hour,
Which I have wondered at. In hope it shall not,
Most freely I confess, myself and Toby
Set this device against Malvolio here,
Upon some stubborn and uncourteous parts
We had conceived against him. Maria writ
The letter at Sir Toby's great importance:
In recompense whereof, he hath married her.
How with a sportful malice it was followed
May rather pluck on laughter than revenge,
If that the injuries be justly weighed
That have on both sides passed.
Oli. Alas, poor fool, how have they baffled thee!

Clo. Why, "some are born great, some achieve greatness, and some have greatness thrown upon them." I was one, sir, in this interlude,—one Sir Topas, sir; but that's all one.—"By the Lord, fool, I am not mad."—But do you remember? "Madam, why laugh you at such a barren rascal? an you smile not, he's gagged:"—and thus the whirligig of time brings in his revenges.

Mal. I'll be revenged on the whole pack of you.

[Exit

Oli. He hath been most notoriously abused.

Duke. Pursue him, and entreat him to a peace,
He hath not told us of the captain yet:
When that is known, and golden time convents,
A solemn combination shall be made
Of our dear souls. Meantime, sweet sister,
We will not part from hence.—Cesario, come;
For so you shall be, while you are a man;
But when in other habits you are seen,
Orsino's mistress and his fancy's queen.

[Exeunt all, except Clown

Clown *sings*

> *When that I was and a little tiny boy,*
> *With hey, ho, the wind and the rain,*
> *A foolish thing was but a toy,*
> *For the rain it raineth every day.*

> *But when I came to man's estate,*
> *With hey, ho, the wind and the rain,*
> *'Gainst knaves and thieves men shut their gate,*
> *For the rain it raineth every day.*

> *But when I came, alas! to wive,*
> *With hey, ho, the wind and the rain,*
> *By swaggering could I never thrive,*
> *For the rain it raineth every day.*

> *But when I came unto my beds,*
> *With hey, ho, the wind and the rain,*
> *With toss-pots still had drunken heads,*
> *For the rain it raineth every day.*

> *A great while ago the world begun,*
> *With hey, ho, the wind and the rain :—*
> *But that's all one, our play is done,*
> *And we'll strive to please you every day.*

[Exit

151

THE TWO GENTLEMEN OF VERONA

DRAMATIS PERSONÆ

DUKE OF MILAN, *father to Silvia*
VALENTINE⎫
PROTEUS ⎭ *the two Gentlemen*
ANTONIO, *father to Proteus*
THURIO, *a foolish Rival to Valentine*
EGLAMOUR, *agent for Silvia in her escape*
SPEED, *a clownish servant to Valentine*
LAUNCE, *the like to Proteus*
PANTHINO, *servant to Antonio*
HOST, where Julia lodges
Outlaws with Valentine

JULIA, *beloved of Proteus*
SILVIA, *beloved of Valentine*
LUCETTA, *waiting-woman to Julia*
Servants, Musicians

SCENE.—*In Verona; in Milan; and in a Forest near Milan*

THE TWO GENTLEMEN OF VERONA

ACT ONE

Scene I.—Verona. An open Place in the City

Enter Valentine *and* Proteus

Val.   Cease to persuade, my loving Proteus;
Home-keeping youth have ever homely wits.
Were 't not affection chains thy tender days
To the sweet glance of thy honoured love,
I rather would entreat thy company
To see the wonders of the world abroad,
Than, living dully sluggardised at home,
Wear out thy youth with shapeless idleness.
But since thou lov'st, love still, and thrive therein,
Even as I would, when I to love begin.
Pro.   Wilt thou be gone?   Sweet Valentine, adieu!
Think on thy Proteus when thou haply seest
Some rare noteworthy object in thy travel:
Wish me partaker in thy happiness
When thou dost meet good hap; and in thy danger,
If ever danger do environ thee,
Commend thy grievance to my holy prayers,
For I will be thy beadsman, Valentine.
Val.   And on a love-book pray for my success.
Pro.   Upon some book I love, I'll pray for thee.
Val.   That 's on some shallow story of deep love;
How young Leander crossed the Hellespont.
Pro.   That 's a deep story of a deeper love;
For he was more than over shoes in love.
Val.   'Tis true; for you are over boots in love,
And yet you never swam the Hellespont.
Pro.   Over the boots! nay, give me not the boots.
Val.   No, I will not, for 't boots not.
Pro.   What?
Val.   To be
In love: where scorn is bought with groans; coy looks,
With heart-sore sighs; one fading moment's mirth,
With twenty watchful, weary, tedious nights:
If haply won, perhaps, a hapless gain;
If lost, why then a grievous labour won:
However, but a folly bought with wit,

Or else a wit by folly vanquishéd.

    Pro.   So by your circumstance you call me fool.
    Val.   So, by your circumstance, I fear you 'll prove.
    Pro.   'T is love you cavil at; I am not Love.
    Val.   Love is your master, for he masters you;
And he that is yokéd by a fool,
Methinks, should not be chronicled for wise.
    Pro.   Yet writers say, as in the sweetest bud
The eating canker dwells, so eating love
Inhabits in the finest wits of all.
    Val.   And writers say, as the most forward bud
Is eaten by the canker ere it blow,
Even so by love the young and tender wit
Is turned to folly; blasting in the bud,
Losing his verdure even in the prime,
And all the fair effects of future hopes.
But wherefore waste I time to counsel thee
That art a votary to fond desire?
Once more, adieu! My father at the road
Expects my coming, there to see me shipped.
    Pro.   And thither will I bring thee, Valentine.
    Val.   Sweet Proteus, no; now let us take our leave.
To Milan let me hear from thee by letters
Of thy success in love, and what news else
Betideth here in absence of thy friend:
And I likewise will visit thee with mine.
    Pro.   All happiness bechance to thee in Milan!
    Val.   As much to you at home! and so, farewell.   [*Exit*
    Pro.   He after honour hunts, I after love:
He leaves his friends to dignify them more;
I leave myself, my friends, and all, for love.
Thou, Julia, thou hast metamorphosed me,—
Made me neglect my studies, lose my time,
War with good counsel, set the world at naught;
Made wit with musing weak, heart sick with thought.

Enter SPEED

    Speed.   Sir Proteus, save you! Saw you my master?
    Pro.   But now he parted hence to embark for Milan.
    Speed.   Twenty to one then, he is shipped already,
And I have played the sheep in losing him.
    Pro.   Indeed, a sheep doth very often stray,
An if the shepherd be awhile away.
    Speed.   You conclude that my m ter is a shepherd
then, and I a sheep?
    Pro.   I do.
    Speed.   Why, then, my horns are his horns, whether
wake or sleep.

Pro. A silly answer, and fitting well a sheep.

Speed. This proves me still a sheep.

Pro. True; and thy master a shepherd.

Speed. Nay, that I can deny by a circumstance.

Pro. It shall go hard but I'll prove it by another.

Speed. The shepherd seeks the sheep, and not the sheep the shepherd; but I seek my master, and my master seeks not me: therefore, I am no sheep.

Pro. The sheep for fodder follow the shepherd, the shepherd for food follows not the sheep; thou for wages followest thy master, thy master for wages follows not thee: therefore, thou art a sheep.

Speed. Such another proof will make me cry 'baa.'

Pro. But dost thou hear? gav'st thou my letter to Julia?

Speed. Ay, sir: I, a lost mutton, gave your letter to her, a laced mutton; and she, a laced mutton, gave me, a lost mutton, nothing for my labour.

Pro. Here 's too small a pasture for such store of muttons.

Speed. If the ground be overcharged, you were best stick her.

Pro. Nay, in that you are a stray, 't were best pound you.

Speed. Nay, sir, less than a pound shall serve me for carrying your letter.

Pro. You mistake; I mean the pound,—a pinfold.

Speed. From a pound to a pin? fold it over and over. 'T is threefold too little for carrying a letter to your lover.

Pro. What said she? [*Speed nods*] Did she nod?

Speed. Ay.

Pro. Nod, Ay! why, that's noddy.

Speed. You mistook, sir; I say she did nod; and you ask me, if she did nod; and I say, Ay.

Pro. And that set together, is "noddy."

Speed. Now you have taken the pains to set it together, take it for your pains.

Pro. No, no; you shall have it for bearing the letter.

Speed. Well, I perceive I must be fain to bear with you.

Pro. Why, sir, how do you bear with me?

Speed. Marry, sir, the letter very orderly; having nothing but the word "noddy" for my pains.

Pro. Beshrew me, but you have a quick wit.

Speed. And yet it cannot overtake your slow purse.

Pro. Come, come; open the matter in brief; what said she?

Speed. Open your purse, that the money and the matter may be both at once delivered.

Pro. Well, sir, here is for your pains. What said she?

Speed.   Truly, sir, I think you 'll hardly win her.
Pro.   Why?   Couldst thou perceive so much from her?
Speed.   Sir, I could perceive nothing at all from her;
no, not so much as a ducat for delivering your letter.
And being so hard to me that brought your mind, I
fear she'll prove as hard to you in telling your mind.   Give
her no token but stones, for she's as hard as steel.
Pro.   What! said she nothing?
Speed.   No, not so much as—"Take this for thy pains."
To testify your bounty, I thank you, you have testerned
me; in requital whereof, henceforth carry your letters
yourself.   And so, sir, I 'll commend you to my master.
Pro.   Go, go, be gone, to save your ship from wreck,
Which cannot perish, having thee aboard,
Being destined to a drier death on shore.—

                                                    [*Exit Speed*

I must go send some better messenger:
I fear my Julia would not deign my lines,
Receiving them from such a worthless post.   [*Exit*

SCENE II.—Verona.   JULIA's Garden

Enter JULIA *and* LUCETTA

Jul.   But say, Lucetta, now we are alone,
Wouldst thou then counsel me to fall in love?
Luc.   Ay, madam; so you stumble not unheedfully.
Jul.   Of all the fair resort of gentlemen
That every day with parle encounter me,
In thy opinion which is worthiest love?
Luc.   Please you, repeat their names, I'll show my mind
According to my shallow simple skill.
Jul.   What think'st thou of the fair Sir Eglamour?
Luc.   As of a knight well-spoken, neat and fine;
But, were I you, he never should be mine.
Jul.   What think'st thou of the rich Mercatio?
Luc.   Well of his wealth; but of himself, so, so.
Jul.   What think'st thou of the gentle Proteus?
Luc.   Lord, Lord! to see what folly reigns in us!
Jul.   How now! what means this passion at his name?
Luc.   Pardon, dear madam: 't is a passing shame
That I, unworthy body as I am,
Should censure thus on lovely gentlemen.
Jul.   Why not on Proteus, as of all the rest?
Luc.   Then thus,—of many good I think him best.
Jul.   Your reason?
Luc.   I have no other but a woman's reason.   I think
him so, because I think him so.

Jul.　And wouldst thou have me cast my love on him?
Luc.　Ay, if you thought your love not cast away.
Jul.　Why, he of all the rest hath never moved me.
Luc.　Yet he of all the rest, I think, best loves ye.
Jul.　His little speaking shows his love but small.
Luc.　Fire that's closest kept burns most of all.
Jul.　They do not love that do not show their love.
Luc.　O, they love least, that let men know their love.
Jul.　I would I knew his mind.
Luc.　　　　　　　　Peruse this paper, madam.
Jul.　'To Julia.'　Say, from whom?
Luc.　　　　　　　　That the contents will show.
Jul.　Say, say, who gave it thee?
Luc.　Sir Valentine's page; and sent, I think, from
　　　Proteus.
He would have given it to you, but I, being in the way,
Did in your name receive it: pardon the fault, I pray.
Jul.　Now, by my modesty, a goodly broker!
Dare you presume to harbour wanton lines?
To whisper and conspire against my youth?
Now, trust me, 't is an office of great worth,
And you an officer fit for the place.
There, take the paper: see it be returned;
Or else return no more into my sight.
Luc.　To plead for love deserves more fee than hate.
Jul.　Will ye be gone?
Luc.　　　　　　　　That you may ruminate.　[*Exit*
Jul.　And yet I would I had o'erlooked the letter.
It were a shame to call her back again,
And pray her to a fault for which I chid her.
What fool is she, that knows I am a maid
And would not force the letter to my view,—
Since maids, in modesty, say 'No' to that
Which they would have the profferer construe, 'Ay.'
Fie, fie, how wayward is this foolish love,
That, like a testy babe, will scratch the nurse,
And presently, all humbled, kiss the rod.
How churlishly I chid Lucetta hence,
When willingly I would have had her here!
How angerly I taught my brow to frown,
When inward joy enforced my heart to smile!
My penance is, to call Lucetta back,
And ask remission for my folly past.—
What, ho! Lucetta!

Re-enter LUCETTA

Luc.　　　　　　　　What would your ladyship?
Jul.　Is it near dinner-time?
Luc.　　　　　　　　I would it were;

That you might kill your stomach on your meat
And not upon your maid.

 Jul. What is 't that you took up so gingerly?

 Luc. Nothing.

 Jul. Why didst thou stoop then?

 Luc.   To take a paper up
That I let fall.

 Jul.   And is that paper nothing?

 Luc. Nothing concerning me.

 Jul. Then let it lie for those that it concerns.

 Luc. Madam, it will not lie where it concerns,
Unless it have a false interpreter.

 Jul. Some love of yours hath writ to you in rhyme.

 Luc. That I might sing it, madam, to a tune.
Give me a note: your ladyship can set.

 Jul. As little by such toys as may be possible:
Best sing it to the tune of 'Light o' love.'

 Luc. It is too heavy for so light a tune.

 Jul. Heavy? belike, it hath some burden, then.

 Luc. Ay; and melodious were it, would you sing it.

 Jul. And why not you?

 Luc.   I cannot reach so high.

 Jul. Let 's see your song.—[*Takes the letter*]—How
now, minion!

 Luc. Keep tune there still, so you will sing it out:
And yet, methinks, I do not like this tune.

 Jul. You do not?

 Luc.   No madam; it is too sharp.

 Jul. You, minion, are too saucy.

 Luc.   Nay, now you are too flat,
And mar the concord with too harsh a descant:
There wanteth but a mean to fill your song.

 Jul. The mean is drowned with your unruly base.

 Luc. Indeed, I bid the base for Proteus.

 Jul. This babble shall not henceforth trouble me:—
Here is a coil with protestation!—   [*Tears the letter*
Go, get you gone, and let the papers lie:
You would be fingering them, to anger me.

 Luc. She makes it strange, but she would be best
   pleased
To be so angered with another letter.   [*Exit*

 Jul. Nay, would I were so angered with the same!
O hateful hands! to tear such loving words:
Injurious wasps, to feed on such sweet honey,
And kill the bees that yield it with your stings?
I'll kiss each several paper for amends.
Look, here is writ—"kind Julia."—Unkind Julia!
As in revenge of thy ingratitude,
I throw thy name against the bruising stones,

Trampling contemptuously on thy disdain.
And here is writ—"love-wounded Proteus."—
Poor wounded name! my bosom, as a bed,
Shall lodge thee, till thy wound be thoroughly healed;
And thus I search it with a sovereign kiss.
But twice or thrice was Proteus written down:
Be calm, good wind, blow not a word away,
Till I have found each letter in the letter,
Except mine own name: that some whirlwind bear
Unto a ragged, fearful-hanging rock,
And throw it thence into the raging sea!
Lo, here in one line is his name twice writ,—
"Poor forlorn Proteus; passionate Proteus
To the sweet Julia:"—that I'll tear away;—
And yet I will not, sith so prettily
He couples it to his complaining names.
Thus will I fold them one upon another:
Now kiss, embrace, contend, do what you will.

Re-enter LUCETTA

Luc.   Madam,
Dinner is ready, and your father stays.
Jul.   Well, let us go.
Luc.   What, shall these papers lie like tell-tales here?
Jul.   If you respect them, best to take them up.
Luc.   Nay, I was taken up for laying them down;
Yet here they shall not lie, for catching cold.
Jul.   I see, you have a month's mind to them.
Luc.   Ay, madam, you may say what sights you see;
I see things too, although you judge I wink.
Jul.   Come, come; will 't please you go?   [*Exeunt*

SCENE III.—Verona.   A Room in ANTONIO's House

Enter ANTONIO *and* PANTHINO

Ant.   Tell me, Panthino, what sad talk was that
Wherewith my brother held you in the cloister?
Pant.   'T was of his nephew Proteus, your son.
Ant.   Why, what of him?
Pant.   He wondered, that your lordship
Would suffer him to spend his youth at home,
While other men, of slender reputation,
Put forth their sons to seek preferment out:
Some, to the wars, to try their fortunes there;
Some, to discover islands far away;
Some, to the studious universities.
For any or for all these exercises

He said that Proteus your son was meet,
And did request me to importune you
To l t him spend his time no more at home,
Wh h would be great impeachment to his age,
In aving known no travel in his youth.
    Ant. Nor need'st thou much impórtune me to that
Whereon this month I have been hammering.
I have considered well his loss of time,
And how he cannot be a perfect man,
Not being tried and tutored in the world:
Experience is by industry achieved,
And perfected by the swift course of time.
Then, tell me, whither were I best to send him?
    Pant. I think your lordship is not ignorant
How his companion, youthful Valentine,
Attends the emperor in his royal court.
    Ant. I know it well.
    Pant. 'T were good, I think, your lordship sent him
           thither.
There shall he practise tilts and tournaments,
Hear sweet discourse, converse with noblemen,
And be in eye of every exercise
Worthy his youth and nobleness of birth.
    Ant. I like thy counsel; well hast thou advised;
And, that thou may'st perceive how well I like it,
The execution of it shall make known.
Even with the speediest expedition
I will despatch him to the emperor's court.
    Pant. To-morrow, may it please you, Don Alphonso,
With other gentlemen of good esteem,
Are journeying to salute the emperor,
And to commend their service to his will.
    Ant. Good company; with them shall Proteus go:
And,—in good time.—Now will we break with him.

Enter PROTEUS

    Pro. Sweet love! sweet lines! sweet life!
Here is her hand, the agent of her heart;
Here is her oath for love, her honour's pawn.
O, that our fathers would applaud our loves.
To seal our happiness with their consents!
O heavenly Julia!
    Ant. How now! what letter are you reading there?
    Pro. May 't please your lordship, 't is a word or two
Of commendations sent from Valentine,
Delivered by a friend that came from him.
    Ant. Lend me the letter; let me see what news.
    Pro. There is no news, my lord, but that he writes

How happily he lives, how well beloved.
And daily gracéd by the emperor;
Wishing me with him, partner of his fortune.
    Ant.   And how stand you affected to his wish?
    Pro.   As one relying on your lordship's will,
And not depending on his friendly wish.
    Ant.   My will is something sorted with his wish.
Muse not that I thus suddenly proceed,
For what I will, I will, and there an end.
I am resolved that thou shalt spend some time
With Valentinus in the emperor's court:
What maintenance he from his friends receives,
Like exhibition thou shalt have from me.
To-morrow be in readiness to go:
Excuse it not; for I am peremptory.
    Pro.   My lord, I cannot be so soon provided:
Please you, deliberate a day or two.
    Ant.   Look, what thou want'st shall be sent after thee:
No more of stay; to-morrow thou must go—
Come on Panthino: you shall be employed
To hasten on his expedition.

                 [Exeunt Antonio and Panthino
    Pro.   Thus have I shunned the fire for fear of burning,
And drenched me in the sea, where I am drowned.
I feared to show my father Julia's letter,
Lest he should take exceptions to my love;
And, with the vantage of mine own excuse
Hath he excepted most against my love.
O, how this spring of love resembleth
    The uncertain glory of an April day,
Which now shows all the beauty of the sun,
    And by-and-by a cloud takes all away.

Re-enter PANTHINO

    Pant.   Sir Proteus, your father calls for you:
        He is in haste; therefore, I pray you, go.
    Pro.   Why, this it is,—my heart accords thereto,
        And yet a thousand times it answers, No.

                        [Exeunt

ACT TWO

SCENE I.—Milan.   A Room in the DUKE'S Palace

Enter VALENTINE *and* SPEED

Speed [*picking up a glove*].   Sir, your glove.
Val.   Not mine; my gloves are on.
Speed.   Why, then this may be yours, for this is but one.

Val. Ha! let me see: ay, give it me, it 's mine.—
Sweet ornament, that decks a thing divine!
Ah, Silvia, Silvia!
          Speed [*calling*].   Madam Silvia, Madam Silvia!
          Val.   How now, sirrah?
          Speed.   She is not within hearing, sir.
          Val.   Why, sir, who bade you call her?
          Speed.   Your worship, sir; or else I mistook.
          Val.   Well, you 'll still be too forward.
          Speed.   And yet I was last chidden for being too slow.
          Val.   Go to, sir; tell me, do you know Madam Silvia?
          Speed.   She that your worship loves?
          Val.   Why, how know you that I am in love?
          Speed.   Marry, by these special marks: first, you have
learned, like Sir Proteus, to wreath your arms, like a
malcontent; to relish a love-song, like a robin-redbreast;
to walk alone, like one that had the pestilence; to sigh,
like a school-boy that had lost his A B C; to weep, like
a young wench that had buried her grandam; to fast,
like one that takes diet; to watch, like one that fears
robbing; to speak puling, like a beggar at Hallowmas.
You were wont, when you laughed, to crow like a cock;
when you walked, to walk like one of the lions; when you
fasted, it was presently after dinner; when you looked
sadly, it was for want of money; and now you are metamorphosed with a mistress, that, when I look on you, I can
hardly think you my master.
          Val.   Are all these things perceived in me?
          Speed.   They are all perceived without ye.
          Val.   Without me? they cannot.
          Speed.   Without you? nay, that 's certain; for, without
you were so simple, none else would: but you are so
without these follies, that these follies are within you, and
shine through you like the water in an urinal, that not an
eye that sees you but is a physician to comment on your
malady.
          Val.   But, tell me, dost thou know my lady Silvia?
          Speed.   She that you gaze on so, as she sits at supper?
          Val.   Hast thou observed that? even she I mean.
          Speed.   Why, sir, I know her not.
          Val.   Dost thou know her by my gazing on her, and yet
knowest her not?
          Speed.   Is she not hard-favoured, sir?
          Val.   Not so fair, boy, as well-favoured.
          Speed.   Sir, I know that well enough.
          Val.   What dost thou know?
          Speed.   That she is not so fair as, of you, well-favoured.
          Val.   I mean, that her beauty is exquisite, but her
favour infinite.

Speed. That's because the one is painted, and the other out of all count.

Val. How painted? and how out of count?

Speed. Marry, sir, so painted to make her fair, that no man counts of her beauty.

Val. How esteem'st thou me? I account of her beauty.

Speed. You never saw her since she was deformed.

Val. How long hath she been deformed?

Speed. Ever since you loved her.

Val. I have loved her ever since I saw her, and still I see her beautiful.

Speed. If you love her, you cannot see her.

Val. Why?

Speed. Because love is blind. O, that you had mine eyes; or your own eyes had the lights they were wont to have, when you chid at Sir Proteus for going ungartered!

Val. What should I see then?

Speed. Your own present folly, and her passing deformity; for he, being in love, could not see to garter his hose; and you, being in love, cannot see to put on your hose.

Val. Belike, boy, then you are in love; for last morning you could not see to wipe my shoes.

Speed. True, sir; I was in love with my bed. I thank you, you swinged me for my love, which makes me the bolder to chide you for yours.

Val. In conclusion, I stand affected to her.

Speed. I would you were set; so your affection would cease.

Val. Last night she enjoined me to write some lines to one she loves.

Speed. And have you?

Val. I have.

Speed. Are they not lamely writ?

Val. No, boy, but as well as I can do them.—Peace! here she comes.

Speed. O excellent motion! O exceeding puppet! Now will he interpret to her.

Enter SILVIA

Val. Madam and mistress, a thousand good-morrows.

Speed. O, give ye good even: here 's a million of manners.

Sil. Sir Valentine and servant, to you two thousand.

Speed. He should give her interest, and she gives it him.

Val. As you enjoined me, I have writ your letter
Unto the secret nameless friend of yours;

165

Which I was much unwilling to proceed in,
But for my duty to your ladyship.   [*Gives a letter*
   Sil. I thank you, gentle servant: 't is very clerkly done.
   Val. Now trust me, madam, it came hardly off;
For, being ignorant to whom it goes,
I writ at random, very doubtfully.
   Sil. Perchance you think too much of so much pains?
   Val. No, madam: so it stead you, I will write,
Please you command, a thousand times as much.
And yet,—
   Sil. A pretty period. Well, I guess the sequel;
And yet I will not name't;—and yet I care not;—
And yet take this again;—and yet I thank you,
Meaning henceforth to trouble you no more.
   Speed. And yet you will; and yet another yet.
   Val. What means your ladyship; do you not like it?
   Sil. Yes, yes; the lines are very quaintly writ,
But since unwillingly, take them again:
Nay, take them.   [*Gives back the letter*
   Val. Madam, they are for you.
   Sil. Ay, ay, you writ them, sir, at my request;
But I will none of them. They are for you:
I would have had them writ more movingly.
   Val. Please you, I'll write your ladyship another.
   Sil. And when it's writ, for my sake read it over:
And, if it please you, so: if not, why, so.
   Val. If it please me, madam; what then?
   Sil. Why, if it please you, take it for your labour.
And so good-morrow, servant.   [*Exit*
   Speed. O jest unseen, inscrutable, invisible,
As a nose on a man's face, or a weathercock on a steeple!
My master sues to her, and she hath taught her suitor,
He being her pupil, to become her tutor.
O excellent device! was there ever heard a better,
That my master, being scribe, to himself should write the
       letter?
   Val. How now, sir! what, are you reasoning with
yourself?
   Speed. Nay, I was rhyming: 't is you that have the
reason.
   Val. To do what?
   Speed. To be a spokesman from Madame Silvia.
   Val. To whom?
   Speed. To yourself. Why, she woos you by a figure.
   Val. What figure?
   Speed. By a letter, I should say.
   Val. Why, she hath not writ to me?
   Speed. What need she, when she hath made you write
to yourself? Why, do you not perceive the jest?

Val. No, believe me.

Speed. No believing you, indeed, sir: but did you perceive her earnest?

Val. She gave me none, except an angry word.

Speed. Why, she hath given you a letter.

Val. That 's the letter I writ to her friend.

Speed. And that letter hath she delivered, and there an end.

Val. I would it were no worse!

Speed. I 'll warrant you, 't is as well:
For often have you writ to her, and she, in modesty,
Or else for want of idle time, could not again reply;
Or fearing else some messenger that might her mind discover,
Herself hath taught her love himself to write unto her lover,
All this I speak in print, for in print I found it.—
Why muse you, sir? 't is dinner-time.

Val. I have dined.

Speed. Ay, but hearken, sir: though the chameleon Love can feed on the air, I am one that am nourished by my victuals, and would fain have meat. O, be not like your mistress; be moved, be moved.   [*Exeunt*

SCENE II.—Verona.   A Room in JULIA'S House

Enter PROTEUS *and* JULIA

Pro. Have patience, gentle Julia.

Jul. I must, where is no remedy.

Pro. When possibly I can, I will return.

Jul. If you turn not, you will return the sooner.
Keep this remembrance for thy Julia's sake.
                              [*Gives him a ring*

Pro. Why, then we 'll make exchange: here, take you this.   [*Gives her a ring*

Jul. And seal the bargain with a holy kiss.

Pro. Here is my hand for my true constancy;
And when that hour o'erslips me in the day
Wherein I sigh not, Julia, for thy sake,
The next ensuing hour some foul mischance
Torment me for my love's forgetfulness.
My father stays my coming; answer not.
The tide is now: nay, not thy tide of tears;
That tide will stay me longer than I should.
Julia, farewell.   [*Exit Julia*
              What! gone without a word?
Ay, so true love should do: it cannot speak;
For truth hath better deeds than words to grace it.

Enter PANTHINO

Pant.   Sir Proteus, you are stayed for.
Pro.   Go; I come, I come.—
Alas! this parting strikes poor lovers dumb!   [*Exeunt*

SCENE III.—Verona.   A Street

Enter LAUNCE, *leading a dog*

Launce.   Nay, 't will be this hour ere I have done
weeping; all the kind of the Launces have this very
fault.   I have received my proportion, like the prodigious
son, and am going with Sir Proteus to the imperial's
court.   I think Crab, my dog, be the sourest-natured dog
that lives: my mother weeping, my father wailing, my
sister crying, our maid howling, our cat wringing her
hands, and all our house in a great perplexity, yet did not
this cruel-hearted cur shed one tear.   He is stone, a very
pebble stone, and has no more pity in him than a dog: a
Jew would have wept to have seen our parting; why, my
grandam, having no eyes, look you, wept herself blind
at my parting.   Nay, I 'll show you the manner of it.
This shoe is my father:—no, this left shoe is my father;
—no, no, this left shoe is my mother;—nay, that cannot
be so, neither;—yes, it is so, it is so; it hath the worser
sole.   This shoe with the hole in it is my mother, and this
my father.   A vengeance on 't! there 't is: now, sir,
this staff is my sister; for, look you, she is as white as a
lily, and as small as a wand: this hat is Nan, our maid:
I am the dog;—no, the dog is himself, and I am the dog,
—O, the dog is me, and I am myself: ay, so, so.   Now
come I to my father; 'Father, your blessing!' now should
not the shoe speak a word for weeping: now should I
kiss my father; well, he weeps on.   Now come I to my
mother;—O, that she could speak now, like a wood
woman!—well, I kiss her; why, there 't is, here 's my
mother's breath up and down.   Now come I to my sister;
mark the moan she makes.   Now, the dog all this while
sheds not a tear, nor speaks a word; but see how I lay
the dust with my tears.

Enter PANTHINO

Pant.   Launce, away, away, aboard: thy master is
shipped, and thou art to post after with oars.   What 's
the matter? why weep'st thou, man?   Away, ass! you 'll
lose the tide, if you tarry any longer.
Launce.   It is no matter if the tied were lost; for it
is the unkindest tied that ever any man tied.

Pant. What 's the unkindest tide?

Launce. Why, he that 's tied here, Crab, my dog.

Pant. Tut, man, I mean thou 'lt lose the flood; and, in losing the flood, lose thy voyage; and, in losing thy voyage, lose thy master; and, in losing thy master, lose thy service; and, in losing thy service,—Why dost thou stop my mouth?

Launce. For fear thou shouldst lose thy tongue.

Pant. Where should I lose my tongue?

Launce. In thy tale.

Pant. In my tail?

Launce. Lose the tide, and the voyage, and the master, and the service and the tied! Why, man, if the river were dry, I am able to fill it with my tears; if the wind were down, I could drive the boat with my sighs.

Pant. Come, come, away, man: I was sent to call thee.

Launce. Sir, call me what thou darest.

Pant. Wilt thou go?

Launce. Well, I will go.   [*Exeunt*

SCENE IV.—Milan. A Room in the DUKE's Palace

Enter VALENTINE, SILVIA, THURIO, *and* SPEED

Sil. Servant,—

Val. Mistress?

Speed. Master, Sir Thurio frowns on you.

Val. Ay, boy, it 's for love.

Speed. Not of you.

Val. Of my mistress then.

Speed. 'T were good you knocked him.

Sil. Servant, you are sad.

Val. Indeed, madam, I seem so.

Thu. Seem you that you are not?

Val. Haply, I do.

Thu. So do counterfeits.

Val. So do you.

Thu. What seem I that I am not?

Val. Wise.

Thu. What instance of the contrary?

Val. Your folly.

Thu. And how quote you my folly?

Val. I quote it in your jerkin.

Thu. My jerkin is a doublet.

Val. Well, then, I 'll double your folly.

Thu. How?

Sil. What, angry, Sir Thurio! do you change colour?

Val. Give him leave, madam; he is a kind of chameleon.

169

Thu. That hath more mind to feed on your blood, than live in your air.

Val. You have said, sir.

Thu. Ay, sir, and done too, for this time.

Val. I know it well, sir: you always end ere you begin.

Sil. A fine volley of words, gentlemen, and quickly shot off.

Val. 'T is indeed, madam, we thank the giver.

Sil. Who is that, servant?

Val. Yourself, sweet lady; for you gave the fire. Sir Thurio borrows his wit from your ladyship's looks, and spends what he borrows kindly in your company.

Thu. Sir, if you spend word for word with me, I shall make your wit bankrupt.

Val. I know it well, sir: you have an exchequer of words, and, I think, no other treasure to give your followers; for it appears by their bare liveries, that they live by your bare words.

Sil. No more, gentlemen, no more:—Here comes my father.

Enter the DUKE

Duke. Now, daughter Silvia, you are hard beset.
Sir Valentine, your father's in good health:
What say you to a letter from your friends
Of much good news?

Val.   My lord, I will be thankful
To any happy messenger from thence.

Duke. Know you Don Antonio, your countryman?

Val. Ay, my good lord; I know the gentleman
To be of worth, and worthy estimation,
And not without desert so well reputed.

Duke. Hath he not a son?

Val. Ay, my good lord; a son, that well deserves
The honour and regard of such a father.

Duke. You know him well?

Val. I know him as myself; for from our infancy
We have conversed, and spent our hours together:
And though myself have been an idle truant,
Omitting the sweet benefit of time
To clothe mine age with angel-like perfection,
Yet hath Sir Proteus, for that's his name,
Made use and fair advantage of his days;
His years but young, but his experience old;
His head unmellowed, but his judgment ripe:
And, in a word,—for far behind his worth
Come all the praises that I now bestow,—
He is complete in feature and in mind

With all good grace to grace a gentleman.
    Duke.   Beshrew me, sir, but, if he make this good,
He is as worthy for an empress' love
As meet to be an emperor's counsellor.
Well, sir, this gentleman is come to me
With commendation from great potentates:
And here he means to spend his time awhile:
I think, 't is no unwelcome news to you.
    Val.   Should I have wished a thing, it had been he.
    Duke.   Welcome him then according to his worth.
Volia, I speak to you; and you, Sir Thurio:—
Sir Valentine, I need not cite him to it.
I 'll send him hither to you presently.   *[Exit*
    Val.   This is the gentleman, I told your ladyship
Had come along with me, but that his mistress
Did hold his eyes locked in her crystal looks.
    Sil.   Belike, that now she hath enfranchised them,
Upon some other pawn for fealty.
    Val.   Nay, sure, I think she holds them prisoners still.
    Sil.   Nay, then, he should be blind; and, being blind,
How could he see his way to seek out you?
    Val.   Why, lady, Love hath twenty pair of eyes.
    Thu.   They say, that Love hath not an eye at all.
    Val.   To see such lovers, Thurio, as yourself:
Upon a homely object Love can wink.

Enter PROTEUS

    Sil.   Have done, have done; here comes the gentleman.
    Val.   Welcome, dear Proteus!—Mistress, I beseech you,
Confirm his welcome with some special favour.
    Sil.   His worth is warrant for his welcome hither,
If this be he you oft have wished to hear from.
    Val.   Mistress, it is; sweet lady, entertain him
To be my fellow-servant to your ladyship.
    Sil.   Too low a mistress for so high a servant.
    Pro.   Not so, sweet lady; but too mean a servant
To have a look of such a worthy mistress.
    Val.   Leave off discourse of disability:—
Sweet lady, entertain him for your servant.
    Pro.   My duty will I boast of, nothing else.
    Sil.   And duty never yet did want his meed.
Servant, you 're welcome to a worthless mistress.
    Pro.   I 'll die on him that says so, but yourself.
    Sil.   That you are welcome?
    Pro.   That you are worthless.

Enter a Servant

    Serv.   Madam, my lord, your father, would speak with
you.

Sil.   I wait upon his pleasure.   [*Exit Serv.*
                                                  Come, Sir Thurio,
Go you with me.—Once more, new servant, welcome:
I 'll leave you to confer of home-affairs;
When you have done, we look to hear from you.
    Pro.   We 'll both attend upon your ladyship.
                                          [*Exeunt Silvia and Thurio*
    Val.   Now, tell me, how do all from whence you came?
    Pro.   Your friends are well, and have them much
          commended.
    Val.   And how do yours?
    Pro.   I left them all in health.
    Val.   How does your lady, and how thrives your love?
    Pro.   My tales of love were wont to weary you;
I know you joy not in a love-discourse.
    Val.   Ay, Proteus, but that life is altered now.
I have done penance for contemning Love:
Whose high imperious thoughts have punished me
With bitter fasts, with penitential groans,
With nightly tears, and daily heart-sore sighs;
For, in revenge of my contempt of Love,
Love hath chased sleep from my enthralled eyes,
And made them watchers of mine own heart's sorrow.
O gentle Proteus, Love 's a mighty lord,
And hath so humbled me, as, I confess,
There is no woe to his correction,
Nor to his service no such joy on earth!
Now no discourse, except it be of love;
Now can I break my fast, dine, sup, and sleep,
Upon the very naked name of love.
    Pro.   Enough; I read your fortune in your eye.
Was this the idol that you worship so?
    Val.   Even she; and is she not a heavenly saint?
    Pro.   No; but she is an earthly paragon.
    Val.   Call her divine.
    Pro.   I will not flatter her.
    Val.   O, flatter me; for love delights in praises.
    Pro.   When I was sick, you gave me bitter pills;
And I must minister the like to you.
    Val.   Then speak the truth by her: if not divine,
Yet let her be a principality,
Sovereign to all the creatures on the earth.
    Pro.   Except my mistress.
    Val.   Sweet, except not any;
Except thou wilt except against my love.
    Pro.   Have I not reason to prefer mine own?
    Val.   And I will help thee to prefer her too:
She shall be dignified with this high honour,—
To bear my lady's train, lest the base earth

Should from her vesture chance to steal a kiss,
And, of so great a favour growing proud,
Disdain to root the summer-swelling flower,
And make rough winter everlastingly.
    Pro. Why, Valentine, what braggardism is this?
    Val. Pardon me, Proteus; all I can, is nothing
To her, whose worth makes other worthies nothing.
She is alone.
    Pro.   Then let her alone.
    Val. Not for the world: why, man, she is mine own,
And I as rich in having such a jewel
As twenty seas, if all their sand were pearl,
The water nectar, and the rocks pure gold.
Forgive me, that I do not dream on thee,
Because thou seest me dote upon my love.
My foolish rival, that her father likes
Only for his possessions are so huge,
Is gone with her along; and I must after,
For love, thou know'st, is full of jealousy.
    Pro. But she loves you?
    Val. Ay,
And we are betrothed; nay, more, our marriage-hour,
With all the cunning manner of our flight,
Determined of: how I must climb her window,
The ladder made of cords, and all the means
Plotted and 'greed on, for my happiness.
Good Proteus, go with me to my chamber,
In these affairs to aid me with thy counsel.
    Pro. Go on before; I shall enquire you forth.
I must unto the road, to disembark
Some necessaries that I needs must use,
And then I 'll presently attend you.
    Val. Will you make haste?
    Pro. I will.—   *[Exeunt Valentine and Speed*
Even as one heat another heat expels,
Or as one nail by strength drives out another,
So the remembrance of my former love
Is by a newer object quite forgotten.
Is it mine eye, or Valentinus' praise,
Her true perfection, or my false transgression,
That makes me, reasonless, to reason thus?
She 's fair, and so is Julia that I love,—
That I did love, for now my love is thawed,
Which, like a waxen image 'gainst a fire,
Bears no impression of the thing it was.
Methinks, my zeal to Valentine is cold,
And that I love him not as I was wont:
O, but I love his lady too too much;
And that 's the reason I love him so little.

How shall I dote on her with more advice,
That thus without advice begin to love her?
'T is but her picture I have yet beheld,
And that hath dazzléd my reason's light;
But when I look on her perfections,
There is no reason but I shall be blind.
If I can check my erring love, I will;
If not, to compass her I 'll use my skill.   [*Exit*

SCENE V.—Milan.   A Street

Enter SPEED *and* LAUNCE

Speed.   Launce! by mine honesty, welcome to Milan!
Launce.   Forswear not thyself, sweet youth, for I am not welcome.   I reckon this always, that a man is never undone till he be hanged; nor never welcome to a place till some certain shot be paid, and the hostess say, 'Welcome!'
Speed.   Come on, you madcap, I 'll to the ale-house with you presently; where for one shot of five-pence thou shalt have five thousand welcomes.   But, sirrah, how did thy master part with Madam Julia?
Launce.   Marry, after they closed in earnest, they parted very fairly in jest.
Speed.   But shall she marry him?
Launce.   No.
Speed.   How then? Shall he marry her?
Launce.   No, neither.
Speed.   What, are they broken?
Launce.   No, they are both as whole as a fish.
Speed.   Why then, how stands the matter with them?
Launce.   Marry, thus: when it stands well with him, it stands well with her.
Speed.   What an ass art thou! I understand thee not.
Launce.   What a block art thou, that thou canst not. My staff understands me.
Speed.   What thou say'st?
Launce.   Ay, and what I do too: look thee, I 'll but lean, and my staff understands me.
Speed.   It stands under thee, indeed.
Launce.   Why, stand-under and under-stand is all one.
Speed.   But tell me true, will 't be a match?
Launce.   Ask my dog: if he say, ay, it will; if he say, no, it will; if he shake his tail and say nothing, it will.
Speed.   The conclusion is then, that it will.
Launce.   Thou shalt never get such a secret from me but by a parable.

174

Speed. 'T is well that I get it so. But, Launce, how say'st thou, that my master is become a notable lover?

Launce. I never knew him otherwise.

Speed. Than how?

Launce. A notable lubber, as thou reportest him to be.

Speed. Why, thou whoreson ass, thou mistakest me.

Launce. Why, fool, I meant not thee; I meant thy master.

Speed. I tell thee, my master is become a hot lover.

Launce. Why, I tell thee, I care not though he burn himself in love. If thou wilt go with me to the ale-house, so; if not, thou art an Hebrew, a Jew, and not worth the name of a Christian.

Speed. Why?

Launce. Because thou hast not so much charity in thee as to go to the ale with a Christian. Wilt thou go?

Speed. At thy service. [*Exeunt*

SCENE VI.—Milan. A room in the DUKE's Palace

Enter PROTEUS

Pro. To leave my Julia, shall I be forsworn;
To love fair Silvia, shall I be forsworn;
To wrong my friend, I shall be much forsworn;
And even that power which gave me first my oath
Provokes me to this threefold perjury:
Love bade me swear, and Love bids me forswear.
O Sweet-suggesting Love, if thou hast sinned,
Teach me, thy tempted subject, to excuse it!
At first I did adore a twinkling star,
But now I worship a celestial sun.
Unheedful vows may heedfully be broken;
And he wants wit that wants resolvéd will
To learn his wit to exchange the bad for better.—
Fie, fie, unreverend tongue! to call her bad
Whose sovereignty so oft thou hast preferred
With twenty thousand soul-confirming oaths.
I cannot leave to love, and yet I do;
But there I leave to love where I should love.
Julia I lose, and Valentine I lose:
If I keep them, I needs must lose myself;
If I lose them, thus find I, by their loss,
For Valentine, myself; for Julia, Silvia.
I to myself am dearer than a friend,
For love is still most precious in itself;
And Silvia—witness Heaven that made her fair!—
Shows Julia but a swarthy Ethiop.

175

I will forget that Julia is alive,
Remembering that my love to her is dead;
And Valentine I 'll hold an enemy,
Aiming at Silvia as a sweeter friend.
I cannot now prove constant to myself
Without some treachery used to Valentine.—
This night, he meaneth with a corded ladder
To climb celestial Silvia's chamber-window;
Myself in counsel, his competitor:
Now presently I 'll give her father notice
Of their disguising and pretended flight;
Who, all enraged, will banish Valentine,
For Thurio he intends shall wed his daughter;
But, Valentine being gone, I 'll quickly cross
By some sly trick blunt Thurio's dull proceeding.
Love, lend me wings, to make my purpose swift,
As thou hast lent me wit to plot this drift!   [*Exit*

SCENE VII.—Verona.   A Room in JULIA's House

Enter JULIA *and* LUCETTA

Jul.   Counsel, Lucetta; gentle girl, assist me;
And, e'en in kind love, I do conjure thee,—
Who are the table, wherein all my thoughts
Are visibly charactered and engraved,—
To lesson me; and tell me some good mean,
How, with my honour, I may undertake
A journey to my loving Proteus.
Luc.   Alas, the way is wearisome and long.
Jul.   A true-devoted pilgrim is not weary
To measure kingdoms with his feeble steps;
Much less shall she that hath Love's wings to fly,
And when the flight is made to one so dear,
Of such divine perfection, as Sir Proteus.
Luc.   Better forbear till Proteus make return.
Jul.   O, know'st thou not his looks are my soul's food?
Pity the dearth that I have pinéd in
By longing for that food so long a time.
Didst thou but know the inly touch of love,
Thou wouldst as soon go kindle fire with snow
As seek to quench the fire of love with words.
Luc.   I do not seek to quench your love's hot fire,
But qualify the fire's extreme rage,
Lest it should burn above the bounds of reason.
Jul.   The more thou damm'st it up, the more it burns.
The current that with gentle murmur glides,
Thou know'st, being stopped, impatiently doth rage;

176

But, when his fair course is not hinderéd,
He makes sweet music with the enamelled stones,
Giving a gentle kiss to every sedge
He overtaketh in his pilgrimage;
And so by many winding nooks he strays
With willing sport to the wild ocean.
Then let me go, and hinder not my course.
I 'll be as patient as a gentle stream,
And make a pastime of each weary step,
Till the last step have brought me to my love;
And there I 'll rest, as, after much turmoil,
A blesséd soul doth in Elysium.

    Luc.   But in what habit will you go along?
    Jul.   Not like a woman; for I would prevent
The loose encounters of lascivious men.
Gentle Lucetta, fit me with such weeds
As may beseem some well-reputed page.
    Luc.   Why, then your ladyship must cut your hair.
    Jul.   No, girl; I 'll knit it up in silken strings
With twenty odd-conceited true-love knots:
To be fantastic, may become a youth
Of greater time than I shall show to be.
    Luc.   What fashion madam, shall I make your
        breeches?
    Jul.   That fits as well as—"Tell me, good my lord,
What compass will you wear your farthingale?"
Why, even what fashion thou best lik'st, Lucetta.
    Luc.   You must needs have them with a codpiece,
        madam.
    Jul.   Out, out, Lucetta! that will be ill-favoured.
    Luc.   A round hose, madam, now 's not worth a pin,
Unless you have a codpiece to stick pins on.
    Jul.   Lucetta, as thou lov'st me, let me have
What thou think'st meet, and is most mannerly.
But tell me, wench, how will the world repute me
For undertaking so unstaid a journey?
I fear me, it will make me scandalised.
    Luc.   If you think so, then stay at home, and go not.
    Jul.   Nay, that I will not.
    Luc.   Then never dream on infamy, but go.
If Proteus like your journey when you come,
No matter who 's displeased when you are gone.
I fear me, he will scarce be pleased withal.
    Jul.   That is the least, Lucetta, of my fear.
A thousand oaths, an ocean of his tears,
And instances as infinite of love,
Warrant me welcome to my Proteus.
    Luc.   All these are servants to deceitful men.
    Jul.   Base men, that use them to so base effect!

But truer stars did govern Proteus' birth:
His words are bonds, his oaths are oracles;
His love sincere, his thoughts immaculate;
His tears pure messengers sent from his heart;
His heart as far from fraud as heaven from earth.
    Luc.   Pray Heaven, he prove so, when you come to him!
    Jul.   Now, as thou lov'st me, do him not that wrong
To bear a hard opinion of his truth:
Only deserve my love by loving him,
And presently go with me to my chamber,
To take a note of what I stand in need of
To furnish me upon my longing journey.
All that is mine I leave at thy dispose,
My goods, my lands, my reputation;
Only, in lieu thereof, dispatch me hence.
Come, answer not, but to it presently:
I am impatient of my tarriance.   *[Exeunt*

ACT THREE

Scene I.—Milan.   An Anteroom in the Duke's Palace

Enter Duke, Thurio, *and* Proteus

    Duke.   Sir Thurio, give us leave, I pray, awhile:
We have some secrets to confer about.—   *[Exit Thurio*
Now, tell me, Proteus, what 's your will with me?
    Pro.   My gracious lord, that which I would discover
The law of friendship bids me to conceal;
But when I call to mind your gracious favours
Done to me, undeserving as I am,
My duty pricks me on to utter that
Which else no worldly good should draw from me.
Know, worthy prince, Sir Valentine, my friend,
This night intends to steal away your daughter;
Myself am one made privy to the plot.
I know you have determined to bestow her
On Thurio, whom your gentle daughter hates;
And should she thus be stolen away from you,
It would be much vexation to your age.
Thus, for my duty's sake, I rather chose
To cross my friend in his intended drift
Than, by concealing it, heap on your head
A pack of sorrows which would press you down,
Being unprevented, to your timeless grave.
    Duke.   Proteus, I thank thee for thine honest care;
Which to requite command me while I live.

This love of theirs myself have often seen,
Haply when they have judged me fast asleep;
And oftentimes have purposed to forbid
Sir Valentine her company and my court;
But, fearing lest my jealous aim might err,
And so unworthily disgrace the man,—
A rashness that I ever yet have shunned,—
I gave him gentle looks; thereby to find
That which thyself hast now disclosed to me.
And, that thou may'st perceive my fear of this,
Know that tender youth is soon suggested,
I nightly lodge her in an upper tower
The key whereof myself have ever kept;
And thence she cannot be conveyed away.
   Pro. Know, noble lord, they have devised a mean
How he her chamber-window will ascend,
And with a corded ladder fetch her down;
For which the youthful lover now is gone,
And this way comes he with it presently,
Where, if it please you, you may intercept him.
But, good my lord, do it so cunningly
That my discovery be not aiméd at;
For love of you, not hate unto my friend,
Hath made me publisher of this pretence.
   Duke. Upon mine honour, he shall never know
That I had any light from thee of this.
   Pro. Adieu, my lord; Sir Valentine is coming.   [*Exit*

Enter VALENTINE

   Duke. Sir Valentine, whither away so fast?
   Val. Please it your grace, there is a messenger
That stays to bear my letters to my friends,
And I am going to deliver them.
   Duke. Be they of much import?
   Val. The tenor of them doth but signify
My health, and happy being at your court.
   Duke. Nay, then, no matter; stay with me awhile.
I am to break with thee of some affairs
That touch me near, wherein thou must be secret.
'T is not unknown to thee that I have sought
To match my friend Sir Thurio to my daughter.
   Val. I know it well, my lord; and, sure, the match
Were rich and honourable; besides, the gentleman
Is full of virtue, bounty, worth, and qualities
Beseeming such a wife as your fair daughter.
Cannot your grace win her to fancy him?
   Duke. No, trust me: she is peevish, sullen, froward,
Proud, disobedient, stubborn, lacking duty;

Neither regarding that she is my child,
Nor fearing me as if I were her father:
And, may I say to thee, this pride of hers,
Upon advice, hath drawn my love from her;
And, where I thought the remnant of mine age
Should have been cherished by her child-like duty,
I now am full resolved to take a wife,
And turn her out to who will take her in:
Then, let her beauty be her wedding-dower;
For me and my possessions she esteems not.

 Val. What would your grace have me to do in this?
 Duke. There is a lady in Milano here,
Whom I affect; but she is nice, and coy,
And nought esteems my agéd eloquence:
Now, therefore, would I have thee to my tutor—
For long agone I have forgot to court;
Besides, the fashion of the time is changed—
How, and which way, I may bestow myself,
To be regarded in her sun-bright eye.

 Val. Win her with gifts, if she respect not words.
Dumb jewels often, in their silent kind,
More than quick words do move a woman's mind.

 Duke. But she did scorn a present that I sent her.
 Val. A woman sometimes scorns what best contents
  her.
Send her another; never give her o'er,
For scorn at first makes after-love the more.
If she do frown, 't is not in hate of you,
But rather to beget more love in you;
If she do chide, 't is not to have you gone,
For why the fools are mad, if left alone.
Take no repulse, whatever she doth say;
For, "get you gone," she doth not mean, "away."
Flatter, and praise, commend, extol their graces;
Though ne'er so black, say they have angels' faces.
That man that hath a tongue, I say, is no man,
If with his tongue he cannot win a woman.

 Duke. But she I mean is promised by her friends
Unto a youthful gentleman of worth,
And kept severely from resort of men,
That no man hath access by day to her.

 Val. Why, then I would resort to her by night.
 Duke. Ay, but the doors be locked, and keys kept safe,
That no man hath recourse to her by night.

 Val. What lets but one may enter at her window?
 Duke. Her chamber is aloft, far from the ground,
And built so shelving, that one cannot climb it
Without apparent hazard of his life.

 Val. Why, then, a ladder quaintly made of cords,

To cast up, with a pair of anchoring hooks,
Would serve to scale another Hero's tower,
So bold Leander would adventure it.
   Duke.   Now, as thou art a gentleman of blood,
Advise me where I may have such a ladder.
   Val.   When would you use it? pray, sir, tell me that.
   Duke.   This very night; for Love is like a child,
That longs for everything that he can come by.
   Val.   By seven o'clock I 'll get you such a ladder.
   Duke.   But hark thee; I will go to her alone.
How shall I best convey the ladder thither?
   Val.   It will be light, my lord, that you may bear it
Under a cloak that is of any length.
   Duke.   A cloak as long as thine will serve the turn?
   Val.   Ay, my good lord.
   Duke.   Then, let me see thy cloak;
I 'll get me one of such another length.
   Val.   Why, any cloak will serve the turn, my lord.
   Duke.   How shall I fashion me to wear a cloak?—
I pray thee, let me feel thy cloak upon me.—
What letter is this same? What 's here?—"To Silvia!"
And here an engine fit for my proceeding!
I 'll be so bold to break the seal for once.   [*Reads*

" My thoughts do harbour with my Silvia nightly :
   And slaves they are to me, that send them flying :
O, could their master come and go as lightly,
   Himself would lodge where senseless they are lying.
My herald thoughts in thy pure bosom rest them :
   While I, their king, that thither them importune,
Do curse the grace that with such grace hath blessed them,
   Because myself do want my servants' fortune :
I curse myself, for they are sent by me,
That they should harbour where their lord should be."

What 's here?

" Silvia, this night I will enfranchise thee."

'T is so; and here 's the ladder for the purpose.
Why, Phaethon,—for thou art Merops' son,—
Wilt thou aspire to guide the heavenly car,
And with thy daring folly burn the world?
Wilt thou reach stars, because they shine on thee?
Go, base intruder! overweening slave!
Bestow thy fawning smiles on equal mates,
And think my patience, more than thy desert,
Is privilege for thy departure hence.
Thank me for this more than for all the favours
Which, all too much, I have bestowed on thee:
But if thou linger in my territories

Longer than swiftest expedition
Will give thee time to leave our royal court,
By Heaven, my wrath shall far exceed the love
I ever bore my daughter or thyself.
Be gone: I will not hear thy vain excuse;
But, as thou lov'st thy life, make speed from hence.

[*Exit Duke*

Val.   And why not death, rather than living torment?
To die is to be banished from myself;
And Silvia is myself: banished from her,
Is self from self; a deadly banishment.
What light is light, if Silvia be not seen?
What joy is joy, if Silvia be not by?
Unless it be to think that she is by,
And feed upon the shadow of perfection.
Except I be by Silvia in the night,
There is no music in the nightingale;
Unless I look on Silvia in the day,
There is no day for me to look upon.
She is my essence; and I leave to be,
If I be not by her fair influence
Fostered, illumined, cherished, kept alive.
I fly not death, to fly his deadly doom:
Tarry I here, I but attend on death;
But, fly I hence, I fly away from life.

Enter PROTEUS *and* LAUNCE

Pro.   Run, boy, run, run, and seek him out.
Launce.   So-ho! so-ho!
Pro.   What seest thou?
Launce.   Him we go to find: there 's not a hair on 's
            head, but 't is a Valentine.
Pro.   Valentine!
Val.   No.
Pro.   Who then? his spirit?
Val.   Neither.
Pro.   What then?
Val.   Nothing.
Launce.   Can nothing speak? master, shall I strike?
Pro.   Who wouldst thou strike?
Launce.   Nothing.
Pro.   Villain, forbear.
Launce.   Why, sir I 'll strike nothing: I pray you,—
Pro.   Sirrah, I say, forbear.—Friend Valentine, a word.
Val.   My ears are stopped, and cannot hear good news.
So much of bad already hath possessed them.
Pro.   Then in dumb silence will I bury mine,
For they are harsh, untuneable, and bad.

Val.   Is Silvia dead?

Pro.   No, Valentine.

Val.   No Valentine, indeed, for sacred Silvia!—
Hath she forsworn me?

Pro.   No, Valentine.

Val.   No Valentine, if Silvia hath forsworn me!—
What is your news?

Launce.   Sir, there is a proclamation that you are
vanished.

Pro.   That thou art banishéd: O, that 's the news,
From hence, from Silvia, and from me, thy friend.

Val.   O, I have fed upon this woe already,
And now excess of it will make me surfeit.
Doth Silvia know that I am banishéd?

Pro.   Ay, ay; and she hath offered to the doom—
Which, unreversed, stands in effectual force—
A sea of melting pearl, which some call tears:
Those at her father's churlish feet she tendered,
With them, upon her knees, her humble self,
Wringing her hands, whose whiteness so became them
As if but now they waxéd pale for woe:
But neither bended knees, pure hands held up,
Sad sighs, deep groans, nor silver-shedding tears,
Could penetrate her uncompassionate sire;
But Valentine, if he be ta'en, must die.
Besides, her intercession chafed him so,
When she for thy repeal was suppliant,
That to close prison he commanded her,
With many bitter threats of biding there.

Val.   No more; unless the next word that thou speak'st
Have some malignant power upon my life:
If so, I pray thee, breathe it in mine ear,
As ending anthem of my endless dolour.

Pro.   Cease to lament for that thou canst not help.
And study help for that which thou lament'st.
Time is the nurse and breeder of all good.
Here if thou stay, thou canst not see thy love;
Besides, thy staying will abridge thy life.
Hope is a lover's staff; walk hence with that,
And manage it against despairing thoughts.
Thy letters may be here, though thou art hence,
Which, being writ to me, shall be delivered
Even in the milk-white bosom of thy love.
The time now serves not to expostulate;
Come, I 'll convey thee through the city-gate,
And, ere I part with thee, confer at large
Of all that may concern thy love-affairs.
As thou lov'st Silvia, though not for thyself,
Regard thy danger, and along with me!

Val.   I pray thee, Launce, an if thou seest my boy,
Bid him make haste, and meet me at the north gate.
    Pro.   Go, sirrah, find him out.   Come, Valentine.
    Val.   O my dear Silvia!—hapless Valentine!
                                    [*Exeunt Valentine and Proteus*
    Launce.   I am but a fool, look you, and yet I have the
wit to think my master is a kind of a knave; but that 's
all one, if he be but one knave.   He lives not now that
knows me to be in love: yet I am in love; but a team of
horse shall not pluck that from me, nor who 't is I love;
and yet 't is a woman; but what woman, I will not tell
myself; and yet 't is a milk-maid; yet 't is not a maid,
for she hath had gossips; yet 't is a maid, for she is her
master's maid, and serves for wages.   She hath more
qualities than a water-spaniel,—which is much in a bare
Christian.   Here is the cate-log [*pulling out a paper*] of her
conditions.   Imprimis, "She can fetch and carry."   Why,
a horse can do no more: nay, a horse cannot fetch, but
only carry; therefore is she better than a jade.   Item,
"She can milk;" look you, a sweet virtue in a maid with
clean hands.

Enter Speed

    Speed.   How now, Signior Launce, what news with your
mastership?
    Launce.   With my master's ship? why, it is at sea.
    Speed.   Well, your old vice still; mistake the word.
What news, then, in your paper?
    Launce.   The blackest news that ever thou heardest.
    Speed.   Why, man, how black?
    Launce.   Why, as black as ink.
    Speed.   Let me read them.
    Launce.   Fie on thee, jolthead! thou canst not read.
    Speed.   Thou liest; I can.
    Launce.   I will try thee.   Tell me this: who begot
thee?
    Speed.   Marry, the son of my grandfather.
    Launce.   O illiterate loiterer! it was the son of thy
grandmother.   This proves that thou canst not read.
    Speed.   Come, fool, come; try me in thy paper.
    Launce.   There, and Saint Nicholas be thy speed!
    Speed.   [*Reads*] "Imprimis, She can milk."
    Launce.   Ay, that she can.
    Speed.   "Item, She brews good ale."
    Launce.   And thereof comes the proverb,—Blessing of
your heart, you brew good ale.
    Speed.   "Item, She can sew."
    Launce.   That 's as much as to say, Can she so?
    Speed.   "Item, She can knit."

Launce. What need a man care for a stock with a wench, when she can knit him a stock?

Speed. "Item, She can wash and scour."

Launce. A special virtue; for then she need not be washed and scoured.

Speed. "Item, She can spin."

Launce. Then may I set the world on wheels, when she can spin for her living.

Speed. "Item, She hath many nameless virtues."

Launce. That 's as much as to say, bastard virtues; that, indeed, know not their fathers, and therefore have no names.

Speed. Here follow her vices.

Launce. Close at the heels of her virtues.

Speed. "Item, She is not to be kissed fasting, in respect of her breath."

Launce. Well, that fault may be mended with a breakfast. Read on.

Speed. "Item, She hath a sweet mouth."

Launce. That makes amends for her sour breath.

Speed. "Item, She doth talk in her sleep."

Launce. It 's no matter for that, so she sleep not in her talk.

Speed. "Item, She is slow in words."

Launce. O villain, that set this down among her vices! To be slow in words is a woman's only virtue. I pray thee, out with 't, and place it for her chief virtue.

Speed. "Item, She is proud."

Launce. Out with that too: it was Eve's legacy, and cannot be ta'en from her.

Speed. "Item, She hath no teeth."

Launce. I care not for that neither, because I love crusts.

Speed. "Item, She is curst."

Launce. Well; the best is, she hath no teeth to bite.

Speed. "Item, She will often praise her liquor."

Launce. If her liquor be good, she shall: if she will not, I will; for good things should be praised.

Speed. "Item, She is too liberal."

Launce. Of her tongue she cannot, for that 's writ down she is slow of; of her purse she shall not, for that I 'll keep shut; now, of another thing she may, and that cannot I help. Well, proceed.

Speed. "Item, She hath more hair than wit, and more faults than hairs, and more wealth than faults."

Launce. Stop there; I 'll have her: she was mine, and not mine, twice or thrice in that last article. Rehearse that once more.

Speed. "Item, She hath more hair than wit,"—

Launce. More hair than wit,—it may be; I 'll prove it: the cover of the salt hides the salt, and therefore it is more than the salt: the hair, that covers the wit, is more than the wit, for the greater hides the less. What 's next?

Speed. "And more faults than hairs,"—

Launce. That 's monstrous: O, that that were out!

Speed. "And more wealth than faults."

Launce. Why, that word makes the faults gracious. Well, I 'll have her; and if it be a match, as nothing is impossible,—

Speed. What then?

Launce. Why, then will I tell thee—that thy master stays for thee at the north gate.

Speed. For me?

Launce. For thee! ay; who art thou? he hath stayed for a better man than thee.

Speed. And must I go to him?

Launce. Thou must run to him, for thou hast stayed so long, that going will scarce serve the turn.

Speed. Why didst not tell me sooner? pox of your love-letters!   [*Exit*

Launce. Now will he be swinged for reading my letter. An unmannerly slave, that will thrust himself into secrets. —I 'll after, to rejoice in the boy's correction.   [*Exit*

SCENE II.—Milan.—An Apartment in the DUKE'S Palace

Enter DUKE *and* THURIO

Duke. Sir Thurio, fear not but that she will love you Now Valentine is banished from her sight.

Thu. Since his exile she hath despised me most; Forsworn my company, and railed at me, That I am desperate of obtaining her.

Duke. This weak impress of love is as a figure Trenchéd in ice, which with an hour's heat Dissolves to water and doth lose his form. A little time will melt her frozen thoughts, And worthless Valentine shall be forgot.—

Enter PROTEUS

How now, Sir Proteus? Is your countryman, According to our proclamation, gone?

Pro. Gone, my good lord.

Duke. My daughter takes his going grievously.

Pro. A little time, my lord, will kill that grief.

Duke. So I believe; but Thurio thinks not so.

Proteus, the good conceit I hold of thee—
For thou hast shown some sign of good desert—
Makes me the better to confer with thee.

Pro.   Longer than I prove loyal to your grace,
Let me not live to look upon your grace.

Duke.   Thou know'st how willingly I would effect
The match between Sir Thurio and my daughter.

Pro.   I do, my lord.

Duke.   And also, I think, thou art not ignorant
How she opposes her against my will.

Pro.   She did, my lord, when Valentine was here.

Duke.   Ay, and perversely she persévers so.
What might we do to make the girl forget
The love of Valentine, and love Sir Thurio?

Pro.   The best way is, to slander Valentine
With falsehood, cowardice, and poor descent;
Three things that women highly hold in hate.

Duke.   Ay, but she 'll think that it is spoke in hate.

Pro.   Ay, if his enemy deliver it:
Therefore, it must, with circumstance, be spoken
By one whom she esteemeth as his friend.

Duke.   Then you must undertake to slander him.

Pro.   And that, my lord, I shall be loth to do:
'T is an ill office for a gentleman,
Especially against his very friend.

Duke.   Where your good word cannot advantage him
Your slander never can endamage him:
Therefore the office is indifferent,
Being entreated to it by your friend.

Pro.   You have prevailed, my lord.   If I can do it
By aught that I can speak in his dispraise,
She shall not long continue love to him.
But say, this weed her love from Valentine,
It follows not that she will love Sir Thurio.

Thu.   Therefore, as you unwind her love from him,
Lest it should ravel and be good to none,
You must provide to bottom it on me;
Which must be done by praising me as much
As you in worth dispraise Sir Valentine.

Duke.   And, Proteus, we dare trust you in this kind,
Because we know, on Valentine's report,
You are already Love's firm votary,
And cannot soon revolt and change your mind.
Upon this warrant shall you have access
Where you with Silvia may confer at large;—
For she is lumpish, heavy, melancholy,
And for your friend's sake, will be glad of you;—
Where you may temper her, by your persuasion,
To hate young Valentine and love my friend.

Pro. As much as I can do I will effect.
But you, Sir Thurio, are not sharp enough;
You must lay lime to tangle her desires
By wailful sonnets, whose composéd rhymes
Should be full fraught with serviceable vows.
  Duke. Ay,
Much is the force of heaven-bred poesy.
  Pro. Say, that upon the altar of her beauty
You sacrifice your tears, your sighs, your heart;
Write till your ink be dry, and with your tears
Moist it again; and frame some feeling line
That may discover such integrity:
For Orpheus' lute was strung with poet's sinews,
Whose golden touch could soften steel and stones,
Make tigers tame, and huge leviathans
Forsake unsounded deeps to dance on sands.
After your dire-lamenting elegies,
Visit by night your lady's chamber-window
With some sweet concert: to their instruments
Tune a deploring dump; the night's dead silence
Will well become such sweet-complaining grievance.
This, or else nothing, will inherit her.
  Duke. This discipline shows thou hast been in love.
  Thu. And thy advice this night I'll put in practice.
Therefore, sweet Proteus, my direction-giver,
Let us into the city presently
To sort some gentlemen well skilled in music.
I have a sonnet that will serve the turn
To give the onset to thy good advice.
  Duke. About it, gentlemen.
  Pro. We'll wait upon your grace till after supper,
And afterward determine our proceedings.
  Duke. Even now about it; I will pardon you. [*Exeunt*

ACT FOUR

SCENE I.—A Forest near Milan
Enter certain Outlaws

  First Out. Fellows, stand fast; I see a passenger.
  Second Out. If there be ten, shrink not, but down with
      'em.
Enter VALENTINE *and* SPEED

  Third Out. Stand, sir, and throw us that you have
      about ye;
If not, we'll make you sit, and rifle you.
  Speed. O, sir, we are undone! These are the villains
That all the travellers do fear so much.

Val. My friends,—
First Out. That 's not so, sir,—we are your enemies.
Second Out. Peace! we 'll hear him.
Third Out. Ay, by my beard, will we;
For he is a proper man.
Val. Then know that I have little wealth to lose.
A man I am crossed with adversity;
My riches are these poor habiliments,
Of which if you should here disfurnish me.
You take the sum and substance that I have.
Second Out. Whither travel you?
Val. To Verona.
First Out. Whence came you?
Val. From Milan.
Third Out. Have you long sojourned there?
Val. Some sixteen months; and longer might have
        stayed,
If crookéd fortune had not thwarted me.
First Out. What, were you banished thence?
Val. I was.
Second Out. For what offence?
Val. For that which now torments me to rehearse:
I killed a man, whose death I much repent;
But yet I slew him manfully in fight,
Without false vantage or base treachery.
First Out. Why, ne'er repent it, if it were done so.
But were you banished for so small a fault?
Val. I was, and held me glad of such a doom.
Second Out. Have you the tongues?
Val. My youthful travel therein made me happy,
Or else I often had been miserable.
Third Out. By the bare scalp of Robin Hood's fat friar,
This fellow were a king for our wild faction.
First Out. We 'll have him. Sirs, a word.
Speed. Master, be one of them:
It is an honourable kind of thievery.
Val. Peace, villain!
Second Out. Tell us this: have you anything to take
        to?
Val. Nothing, but my fortune.
Third Out. Know then, that some of us are gentlemen
Such as the fury of ungoverned youth
Thrust from the company of awful men:
Myself was from Verona banishéd
For practising to steal away a lady,
An heir, and near allied unto the duke.
Second Out. And I from Mantua, for a gentleman,
Who, in my mood, I stabbed unto the heart.
First Out. And I for such-like petty crimes as these.

But to the purpose,—for we cite our faults,
That they may hold excused our lawless lives;
And, partly, seeing you are beautified
With goodly shape, and by your own report
A linguist, and a man of such perfection
As we do in our quality much want—
    Second Out.   Indeed, because you are a banished man,
Therefore, above the rest, we parley to you.
Are you content to be our general?
To make a virtue of necessity,
And live, as we do, in this wilderness?
    Third Out.   What say'st thou? wilt thou be of our con-
        sort?
Say, ay, and be the captain of us all.
We 'll do thee homage, and be ruled by thee,
Love thee as our commander and our king.
    First Out.   But if thou scorn our courtesy, thou diest.
    Second Out.   Thou shalt not live to brag what we have
        offered.
    Val.   I take your offer, and will live with you;
Provided that you do no outrages
On silly women or poor passengers.
    Third Out.   No, we detest such vile, base practices.
Come, go with us, we 'll bring thee to our cave,
And show thee all the treasure we have got,
Which, with ourselves, shall rest at thy dispose.   [*Exeunt*

SCENE II.—Milan.   The Court of the Palace

Enter PROTEUS

    Pro.   Already have I been false to Valentine,
And now I must be as unjust to Thurio.
Under the colour of commending him,
I have access my own love to prefer;
But Silvia is too fair, too true, too holy,
To be corrupted with my worthless gifts.
When I protest true loyalty to her,
She twits me with my falsehood to my friend;
When to her beauty I commend my vows,
She bids me think how I have been forsworn,
In breaking faith with Julia whom I loved:
And notwithstanding all her sudden quips,
The least whereof would quell a lover's hope,
Yet, spaniel-like, the more she spurns my love,
The more it grows, and fawneth on her still.
But here comes Thurio.   Now must we to her window,
And give some evening music to her ear.

Enter THURIO, *and Musicians*

Thu.   How now, Sir Proteus? are you crept before us?
Pro.   Ay, gentle Thurio; for you know that love
Will creep in service where it cannot go.
Thu.   Ay, but I hope, sir, that you love not here.
Pro.   Sir, but I do; or else I would be hence.
Thu.   Who? Silvia?
Pro.   Ay, Silvia,—for your sake.
Thu.   I thank you for your own.   Now, gentlemen,
Let 's tune, and to it lustily awhile.

Enter at a distance Host, and JULIA *in boy's clothes*

Host.   Now, my young guest; methinks you 're alli-
cholly: I pray you, why is it?
Jul.   Marry, mine host, because I cannot be merry.
Host.   Come, we 'll have you merry.   I 'll bring you
where you shall hear music, and see the gentleman that
you asked for.
Jul.   But shall I hear him speak?
Host.   Ay, that you shall.
Jul.   That will be music.   [*Music plays*
Host.   Hark! hark!
Jul.   Is he among these?
Host.   Ay; but peace! let 's hear 'em.

SONG

Who is Silvia? what is she,
    That all our swains commend her?
Holy, fair, and wise is she;
    The heaven such grace did lend her
That she might admirèd be.

Is she kind, as she is fair?
    For beauty lives with kindness:
Love doth to her eyes repair,
    To help him of his blindness;
And, being helped, inhabits there.

Then to Silvia let us sing,
    That Silvia is excelling;
She excels each mortal thing
    Upon the dull earth dwelling;
To her let us garlands bring.

Host.   How now! are you sadder than you were before?
How do you, man? the music likes you not.
Jul.   You mistake: the musician likes me not.
Host.   Why, my pretty youth?
Jul.   He plays false, father.

191

Host. How? out of tune on the strings?
Jul. Not so; but yet so false, that he grieves my very heartstrings.
Host. You have a quick ear.
Jul. Ay, I would I were deaf! it makes me have a slow heart.
Host. I perceive, you delight not in music.
Jul. Not a whit, when it jars so.
Host. Hark, what fine change is in the music.
Jul. Ay, that change is the spite.
Host. You would have them always play but one thing?
Jul. I would always have one play but one thing.
But, host, doth this Sir Proteus that we talk on
Often resort unto this gentlewoman?
Host. I tell you what Launce, his man, told me,—he loved her out of all nick.
Jul. Where is Launce?
Host. Gone to seek his dog; which, to-morrow, by his master's command, he must carry for a present to his lady.
Jul. Peace! stand aside: the company parts.
Pro. Sir Thurio, fear not you: I will so plead
That you shall say my cunning drift excels.
Thu. Where meet we?
Pro.   At Saint Gregory's well.
Thu.   Farewell.
            [*Exeunt Thurio and Musicians*

Enter SILVIA *above, at her window*

Pro. Madam, good even to your ladyship.
Sil. I thank you for your music, gentlemen.
Who is that that spake?
Pro. One, lady, if you knew his pure heart's truth,
You would quickly learn to know him by his voice.
Sil. Sir Proteus, as I take it.
Pro. Sir Proteus, gentle lady, and your servant.
Sil. What is your will?
Pro.   That I may compass yours.
Sil. You have your wish: my will is even this,
That presently you hie you home to bed.
Thou subtle, perjured, false, disloyal man!
Think'st thou, I am so shallow, so conceitless,
To be seducéd by thy flattery,
That hast deceived so many with thy vows?
Return, return, and make thy love amends.
For me, by this pale queen of night I swear,
I am so far from granting thy request
That I despise thee for thy wrongful suit,
And by-and-by intend to chide myself
Even for this time I spend in talking to thee.

192

Pro. I grant, sweet love, that I did love a lady,
But she is dead.
Jul. [*Aside*] 'T were false, if I should speak it;
For, I am sure, she is not buriéd.
Sil. Say, that she be; yet Valentine, thy friend,
Survives, to whom, thyself art witness,
I am betrothed; and art thou not ashamed
To wrong him with thy importúnacy?
Pro. I likewise hear, that Valentine is dead.
Sil. And so, suppose, am I; for in his grave,
Assure thyself, my love is buriéd.
Pro. Sweet lady, let me rake it from the earth.
Sil. Go to thy lady's grave, and call hers thence;
Or, at the least, in hers sepúlchre thine.
Jul. [*Aside*] He heard not that.
Pro. Madam, if your heart be so obdurate,
Vouchsafe me yet your picture for my love,
The picture that is hanging in your chamber:
To that I 'll speak, to that I 'll sigh and weep;
For, since the substance of your perfect self
Is else devoted, I am but a shadow,
And to your shadow will I make true love.
Jul. [*Aside*] If 't were a substance, you would, sure,
            deceive it,
And make it but a shadow, as I am.
Sil. I am very loth to be your idol, sir;
But, since your falsehood shall become you well
To worship shadows, and adore false shapes,
Send to me in the morning, and I 'll send it:
And so, good rest.
Pro.   As wretches have o'ernight,
That wait for execution in the morn.
                              [*Exeunt Proteus and Silvia*
Jul. Host, will you go?
Host. By my halidom, I was fast asleep.
Jul. Pray you, where lies Sir Proteus?
Host. Marry, at my house. Trust me, I think, 't is
almost day.
Jul. Not so; but it hath been the longest night
That e'er I watched, and the most heaviest.   [*Exeunt*

SCENE III.—The Same

Enter EGLAMOUR

Egl. This is the hour that Madam Silvia
Entreated me to call and know her mind.
There 's some great matter she 'd employ me in.—
Madam, madam!

193

Enter SILVIA *above, at her window*

Sil.   Who calls?

Egl.   Your servant and your friend;
One that attends your ladyship's command.

Sil.   Sir Eglamour, a thousand times good morrow.

Egl.   As many, worthy lady, to yourself.
According to your ladyship's impose,
I am thus early come to know what service
It is your pleasure to command me in.

Sil.   O Eglamour, thou art a gentleman—
Think not I flatter, for I swear I do not,—
Valiant, wise, remorseful, well accomplished.
Thou art not ignorant what dear good will
I bear unto the banished Valentine,
Nor how my father would enforce me marry
Vain Thurio, whom my very soul abhors.
Thyself hast loved; and I have heard thee say,
No grief did ever come so near thy heart
As when thy lady and thy true love died,
Upon whose grave thou vow'dst pure chastity.
Sir Eglamour, I would to Valentine,
To Mantua, where I hear he makes abode;
And, for the ways are dangerous to pass,
I do desire thy worthy company,
Upon whose faith and honour I repose.
Urge not my father's anger, Eglamour,
But think upon my grief,—a lady's grief,—
And on the justice of my flying hence,
To keep me from a most unholy match
Which heaven and fortune still rewards with plagues.
I do desire thee, even from a heart
As full of sorrows as the sea of sands,
To bear me company, and go with me:
If not, to hide what I have said to thee,
That I may venture to depart alone.

Egl.   Madam, I pity much your grievances;
Which since I know they virtuously are placed,
I give consent to go along with you;
Recking as little what betideth me,
As much I wish all good befortune you.
When will you go?

Sil.   This evening coming.

Egl.   Where shall I meet you?

Sil.   At Friar Patrick's cell,
Where I intend holy confession.

Egl.   I will not fail your ladyship.
Good morrow, gentle lady.

Sil.   Good morrow, kind Sir Eglamour.

                        [*Exeunt Eglamour, and Silvia above*

SCENE IV.—The Same

Enter LAUNCE *with his dog*

Launce. When a man's servant shall play the cur with him, look you, it goes hard: one that I brought up of a puppy; one that I saved from drowning, when three or four of his blind brothers and sisters went to it. I have taught him, even as one would say precisely, "Thus I would teach a dog." I was sent to deliver him as a present to Mistress Silvia from my master, and I came no sooner into the dining-chamber, but he steps me to her trencher, and steals her capon's leg. O, 't is a foul thing, when a cur cannot keep himself in all companies. I would have, as one should say, one that takes upon him to be a dog indeed; to be, as it were, a dog at all things. If I had not had more wit than he, to take a fault upon me that he did, I think verily, he had been hanged for 't: sure as I live, he had suffered for 't: you shall judge. He thrusts me himself into the company of three or four gentlemen-like dogs under the duke's table: he had not been there (bless the mark) a pissing while, but all the chamber smelt him. "Out with the dog!" says one; "What cur is that?" says another; "Whip him out," says the third; "Hang him up," says the duke. I, having been acquainted with the smell before, knew it was Crab, and goes me to the fellow that whips the dog: "Friend," quoth I, "you mean to whip the dog?" "Ay, marry, do I," quoth he. "You do him the more wrong," quoth I; "'t was I did the thing you wot of." He makes me no more ado, but whips me out of the chamber. How many masters would do this for his servant? Nay, I'll be sworn, I have sat in the stocks for puddings he hath stolen, otherwise he had been executed; I have stood on the pillory for geese he hath killed, otherwise he had suffered for 't: thou think'st not of this now.—Nay, I remember the trick you served me, when I took my leave of Madam Silvia. Did not I bid thee still mark me, and do as I do? When didst thou see me heave up my leg, and make water against a gentlewoman's farthingale? Didst thou ever see me do such a trick?

Enter PROTEUS, *and* JULIA *in boy's clothes*

Pro. Sebastian is thy name? I like thee well,
And will employ thee in some service presently.
Jul. In what you please: I will do what I can.

Pro.   I hope thou wilt.—How now, you whoreson
       peasant!
Where have you been these two days loitering?
    Launce.   Marry, sir, I carried Mistress Silvia the dog
you bade me.
    Pro.   And what says she to my little jewel?
    Launce.   Marry, she says, your dog was a cur; and
tells you, currish thanks is good enough for such a present.
    Pro.   But she received my dog?
    Launce.   No, indeed, did she not.   Here have I brought
him back again.
    Pro.   What! didst thou offer her this from me?
    Launce.   Ay, sir: the other squirrel was stolen from me
by the hangman's boys in the market-place; and then I
offered her mine own, who is a dog as big as ten of yours,
and therefore the gift the greater.
    Pro.   Go get thee hence, and find my dog again,
Or ne'er return again into my sight.
Away, I say! Stay'st thou to vex me here?—
A slave that still an end turns me to shame.—
                             [*Exit Launce*
Sebastian, I have entertainéd thee,
Partly, that I have need of such a youth,
That can with some discretion do my business,
For 't is no trusting to yon foolish lout;
But, chiefly, for thy face, and thy behaviour,
Which—if my augury deceive me not—
Witness good bringing up, fortune, and truth;
Therefore know thou for this I entertain thee.
Go presently, and take this ring with thee:
Deliver it to Madam Silvia.
She loved me well, delivered it to me.
    Jul.   It seems you loved not her, to leave her token.
She 's dead, belike?
    Pro.   Not so: I think, she lives.
    Jul.   Alas!
    Pro.   Why dost thou cry, Alas?
    Jul.   I cannot choose but pity her.
    Pro.   Wherefore shouldst thou pity her?
    Jul.   Because, methinks, that she loved you as well
As you do love your lady Silvia.
She dreams on him that has forgot her love;
You dote on her that cares not for your love.
'T is pity love should be so contrary;
And thinking on it makes me cry, Alas!
    Pro.   Well, well, give her that ring, and there withal
This letter:—that 's her chamber.—Tell my lady,
I claim the promise for her heavenly picture.
Your message done, hie home unto my chamber,

Where thou shalt find me, sad and solitary.   [*Exit*
 Jul.   How many women would do such a message?
Alas, poor Proteus! thou hast entertained
A fox to be the shepherd of thy lambs.
Alas, poor fool! why do I pity him
That with his very heart despiseth me?
Because he loves her, he despiseth me;
Because I love him, I must pity him.
This ring I gave him, when he parted from me,
To bind him to remember my good will;
And now am I—unhappy messenger—
To plead for that which I would not obtain;
To carry that which I would have refused;
To praise his faith, which I would have dispraised.
I am my master's true-confirméd love,
But cannot be true servant to my master
Unless I prove false traitor to myself.
Yet will I woo for him; but yet so coldly
As, heaven it knows, I would not have him speed.—

    Enter SILVIA, *attended*

Gentlewoman, good day.   I pray you, be my mean
To bring me where to speak with Madam Silvia.
 Sil.   What would you with her, if that I be she?
 Jul.   If you be she, I do entreat your patience
To hear me speak the message I am sent on.
 Sil.   From whom?
 Jul.   From my master, Sir Proteus, madam.
 Sil.   O, he sends you for a picture?
 Jul.   Ay, madam.
 Sil.   Ursula, bring my picture there.—
         [*A picture brought*
Go, give your master this: tell him from me,
One Julia, that his changing thoughts forget,
Would better fit his chamber than this shadow.
 Jul.   Madam, please you peruse this letter.
          [*Gives a letter*
Pardon me, madam, I have unadvised
Delivered you a paper that I should not:
This is the letter to your ladyship.   [*Gives another*
 Sil.   I pray thee, let me look on that again.
 Jul.   It may not be; good madam, pardon me.
 Sil.   There, hold.
I will not look upon your master's lines:
I know they are stuffed with protestations,
And full of new-found oaths, which he will break
As easily as I do tear this paper.   [*Tears the second letter*
 Jul.   Madam, he sends your ladyship this ring.

Sil. The more shame for him that he sends it me;
For I have heard him say a thousand times
His Julia gave it him at his departure.
Though his false finger have profaned the ring,
Mine shall not do his Julia so much wrong.
    Jul. She thanks you.
    Sil. What say'st thou?
    Jul. I thank you, madam, that you tender her.
Poor gentlewoman! my master wrongs her much.
    Sil. Dost thou know her?
    Jul. Almost as well as I do know myself.
To think upon her woes, I do protest
That I have wept a hundred several times.
    Sil. Belike she thinks that Proteus hath forsook her.
    Jul. I think she doth, and that's her cause of sorrow.
    Sil. Is she not passing fair?
    Jul. She hath been fairer, madam, than she is.
When she did think my master loved her well,
She, in my judgment, was as fair as you;
But since she did neglect her looking-glass,
And threw her sun-expelling mask away,
The air hath starved the roses in her cheeks,
And pinched the lily-tincture of her face,
That now she is become as black as I.
    Sil. How tall was she?
    Jul. About my stature; for, at Pentecost,
When all our pageants of delight were played,
Our youth got me to play the woman's part,
And I was trimmed in Madam Julia's gown,
Which servéd me as fit, by all men's judgments,
As if the garment had been made for me:
Therefore I know she is about my height.
And at that time I made her weep agood,
For I did play a lamentable part.
Madam, 't was Ariadne, passioning
For Theseus' perjury and unjust flight;
Which I so lively acted with my tears,
That my poor mistress, movéd therewithal,
Wept bitterly, and would I might be dead,
If I in thought felt not her very sorrow.
    Sil. She is beholding to thee, gentle youth.
Alas, poor lady, desolate and left!—
I weep myself, to think upon thy words.
Here, youth; there is my purse: I give thee this
For thy sweet mistress' sake, because thou lov'st her.
Farewell.   [*Exit Silvia, attended*
    Jul. And she shall thank you for 't, if e'er you know
    her.—
A virtuous gentlewoman, mild and beautiful!

I hope my master's suit will be but cold,
Since she respects my mistress' love so much.
Alas, how love can trifle with itself!
Here is her picture: let me see; I think,
If I had such a tire, this face of mine
Were full as lovely as is this of hers;
And yet the painter flattered her a little,
Unless I flatter with myself too much.
Her hair is auburn, mine is perfect yellow;
If that be all the difference in his love,
I'll get me such a coloured periwig.
Her eyes are grey as glass, and so are mine:
Ay, but her forehead 's low, and mine 's as high.
What should it be, that he respects in her,
But I can make respective in myself,
If this fond Love were not a blinded god?
Come, shadow, come, and take this shadow up,
For 't is thy rival.   O thou senseless form!
Thou shalt be worshipped, kissed, loved, and adored,
And, were there sense in his idolatry,
My substance should be statue in thy stead.
I 'll use thee kindly for thy mistress' sake,
That used me so, or else, by Jove I vow,
I should have scratched out your unseeing eyes,
To make my master out of love with thee.   [*Exit*

ACT FIVE

Scene I.—Milan.   An Abbey

Enter Eglamour

Egl.   The sun begins to gild the western sky;
And now it is about the very hour
That Silvia at Friar Patrick's cell should meet me.
She will not fail; for lovers break not hours,
Unless it be to come before their time,
So much they spur their expedition.
See, where she comes.—

Enter Silvia

                    Lady, a happy evening!
  Sil.   Amen, amen! go on, good Eglamour,
Out at the postern by the abbey-wall:
I fear, I am attended by some spies.
  Egl.   Fear not: the forest is not three leagues off;
If we recover that, we are sure enough.   [*Exeunt*

SCENE II.—Milan. A Room in the DUKE's Palace

Enter THURIO, PROTEUS, *and* JULIA *in boy's clothes*

Thu. Sir Proteus, what says Silvia to my suit?
Pro. O, sir, I find her milder than she was;
And yet she takes exceptions at your person.
Thu. What, that my leg is too long?
Pro. No, that it is too little.
Thu. I 'll wear a boot to make it somewhat rounder.
Jul. [*Aside*] But love will not be spurred to what it loathes.
Thu. What says she to my face?
Pro. She said it is a fair one.
Thu. Nay, then the wanton lies; my face is black.
Pro. But pearls are fair, and the old saying is,
Black men are pearls in beauteous ladies' eyes.
Jul. [*Aside*] 'T is true, such pearls as put out ladies' eyes;
For I had rather wink than look on them.
Thu. How likes she my discourse?
Pro. Ill, when you talk of war.
Thu. But well, when I discourse of love and peace?
Jul. [*Aside*] But, indeed, better when you hold your peace.
Thu. What says she to my valour?
Pro. O, sir, she makes no doubt of that.
Jul. [*Aside*] She needs not, when she knows it cowardice.
Thu. What says she to my birth?
Pro. That you are well derived.
Jul. [*Aside*] True; from a gentleman to a fool.
Thu. Considers she my possessions?
Pro. O, ay; and pities them.
Thu. Wherefore?
Jul. [*Aside*] That such an ass should owe them.
Pro. That they are out by lease.
Jul. Here comes the duke.

Enter DUKE

Duke. How now, Sir Proteus! how now, Thurio!
Which of you saw Sir Eglamour of late?
Thu. Not I.
Pro.   Nor I.
Duke.   Saw you my daughter?
Pro.   Neither.
Duke. Why, then, she 's fled unto that peasant Valentine,

And Eglamour is in her company.
'T is true; for Friar Laurence met them both,
As he in penance wandered through the forest;
Him he knew well, and guessed that it was she,
But, being masked, he was not sure of it;
Besides, she did intend confession
At Patrick's cell this even: and there she was not.
These likelihoods confirm her flight from hence.
Therefore, I pray you, stand not to discourse,
But mount you presently; and meet with me,
Upon the rising of the mountain foot
That leads towards Mantua, whither they are fled:
Dispatch, sweet gentlemen, and follow me.   [*Exit*

   Thu.   Why, this it is to be a peevish girl,
That flies her fortune when it follows her.
I 'll after, more to be revenged on Eglamour,
Than for the love of reckless Silvia.   [*Exit*

   Pro.   And I will follow, more for Silvia's love
Than hate of Eglamour that goes with her.   [*Exit*

   Jul.   And I will follow, more to cross that love,
Than hate for Silvia that is gone for love.   [*Exit*

Scene III.—The Forest

Enter Outlaws with Silvia

   First Out.   Come, come;
Be patient; we must bring you to our captain.
   Sil.   A thousand more mischances than this one
Have learned me how to brook this patiently.
   Second Out.   Come, bring her away.
   First Out.   Where is the gentleman that was with her?
   Third Out.   Being nimble-footed, he hath outrun us;
But Moyses and Valerius follow him.
Go thou with her to the west end of the wood;
There is our captain.   We 'll follow him that 's fled;
The thicket is beset, he cannot scape.
   First Out.   Come, I must bring you to our captain's
               cave.
Fear not; he bears an honourable mind,
And will not use a woman lawlessly.
   Sil.   O Valentine, this I endure for thee.   [*Exeunt*

Scene IV.—Another Part of the Forest

Enter Valentine

   Val.   How use doth breed a habit in a man!
This shadowy desert, unfrequented woods,

I better brook than flourishing peopled towns:
Here can I sit alone, unseen of any,
And to the nightingale's complaining notes
Tune my distresses and record my woes.
O thou that dost inhabit in my breast,
Leave not the mansion so long tenantless,
Lest, growing ruinous, the building fall,
And leave no memory of what it was!
Repair me with thy presence, Silvia!
Thou gentle nymph, cherish thy forlorn swain!—
[Noise within

What halloing and what stir is this to-day?
These are my mates, that make their wills their law,
Have some unhappy passenger in chase.
They love me well: yet I have much to do
To keep them from uncivil outrages.
Withdraw thee, Valentine: who's this comes here?
[Steps aside

Enter PROTEUS, SILVIA, *and* JULIA *in boy's clothes*

Pro. Madam, this service I have done for you—
Though you respect not aught your servant doth—
To hazard life, and rescue you from him
That would have forced your honour and your love.
Vouchsafe me, for my meed, but one fair look:
A smaller than this I cannot beg,
And less than this, I am sure, you cannot give.
Val. How like a dream is this I see and hear!
Love, lend me patience to forbear awhile.
Sil. O miserable, unhappy that I am!
Pro. Unhappy were you, madam, ere I came;
But by my coming I have made you happy.
Sil. By thy approach thou mak'st me most unhappy.
Jul. [*Aside*] And me, when he approacheth to your
presence.
Sil. Had I been seizéd by a hungry lion,
I would have been a breakfast to the beast
Rather than have false Proteus rescue me.
O Heaven be judge, how I love Valentine,
Whose life's as tender to me as my soul;
And full as much—for more there cannot be—
I do detest false perjured Proteus.
Therefore be gone; solicit me no more.
Pro. What dangerous action, stood it next to death,
Would I not undergo for one calm look?
O, 't is the curse in love, and still approved,
When women cannot love where they're beloved.
Sil. When Proteus cannot love where he's beloved.

Read over Julia's heart, they first best love,
For whose dear sake thou didst then rend thy faith
Into a thousand oaths; and all those oaths
Descend into perjury to love me.
Thou hast no faith left now, unless thou 'dst two,
And that 's far worse than none; better have none
Than plural faith, which is too much by one.
Thou counterfeit to thy true friend!
    Pro.   **In love**
Who respects friend?
    Sil.   All men but Proteus.
    Pro.   Nay, if the gentle spirit of moving words
Can no way change you to a milder form,
I 'll woo you like a soldier, at arms' end,
And love you 'gainst the nature of love,—force you.
    Sil.   O Heaven!
    Pro.   I 'll force thee yield to my desire.
    Val.   [*Coming forward*] Ruffian, let go that rude un-
        civil touch,—
Thou friend of an ill fashion!
    Pro.   Valentine!
    Val.   Thou common friend, that 's without faith or
        love,—
For such is a friend now;—treacherous man!
Thou hast beguiled my hopes: nought but mine eye
Could have persuaded me. Now I dare not say
I have one friend alive; thou wouldst disprove me.
Who should be trusted, when one's own right hand
Is perjured to the bosom? Proteus,
I am sorry I must never trust thee more,
But count the world a stranger for thy sake.
The private wound is deep'st: time most accurst,
'Mongst all foes that a friend should be the worst!
    Pro.   My shame and guilt confound me.—
Forgive me, Valentine. If hearty sorrow
Be a sufficient ransom for offence,
I tender 't here; I do as truly suffer
As e'er I did commit.
    Val.   Then I am paid;
And once again I do receive thee honest.
Who by repentance is not satisfied
Is nor of Heaven, nor earth; for these are pleased;
By penitence the Eternal's wrath 's appeased:—
And, that my love may appear plain and free,
All that was mine in Silvia I give thee.
    Jul.   O me unhappy!   [*Faints*
    Pro.   Look to the boy.
    Val.   Why, boy! why, wag! how now? what is the
        matter?

Look up; speak.
   Jul.   O good sir! my master charged me
To deliver a ring to Madam Silvia;
Which, out of my neglect, was never done.
   Pro.   Where is that ring, boy?
   Jul.   Here 't is; this is it.   [*Gives a ring*
   Pro.   How! let me see.
Why, this is the ring I gave to Julia.
   Jul.   O, cry you mercy, sir; I have mistook:
This is the ring you sent to Silvia.   [*Shows another ring*
   Pro.   But, how cam'st thou by this ring?
At my depart I gave this unto Julia.
   Jul.   And Julia herself did give it me;
And Julia herself hath brought it hither.
   Pro.   How? Julia!
   Jul.   Behold her that gave aim to all thy oaths,
And entertained them deeply in her heart:
How oft hast thou with perjury cleft the root!
O Proteus, let this habit make thee blush:
Be thou ashamed, that I have took upon me
Such an immodest raiment,—if shame live
In a disguise of love.
It is the lesser blot, modesty finds,
Women to change their shapes than men their minds.
   Pro.   Than men their minds! 't is true. O Heaven, were man
But constant, he were perfect: that one error
Fills him with faults; makes him run through all sins:
Inconstancy falls off, ere it begins.
What is in Sylvia's face but I may spy
More fresh in Julia's, with a constant eye?
   Val.   Come, come, a hand from either.
Let me be blest to make this happy close;
'T were pity two such friends should be long foes.
   Pro.   Bear witness, Heaven, I have my wish for ever.
   Jul.   And I mine.

Enter Outlaws, with DUKE *and* THURIO

   Outlaws.   A prize! a prize! a prize!
   Val.   Forbear,—
Forbear, I say; it is my lord the duke.—
Your grace is welcome to a man disgraced,
Banishéd Valentine.
   Duke.   Sir Valentine!
   Thu.   Yonder is Sylvia; and Silvia 's mine.
   Val.   Thurio, give back, or else embrace thy death;
Come not within the measure of my wrath:

Do not name Silvia thine; if once again,
Milano shall not hold thee. Here she stands;
Take but possession of her with a touch:—
I dare thee but to breathe upon my love.
    Thu. Sir Valentine, I care not for her, I:
I hold him but a fool that will endanger
His body for a girl that loves him not:
I claim her not, and therefore she is thine.
    Duke. The more degenerate and base art thou,
To make such means for her as thou hast done,
And leave her on such slight conditions.—
Now, by the honour of my ancestry,
I do applaud thy spirit, Valentine,
And think thee worthy of an empress' love:
Know, then, I here forget all former griefs,
Cancel all grudge, repeal thee home again.
Plead a new state in thy unrivalled merit,
To which I thus subscribe,—Sir Valentine,
Thou art a gentleman, and well derived:
Take thou thy Silvia, for thou hast deserved her.
    Val. I thank your grace; the gift hath made happy.
I now beseech you, for your daughter's sake,
To grant one boon that I shall ask of you.
    Duke. I grant it for thine own, whate'er it be.
    Val. These banished men, that I have kept withal,
Are men endued with worthy qualities:
Forgive them what they have committed here,
And let them be recalled from their exile.
They are reforméd, civil, full of good,
And fit for great employment, worthy lord.
    Duke. Thou hast prevailed; I pardon them and thee:
Dispose of them as thou know'st their deserts.
Come, let us go: we will include all jars
With triumphs, mirth, and rare solemnity.
    Val. And, as we walk alone, I dare be bold
With our discourse to make your grace to smile.
What think you of this page, my lord?
    Duke. I think the boy hath grace in him; he blushes.
    Val. I warrant you, my lord, more grace than boy.
    Duke. What mean you by that saying?
    Val. Please you, I 'll tell you as we pass along,
That you will wonder what hath fortunéd.—
Come, Proteus, 't is your penance but to hear
The story of your loves discoveréd:
That done, our day of marriage shall be yours;
One feast, one house, one mutual happiness.

                                       [Exeunt

THE WINTER'S TALE

DRAMATIS PERSONÆ

Leontes, *king of Sicilia*
Mamillius, *young prince of Sicilia*
Camillo ⎫
Antigonus ⎬ *lords of Sicilia*
Cleomenes ⎪
Dion ⎭
Rogero, *a gentleman of Sicilia*
Polixenes, *king of Bohemia*
Florizel, *prince of Bohemia*
Archidamus, *a lord of Bohemia*
A Mariner
A Gaoler
An Old Shepherd, reputed father of Perdita
Clown, his Son
Autolycus, *a rogue*

Hermione, *queen to Leontes*
Perdita, *daughter to Leontes and Hermione*
Paulina, *wife to Antigonus*
Emilia, *a lady attending the Queen*
Mopsa ⎫
Dorcas ⎬ *Shepherdesses*

Lords, Ladies and Gentlemen, Officers and Servants, Shepherds
and Shepherdesses, Guards, &c.

Time, as Chorus

SCENE.—*Sometimes in Sicilia, sometimes in Bohemia*

208

THE WINTER'S TALE

ACT ONE

SCENE I.—Sicilia. An Ante-chamber in the Palace
of LEONTES

Enter CAMILLO *and* ARCHIDAMUS

Arch. If you shall chance, Camillo, to visit Bohemia, on
the like occasion whereon my services are now on foot,
you shall see, as I have said, great difference betwixt
our Bohemia and your Sicilia.

Cam. I think this coming summer, the King of Sicilia
means to pay Bohemia the visitation which he justly owes
him.

Arch. Wherein our entertainment shall shame us, we
will be justified in our loves: for, indeed—

Cam. 'Beseech you—

Arch. Verily, I speak it in the freedom of my knowledge: we cannot with such magnificence—in so rare—
I know not what to say.—We will give you sleepy drinks,
that your senses, unintelligent of our insufficience, may,
though they cannot praise us, as little accuse us.

Cam. You pay a great deal too dear for what 's given
freely.

Arch. Believe me, I speak as my understanding instructs
me, and as mine honesty puts it to utterance.

Cam. Sicilia cannot show himself over-kind to Bohemia.
They were trained together in their childhoods; and there
rooted betwixt them then such an affection, which cannot
choose but branch now. Since their more mature dignities
and royal necessities made separation of their society,
their encounters, though not personal, have been royally
attorneyed with interchange of gifts, letters, loving
embassies, that they have seemed to be together though
absent, shook hands as over a vast, and embraced, as it
were, from the ends of opposed winds. The heavens
continue their loves!

Arch. I think there is not in the world either malice
or matter to alter it. You have an unspeakable comfort
of your young Prince Mamillius: it is a gentleman of the
greatest promise that ever came into my note.

Cam. I very well agree with you in the hopes of him.

It is a gallant child; one that, indeed, physics the subject,
makes old hearts fresh: they that went on crutches ere
he was born desire yet their life to see him a man.

Arch.   Would they else be content to die?

Cam.   Yes, if there were no other excuse why they
should desire to live.

Arch.   If the king had no son, they would desire to
live on crutches till he had one.   [*Exeunt*

SCENE II.—Sicilia.   A Room of State in the Palace

Enter LEONTES, POLIXENES, HERMIONE, MAMILLIUS,
CAMILLO, *and Attendants*

Pol.   Nine changes of the watery star have been
The shepherd's note since we have left our throne
Without a burden: time as long again
Would be filled up, my brother, with our thanks,
And yet we should for perpetuity
Go hence in debt: and therefore, like a cipher,
Yet standing in rich place, I multiply
With one 'We thank you' many thousands more
That go before it.

Leon.   Stay your thanks awhile,
And pay them when you part.

Pol.   Sir, that's to-morrow.
I am questioned by my fears of what may chance
Or breed upon our absence; that may blow
No sneaping winds at home to make us say,
'This is put forth too truly!'   Besides, I have stayed
To tire your royalty.

Leon.   We are tougher, brother,
Than you can put us to 't.

Pol.   No longer stay.

Leon.   One seven-night longer.

Pol.   Very sooth, to-morrow.

Leon.   We'll part the time between 's then; and in that,
I'll no gainsaying.

Pol.   Press me not, 'beseech you, so.
There is no tongue that moves, none, none i' the world
So soon as yours, could win me; so it should now
Were there necessity in your request, although
'T were needful I denied it.   My affairs
Do even drag me homeward; which to hinder
Were, in your love, a whip to me, my stay,
To you a charge and trouble: to save both,
Farewell, our brother.

Leon.   Tongue-tied, our queen? speak you

210

Her. I had thought, sir, to have held my peace until
You had drawn oaths from him not to stay. You, sir,
Charge him too coldly: tell him, you are sure
All in Bohemia 's well: this satisfaction
The by-gone day proclaimed. Say this to him,
He 's beat from his best ward.
   Leon.   Well said, Hermione.
   Her. To tell he longs to see his son were strong:
But let him say so then, and let him go;
But let him swear so, and he shall not stay,
We 'll thwack him hence with distaffs.—
[*To Polixenes*] Yet of your royal presence I 'll adventure
The borrow of a week. When at Bohemia
You take my lord, I 'll give him my commission
To let him there a month behind the gest
Prefixed for 's parting: yet, good deed, Leontes,
I love thee not a jar o' the clock behind
What lady she her lord.—You 'll stay?
   Pol.   No, madam.
   Her. Nay, but you will?
   Pol.   I may not, verily.
   Her. Verily!
You put me off with limber vows; but I,
Though you would seek to unsphere the stars with oaths,
Should yet say, "Sir, no going." Verily,
You shall not go: a lady's "verily" is
As potent as a lord's. Will you go yet?
Force me to keep you as a prisoner,
Not like a guest; so you shall pay your fees
When you depart, and save your thanks. How say you?
My prisoner, or my guest? by your dread "verily,"
One of them you shall be.
   Pol.   Your guest then, madam:
To be your prisoner should import offending;
This is for me less easy to commit
Than you to punish.
   Her.   Not your gaoler, then,
But your kind hostess. Come, I 'll question you
Of my lord's tricks and yours, when you were boys;
You were pretty lordings then.
   Pol.   We were, fair queen,
Two lads, that thought there was no more behind
But such a day to-morrow as to-day,
And to be boy eternal.
   Her. Was not my lord the verier wag o' the two?
   Pol. We were as twinned lambs that did frisk i' the sun,
And bleat the one at the other: what we changed,
Was innocence for innocence; we knew not
The doctrine of ill-doing, nor dreamed

That any did.   Had we pursued that life,
And our weak spirits ne'er been higher reared
With stronger blood, we should have answered heaven
Boldly, "not guilty," the imposition cleared,
Hereditary ours.
    Her.   By this we gather,
You have tripped since.
    Pol.   O, my most sacred lady,
Temptations have since then been born to 's; for
In those unfledged days was my wife a girl:
Your precious self had then not crossed the eyes
Of my young playfellow.
    Her.   Grace to boot!
Of this make no conclusion, lest you say
Your queen and I are devils: yet, go on;
The offences we have made you do, we 'll answer
If you first sinned with us, and that with us
You did continue fault, and that you slipped not
With any but with us.
    Leon.   Is he won yet?
    Her. He 'll stay, my lord.
    Leon.   At my request he would not.
Hermione, my dearest, thou ne'er spok'st
To better purpose.
    Her.   Never?
    Leon.   Never, but once.
    Her. What, have I twice said well? when was 't before?
I pr'ythee, tell me.   Cram 's with praise, and make 's
As fat as tame things: one good deed, dying tongueless,
Slaughters a thousand waiting upon that.
Our praises are our wages: you may ride 's
With one soft kiss a thousand furlongs, ere
With spur we heat an acre.   But to the goal:—
My last good deed was to entreat his stay;
What was my first? it has an elder sister,
Or I mistake you: O, 'would her name were Grace!
But once before I spoke to the purpose: when?
Nay, let me have 't; I long.
    Leon.   Why, that was when
Three crabbéd months had soured themselves to death
Ere I could make thee open thy white hand
And clap thyself my love: then didst thou utter,
" I am yours for ever."
    Her.   'T is Grace, indeed.—
Why, lo you now, I have spoke to the purpose twice:
The one for ever earned a royal husband,
The other for some while a friend.
                        [*Giving her hand to Polixenes*

    Leon. [*Aside*]   Too hot, too hot!

To mingle friendship far is mingling bloods.
I have *tremor cordis* on me:—my heart dances,
But not for joy, not joy.—This entertainment
May a free face put on; derive a liberty
From heartiness, from bounty, fertile bosom,
And well become the agent: 't may, I grant;
But to be paddling palms, and pinching fingers,
As now they are; and making practised smiles
As in a looking-glass;—and then to sign, as 't were
The mort o' the deer; O, that is entertainment
My bosom likes not, nor my brows.—Mamillius,
Art thou my boy?
   Mam.   Ay, my good lord.
   Leon.   I' fecks?
Why, that 's my bawcock. What, has smutch'd thy
       nose?—
They say, it is a copy out of mine: Come, captain,
We must be neat; not neat, but cleanly, captain:
And yet the steer, the heifer, and the calf,
Are all called neat.—Still virginalling
Upon his palm?—How now, you wanton calf,
Art thou my calf?
   Mam.   Yes, if you will, my lord.
   Leon. Thou want'st a rough pash, and the shoots that
       I have,
To be full like me:—yet, they say, we are
Almost as like as eggs; women say so,
That will say anything: but were they false
As o'er-dyed blacks, as wind, as waters, false
As dice are to be wished by one that fixes
No bourn 'twixt his and mine; yet were it true
To say this boy were like me.—Come, sir page,
Look on me with your welkin eye: sweet villain,
Most dear'st, my collop,—Can thy dam?—may 't be?—
Affection, thy intention stabs the centre:
Thou dost make possible things not so held,
Communicat'st with dreams;—how can this be?—
With what 's unreal thou co-active art,
And fellow'st nothing. Then, 't is very credent,
Thou may'st co-join with something; and thou dost,—
And that beyond commission; and I find it;
And that to the infection of my brains,
And hardening of my brows.
   Pol.   What means Sicilia?
   Her. He something seems unsettled.
   Pol.   How, my lord!
What cheer? how is 't with you, best brother?
   Her.   You look
As if you held a brow of much distraction:

Are you moved, my lord?
  Leon.   No, in good earnest.—
How sometimes nature will betray its folly,
Its tenderness, and make itself a pastime
To harder bosoms! Looking on the lines
Of my boy's face, methoughts I did recoil
Twenty-three years, and saw myself unbreeched,
In my green velvet coat, my dagger muzzled,
Lest it should bite its master, and so prove,
As ornaments oft do, too dangerous.
How like, methought, I then was to this kernel,
This squash, this gentleman.—Mine honest friend,
Will you take eggs for money?
  Mam. No, my lord, I 'll fight.
  Leon. You will? why, happy man be 's dole!—My
     brother,
Are you so fond of your young prince as we
Do seem to be of ours?
  Pol.   If at home, sir,
He 's all my exercise, my mirth, my matter:
Now my sworn friend, and then mine enemy;
My parasite, my soldier, statesman, all.
He makes a July's day short as December;
And with his varying childness cures in me
Thoughts that would thick my blood.
  Leon.   So stands this squire
Officed with me. We two will walk, my lord,
And leave you to your graver steps.—Hermione,
How thou lov'st us, show in our brother's welcome;
Let what is dear in Sicily, be cheap.
Next to thyself and my young rover, he 's
Apparent to my heart.
  Her.   If you would seek us,
We are yours i' the garden: shall 's attend you there?
  Leon. To your own bents dispose you: you 'll be found,
Be you beneath the sky.—[*Aside*] I am angling now,
Though you perceive me not how I give line.
Go to, go to!
How she holds up the neb, the bill to him;
And arms her with the boldness of a wife
To her allowing husband!
      [*Exeunt Polixenes, Hermione, and Attendants*
      Gone already;
Inch-thick, knee-deep, o'er head and ears a forked one!—
Go play, boy, play;—thy mother plays, and I
Play too, but so disgraced a part, whose issue
Will hiss me to my grave: contempt and clamour
Will be my knell.—Go play, boy, play.—There have been,
Or I am much deceived, cuckolds ere now;

And many a man there is (even at this present,
Now, while I speak this) holds his wife by the arm,
That little thinks she has been sluiced in 's absence,
And his pond fished by his next neighbour, by
Sir Smile, his neighbour.   Nay, there 's comfort in 't
Whiles other men have gates, and those gates opened
As mine, against their will.   Should all despair
That have revolted wives, the tenth of mankind
Would hang themselves.   Physic for 't there is none:
It is a bawdy planet, that will strike
Where 't is predominant: and 't is powerful, think it,
From east, west, north, and south; be it concluded,
No barricado for a belly; know 't;
It will let in and out the enemy,
With bag and baggage.   Many a thousand on 's
Have the disease, and feel 't not.—How now, boy?
     Mam.   I am like you, they say.
     Leon.   Why, that 's some comfort—
What! Camillo there?
     Cam.   Ay, my good lord.
     Leon.   Go play, Mamillius; thou 'rt an honest man.—
                             [*Exit Mamillius*
Camillo, this great sir will yet stay longer.
     Cam.   You had much ado to make his anchor hold:
When you cast out, it still came home.
     Leon.   Didst note it?
     Cam.   He would not stay at your petitions; made
His business more material.
     Leon.   Didst perceive it?—
They're here with me already; whispering, rounding,
"Sicilia is a—so forth."   'T is far gone,
When I shall gust it last.—How came 't, Camillo,
That he did stay?
     Cam.   At the good queen's entreaty.
     Leon.   At the queen's, be 't: good should be pertinent;
But so it is, it is not.   Was this taken
By any understanding pate but thine?
For thy conceit is soaking; will draw in
More than the common blocks: not noted, is 't,
But of the finer natures? by some severals
Of head-piece extraordinary? lower messes,
Perchance, are to this business purblind: say.
     Cam.   Business, my lord?   I think, most understand
Bohemia stays here longer.
     Leon.   Ha?
     Cam.   Stays here longer.
     Leon.   Ay, but why?
     Cam.   To satisfy your highness, and the entreaties
Of our most gracious mistress.

Leon.   Satisfy
The entreaties of your mistress?—satisfy?—
Let that suffice. I have trusted thee, Camillo,
With all the nearest things to my heart, as well
My chamber-councils, wherein, priest-like, thou
Hast cleansed my bosom; I from thee departed
Thy penitent reformed: but we have been
Deceived in thy integrity, deceived
In that which seems so.
    Cam.   Be it forbid, my lord!
    Leon.   To bide upon 't,—thou art not honest; or
If thou inclin'st that way, thou art a coward,
Which hoxes honesty behind, restraining
From course required; or else thou must be counted
A servant grafted in my serious trust,
And therein negligent; or else a fool
That seest a game played home, the rich stake drawn,
And tak'st it all for jest.
    Cam.   My gracious lord,
I may be negligent, foolish, and fearful:
In every one of these no man is free,
But that his negligence, his folly, fear,
Among the infinite doings of the world,
Sometime puts forth. In your affairs, my lord,
If ever I were wilful-negligent,
It was my folly; if industriously
I played the fool, it was my negligence,
Not weighing well the end; if ever fearful
To do a thing where I the issue doubted,
Whereof the execution did cry out
Against the non-performance, 't was a fear
Which oft infects the wisest. These, my lord,
Are such allowed infirmities that honesty
Is never free of. But, 'beseech your grace,
Be plainer with me; let me know my trespass
By its own visage; if I then deny it,
'T is none of mine.
    Leon.   Ha' not you seen, Camillo,—
But that 's past doubt: you have, or your eye-glass
Is thicker than a cuckold's horn—or heard,—
For, to a vision so apparent, rumour
Cannot be mute—or thought,—for cogitation
Resides not in that man that does not think—
My wife is slippery? If thou wilt confess—
Or else be impudently negative,
To have nor eyes, nor thought,—then say
My wife 's a hobbyhorse, deserves a name
As rank as any flax-wench that puts to
Before her troth-plight; say 't, and justify 't.

Cam.   I would not be a stander-by to hear
My sovereign mistress clouded so without
My present vengeance taken. 'Shrew my heart,
You never spoke what did become you less
Than this; which to reiterate were sin
As deep as that, though true.
    Leon.   Is whispering nothing?
Is leaning cheek to cheek? is meeting noses?
Kissing with inside lip? stopping the career
Of laughter with a sigh?—a note infallible
Of breaking honesty—horsing foot on foot?
Skulking in corners? wishing clocks more swift?
Hours, minutes? noon, midnight? and all eyes
Blind with the pin and web, but theirs, theirs only,
That would unseen be wicked?—is this nothing?
Why, then the world and all that's in't is nothing;
The covering sky is nothing; Bohemia nothing;
My wife is nothing; nor nothing have these nothings
If this be nothing.
    Cam.   Good my lord, be cured
Of this diseased opinion, and betimes;
For 't is most dangerous.
    Leon.   Say, it be; 't is true.
    Cam.   No, no, my lord.
    Leon.   It is; you lie, you lie;
I say, thou liest, Camillo, and I hate thee;
Pronounce thee a gross lout, a mindless slave,
Or else a hovering temporiser, that
Canst with thine eyes at once see good and evil,
Inclining to them both; were my wife's liver
Infected as her life, she would not live
The running of one glass.
    Cam.   Who does infect her?
    Leon.   Why, he that wears her like her medal, hanging
About his neck, Bohemia: who, if I
Had servants true about me, that bare eyes
To see alike mine honour as their profits,
Their own particular thrifts, they would do that
Which should undo more doing: ay, and thou,
His cup-bearer, whom I from meaner form
Have benched, and reared to worship; who may'st see,
Plainly as heaven sees earth and earth sees heaven,
How I am gallèd,—might'st bespice a cup,
To give mine enemy a lasting wink;
Which draught to me were cordial.
    Cam.   Sir, my lord!
I could do this, and that with no rash potion,
But with a lingering dram that should not work
Maliciously like poison: but I cannot

Believe this crack to be in my dread mistress,
So sovereignly being honourable.—
I have loved thee.—
    Leon.   Make that thy question, and go rot!
Dost think, I am so muddy, so unsettled,
To appoint myself in this vexation, sully
The purity and whiteness of my sheets,—
Which to preserve is sleep; which, being spotted,
Is goads, thorns, nettles, tails of wasps,—
Give scandal to the blood o' the prince, my son,—
Who, I do think, is mine, and love as mine—
Without ripe moving to 't? Would I do this?
Could man so blench?
    Cam.   I must believe you, sir:
I do; and will fetch off Bohemia for 't;
Provided, that when he 's removed, your highness
Will take again your queen as yours at first,
Even for your son's sake, and thereby for sealing
The injury of tongues, in courts and kingdoms
Known and allied to yours.
    Leon.   Thou dost advise me
Even so as I mine own course have set down.
I 'll give no blemish to her honour, none.
    Cam.   My lord,
Go then; and with a countenance as clear
As friendship wears at feasts, keep with Bohemia
And with your queen. I am his cup-bearer;
If from me he have wholesome beverage,
Account me not your servant.
    Leon.   This is all:
Do 't, and thou hast the one half of my heart;
Do 't not, thou splitt'st thine own.
    Cam.   I 'll do 't, my lord,
    Leon.   I will seem friendly, as thou hast advised me.
                                [Exit

    Cam. O miserable lady!—But, for me,
What case stand I in? I must be the poisoner
Of good Polixenes; and my ground to do 't
Is the obedience to a master; one
Who, in rebellion with himself, will have
All that are his so too.—To do this deed,
Promotion follows. If I could find example
Of thousands that had struck anointed kings
And flourished after, I 'd not do 't; but since
Nor brass, nor stone, nor parchment, bears not one,
Let villainy itself forswear 't. I must
Forsake the court: to do 't, or no, is certain
To me a break-neck. Happy star, reign now!
Here comes Bohemia.

Re-enter POLIXENES

 Pol.   This is strange. Methinks,
My favour here begins to warp. Not speak?—
Good day, Camillo.
 Cam.   Hail, most royal sir!
 Pol. What is the news i' the court?
 Cam.   None rare, my lord.
 Pol. The king hath on him such a countenance
As he had lost some province, and a region
Loved as he loves himself: even now I met him
With customary compliment, when he,
Wafting his eyes to the contrary, and falling
A lip of much contempt, speeds from me, and
So leave me to consider what is breeding
That changes thus his manners.
 Cam. I dare not know, my lord.
 Pol. How! dare not?—Do not?—Do you know, and
   dare not
Be intelligent to me? 'T is thereabouts;
For to yourself what you do know, you must,
And cannot say you dare not. Good Camillo,
Your changed complexions are to me a mirror,
Which shows me mine changed too; for I must be
A party in this alteration, finding
Myself thus altered with 't.
 Cam.   There is a sickness
Which puts some of us in distemper; but
I cannot name the disease, and it is caught
Of you, that yet are well.
 Pol.   How caught of me?
Make me not sighted like the basilisk:
I have looked on thousands, who have sped the better
By my regard, but killed none so. Camillo,—
As you are certainly a gentleman; thereto
Clerk-like experienced, which no less adorns
Our gentry than our parents' noble names
In whose success we are gentle,—I beseech you,
If you know aught which does behove my knowledge
Thereof to be informed, imprison 't not
In ignorant concealment.
 Cam.   I may not answer.
 Pol. A sickness caught of me, and yet I well?
I must be answered.—Dost thou hear, Camillo,
I conjure thee, by all the parts of man
Which honour does acknowledge,—whereof the least
Is not this suit of mine,— that thou declare
What incidency thou dost guess of harm
Is creeping towards me; how far off, how near;

Which way to be prevented, if to be:
If not, how best to bear it.
    Cam.   Sir, I will tell you;
Since I am charged in honour, and by him
That I think honourable. Therefore, mark my counsel,
Which must be even as swiftly followed as
I mean to utter it, or both yourself and me
Cry 'lost,' and so good night.
    Pol.   On, good Camillo.
    Cam.   I am appointed him to murder you.
    Pol.   By whom, Camillo?
    Cam.   By the king.
    Pol.   For what?
    Cam.   He thinks, nay, with all confidence he swears,
As he had seen 't or been an instrument
To vice you to 't,—that you have touched his queen
Forbiddenly.
    Pol.   O, then my best blood turn
To an infected jelly, and my name
Be yoked with his that did betray the Best!
Turn then my fresh reputation to
A savour that may strike the dullest nostril
Where I arrive, and my approach be shunned,
Nay, hated too, worse than the great'st infection
That e'er was heard, or read!
    Cam.   Swear his thought over
By each particular star in heaven and
By all their influences, you may as well
Forbid the sea for to obey the moon,
As, or by oath, remove, or counsel, shake,
The fabric of his folly, whose foundation
Is piled upon his faith, and will continue
The standing of his body.
    Pol.   How should this grow?
    Cam.   I know not; but, I am sure, 't is safer to
Avoid what 's grown than question how 't is born.
If therefore you dare trust my honesty,
That lies encloséd in this trunk which you
Shall bear along impawned, away to-night!
Your followers I will whisper to the business;
And will, by twos and threes, at several posterns,
Clear them o' the city. For myself, I 'll put
My fortunes to your service, which are here
By this discovery lost. Be not uncertain;
For, by the honour of my parents, I
Have uttered truth, which if you seek to prove,
I dare not stand by; nor shall you be safer
Than one condemned by the king's own mouth, thereon
His execution sworn.

Pol.   I do believe thee:
I saw his heart in 's face.   Give me thy hand:
Be pilot to me, and thy places shall
Still neighbour mine.   My ships are ready, and
My people did expect my hence departure
Two days ago.—This jealousy
Is for a precious creature: as she 's rare,
Must it be great; and, as his person 's mighty,
Must it be violent; and, as he does conceive
He is dishonoured by a man which ever
Professed to him, why, his revenge must
In that be made more bitter.   Fear o'ershades me:
Good expedition be my friend, and comfort
The gracious queen, part of his theme, but nothing
Of his ill-ta'en suspicion!   Come, Camillo:
I will respect thee as a father, if
Thou bear'st my life off hence.   Let us avoid.
  Cam.   It is in mine authority to command
The keys of all the posterns.   Please your highness
To take the urgent hour.   Come, sir: away!

                                              [*Exeunt*

ACT TWO

Scene I.—Sicilia.   Within the Palace of Leontes

Enter Hermione, Mamillius, *and Ladies*

  Her.   Take the boy to you: he so troubles me,
'T is past enduring.
  First Lady.   Come, my gracious lord:
Shall I be your playfellow?
  Mam.   No, I 'll none of you.
  First Lady.   Why, my sweet lord?
  Mam.   You 'll kiss me hard, and speak to me as if
I were a baby still.—I love you better.
  Second Lady.   And why so, my lord?
  Mam.   Not for because
Your brows are blacker; yet black brows, they say,
Become some women best, so that there be not
Too much hair there, but in a semicircle
Or a half-moon made with a pen.
  Second Lady.   Who taught you this?
  Mam.   I learned it out of women's faces.—Pray now,
What colour are your eyebrows?
  First Lady.   Blue, my lord.
  Mam.   Nay, that 's a mock: I have seen a lady's nose
That has been blue, but not her eyebrows.

  Second Lady.   Hark ye,
The queen, your mother, rounds apace: we shall
Present our services to a fine new prince
One of these days: and then you 'd wanton with us,
If we would have you.
  First Lady.   She is spread of late
Into a goodly bulk: good time encounter her!
  Her. What wisdom stirs amongst you?   Come, sir;
        now
I am for you again: pray you, sit by us
And tell 's a tale.
  Mam.   Merry, or sad, shall 't be?
  Her. As merry as you will.
  Mam.   A sad tale 's best for winter.
I have one of sprites and goblins.
  Her.   Let's have that, good sir.
Come on, sit down: come on, and do your best
To fright me with your sprites: you 're powerful at it.
  Mam. There was a man,—
  Her.   Nay, come, sit down; then on.
  Mam. Dwelt by a churchyard.—I will tell it softly;
Yond crickets shall not hear it.
  Her.   Come on, then,
And give 't me in mine ear.

    Enter LEONTES, ANTIGONUS, *Lorde, and others*

  Leon. Was he met there? his train? Camillo with
      him?
  First Lord. Behind the tuft of pines I met them: never
Saw I men scour so on their way.   I eyed them
Even to their ships.
  Leon.   How blest am I
In my just censure, in my true opinion!—
Alack, for lesser knowledge! How accursed
In being so blest!—There may be in the cup
A spider steeped, and one may drink, depart,
And yet partake no venom, for his knowledge
Is not infected; but if one present
The abhorred ingredient to his eye made known
How he hath drunk, he cracks his gorge, his sides,
With violent hefts.—I have drunk, and seen the spider.
Camillo was his help in this, his pander!—
There is a plot against my life, my crown:
All 's true that is mistrusted:—that false villain,
Whom I employed, was pre-employed by him.
He had discovered my design, and I
Remain a pinched thing; yea, a very trick
For them to play at will.—How came the posterns
So easily open?

First Lord. By his great authority;
Which often hath no less prevailed than so,
On your command.
　　Leon. I know 't too well.—
　　Give me the boy. [*To Hermione.*] I am glad you did
　　　　not nurse him:
Though he does bear some signs of me, yet you
Have too much blood in him.
　　Her. What is this? sport?
　　Leon. Bear the boy hence; he shall not come about her.
Away with him, and let her sport herself
With that she 's big with, for 't is Polixenes
Has made thee swell thus.
　　Her. But I 'd say he had not,
And, I 'll be sworn, you would believe my saying,
Howe'er you lean to the nayward.
　　Leon. You, my lords,
Look on her, mark her well: be but about
To say, "she is a goodly lady," and
The justice of your hearts will thereto add,
"'T is pity she 's not honest, honourable:"
Praise her but for this her without-door form—
Which, on my faith, deserves high speech—and straight;
The shrug, the hum, or ha, these petty brands
That calumny doth use:—O, I am out,
That mercy does, for calumny will sear
Virtue itself: these shrugs, these hums and ha's,
When you have said, "she 's goodly," come between,
Ere you can say, "she 's honest." But be 't known
From him that has most cause to grieve it should be,
She 's an adult'ress.
　　Her. Should a villain say so,
The most replenished villain in the world,
He were as much more villain: you, my lord,
Do but mistake.
　　Leon. You have mistook, my lady,
Polixenes for Leontes. O thou thing,
Which I 'll not call a creature of thy place,
Lest barbarism, making me the precedent,
Should a like language use to all degrees
And mannerly distinguishment leave out
Betwixt the prince and beggar!—I have said
She 's an adult'ress: I have said with whom:
More, she 's a traitor; and Camillo is
A federary with her, and one that knows
What she should shame to know herself,
But with her most vile principal, that she's
A bed-swerver, even as bad as those
That vulgars give bold'st titles; ay, and privy

To this their late escape.
    Her.   No, by my life,
Privy to none of this.   How will this grieve you,
When you shall come to clearer knowledge, that
You thus have published me?   Gentle, my lord,
You scarce can right me throughly then, to say
You did mistake.
    Leon.   No: if I mistake
In those foundations which I build upon,
The centre is not big enough to bear
A school-boy's top.—Away with her to prison!
He who shall speak for her is afar off guilty,
But that he speaks.
    Her.   There 's some ill planet reigns:
I must be patient, till the heavens look
With an aspect more favourable.—Good my lords,
I am not prone to weeping, as our sex
Commonly are; the want of which vain dew,
Perchance, shall dry your pities; but I have
That honourable grief lodged here which burns
Worse than tears drown.   Beseech you all, lords,
With thoughts so qualified as your charities
Shall best instruct you, measure me: and so
The king's will be performed.
    Leon.   Shall I be heard?
    Her.   Who is 't, that goes with me?—Beseech your
        highness
My women may be with me; for, you see,
My plight requires it.   Do not weep, good fools;
There is no cause: when you shall know your mistress
Has deserved prison, then abound in tears
As I come out: this action I now go on,
Is for my better grace.—Adieu, my lord:
I never wished to see you sorry; now,
I trust I shall.—My women, come; you have leave.
    Leon.   Go, do our bidding: hence!
                        [Exeunt Queen and Ladies
    First Lord. 'Beseech your highness, call the queen
        again.
    Ant.   Be certain what you do, sir, lest your justice
Prove violence, in the which three great ones suffer,
Yourself, your queen, your son.
    First Lord.   For her, my lord,
I dare my life lay down, and will do 't, sir,
Please you to accept it, that the queen is spotless
I' the eyes of heaven and to you; I mean,
In this which you accuse her.
    Ant.   If it prove
She 's otherwise, I 'll keep my stables where

I lodge my wife; I 'll go in couples with her;
Than when I feel and see her, no further trust her;
For every inch of woman in the world,
Ay, every dram of woman's flesh, is false,
If she be.
    Lord.   Hold your peaces!
    First Lord.   Good my lord,—
    Ant.   It is for you we speak, not for ourselves.
You are abused, and by some putter-on,
That will be damned for 't; would I knew the villain,
I would land-damn him. Be she honour-flawed,—
I have three daughters; the eldest is eleven,
The second, and the third, nine, and some five;
If this prove true, they 'll pay for 't; by mine honour,
I 'll geld them all; fourteen they shall not see,
To bring false generations; they are co-heirs;
And I had rather glib myself, than they
Should not produce fair issue.
    Leon.   Cease! no more.
You smell this business with a sense as cold
As is a dead man's nose; but I do see 't, and feel 't,
As you feel doing thus, and see withal
The instruments that feel.
    Ant.   If it be so,
We need no grave to bury honesty:
There 's not a grain of it the face to sweeten
Of the whole dungy earth.
    Leon.   What? lack I credit?
    First Lord.   I had rather you did lack, than I, my lord,
Upon this ground; and more it would content me
To have her honour true, than your suspicion;
Be blamed for 't how you might.
    Leon.   Why, what need we
Commune with you of this, but rather follow
Our forcible instigation? Our prerogative
Calls not your counsels, but our natural goodness
Imparts this; which, if you—or stupefied,
Or seeming so in skill—cannot, or will not,
Relish a truth like us, inform yourselves
We need no more of your advice: the matter,
The loss, the gain, the ordering on 't, is all
Properly ours.
    Ant.   And I wish, my liege,
You had only in your silent judgment tried it,
Without more overture.
    Leon.   How could that be?
Either thou art most ignorant by age,
Or thou wert born a fool. Camillo's flight,
Added to their familiarity—

Which was as gross as ever touched conjecture,
They lacked sight only, naught for approbation,
But only seeing, all other circumstances
Made up to the deed—doth push on this proceeding:
Yet, for a greater confirmation,—
For in an act of this importance 't were
Most piteous to be wild—I have despatched in post,
To sacred Delphos, to Apollo's temple,
Cleomenes and Dion, whom you know
Of stuffed sufficiency. Now, from the oracle
They will bring all; whose spiritual counsel had,
Shall stop, or spur me. Have I done well?
    First Lord. Well done, my lord.
    Leon. Though I am satisfied, and need no more
Than what I know, yet shall the oracle
Give rest to the minds of others such as he
Whose ignorant credulity will not
Come up to the truth. So have we thought it good
From our free person she should be confined,
Lest that the treachery of the two fled hence
Be left her to perform. Come, follow us:
We are to speak in public; for this business
Will raise us all.
    Ant. [*Aside*] To laughter, as I take it,
If the good truth were known.   [*Exeunt*

SCENE II.—*The Same. The outer Room of a Prison*

Enter PAULINA *and Attendants*

    Paul. The keeper of the prison,—call to him;
Let him have knowledge who I am.—Good lady!
                    [*Exit an Attendant*
No court in Europe is too good for thee!
What dost thou then in prison?—

Re-enter Attendant, with the Gaoler

                        Now, good sir,
You know me, do you not?
    Gaoler.   For a worthy lady,
And one whom much I honour.
    Paul.   Pray you, then,
Conduct me to the queen.
    Gaoler. I may not, madam: to the contrary
I have express commandment.
    Paul.   Here 's ado,
To lock up honesty and honour from
The access of gentle visitors!—Is 't lawful,

Pray you, to see her women? any of them?
Emilia?
    Gaoler.   So please you, madam,
To put apart these your attendants, I
Shall bring Emilia forth.
    Paul.   I pray now, call her.—
Withdraw yourselves.   *[Exeunt Attendants*
    Gaoler.   And, madam,
I must be present at your conference.
    Paul.   Well, be 't so, pr'ythee.   *[Exit Gaoler*
Here 's such ado to make no stain a stain
As passes colouring.

         Re-enter Gaoler, with EMILIA

               Dear gentlewoman,
How fares our gracious lady?
    Emil.   As well as one so great and so forlorn
May hold together.   On her frights and griefs—
Which never tender lady hath borne greater—
She is, something before her time, delivered.
    Paul.   A boy?
    Emil.   A daughter; and a goodly babe,
Lusty, and like to live: the queen receives
Much comfort in 't, says, "My poor prisoner,
I am innocent as you."
    Paul.   I dare be sworn:—
These dangerous, unsafe lunes i' the king, beshrew them!
He must be told on 't, and he shall: the office
Becomes a woman best; I 'll take 't upon me.
If I prove honey-mouthed let my tongue blister,
And never to my red-looked anger be
The trumpet any more.—Pray you, Emilia,
Commend my best obedience to the queen;
If she dares trust me with her little babe,
I 'll show 't the king, and undertake to be
Her advocate to the loud'st.   We do not know
How he may soften at the sight o' the child;
The silence often of pure innocence
Persuades, when speaking fails.
    Emil.   Most worthy madam,
Your honour, and your goodness is so evident,
That your free undertaking cannot miss
A thriving issue: there is no lady living
So meet for this great errand.   Please your ladyship
To visit the next room, I 'll presently
Acquaint the queen of your most noble offer,
Who, but to-day, hammered of this design,
But durst not tempt a minister of honour,

Lest she should be denied.
    Paul.   Tell her, Emilia,
I'll use that tongue I have: if wit flow from 't,
As boldness from my bosom, let 't not be doubted
I shall do good.
    Emil.   Now, be you blest for it!
I 'll to the queen.—Please you, come something nearer.
    Gaoler.   Madam, if 't please the queen to send the babe
I know not what I shall incur to pass it,
Having no warrant.
    Paul.   You need not fear it, sir;
The child was prisoner to the womb, and is,
By law and process of great nature, thence
Freed and enfranchised; not a party to
The anger of the king, nor guilty of,
If any be, the trespass of the queen.
    Gaoler. I do believe it.
    Paul. Do not you fear: upon mine honour, I
Will stand betwixt you and danger.   [*Exeunt*

SCENE III.—The Same.   A Room in the Palace

Enter LEONTES, ANTIGONUS, *Lords, and other Attendants*

    Leon. Nor night nor day, no rest.   It is but weakness
To bear the matter thus, mere weakness.   If
The cause were not in being,—part o' the cause,
She, the adult'ress; for the harlot king
Is quite beyond mine arm, out of the blank
And level of my brain, plot-proof; but she,
I can hook to me:—say, that she were gone,
Given to the fire, a moiety of my rest
Might come to me again.—Who 's there?
    First Atten.   My lord.
    Leon. How does the boy?
    First Atten.   He took good rest to-night;
'T is hoped, his sickness is discharged.
    Leon.   To see his nobleness!
Conceiving the dishonour of his mother,
He straight declined, drooped, took it deeply,
Fastened and fixed the shame on 't in himself,
Threw off his spirit, his appetite, his sleep,
And downright languished.—Leave me solely:—
See how he fares. [*Exit Attendant*]—Fie, fie! no thought
       of him:
The very thought of my revenges that way
Recoil upon me: in himself too mighty,
And in his parties, his alliance;—let him be,

Until a time may serve. For present vengeance,
Take it on her. Camillo and Polixenes
Laugh at me; make their pastime at my sorrow:
They should not laugh, if I could reach them; nor
Shall she, within my power.

Enter PAULINA, *with a Child*

   First Lord.   You must not enter.
   Paul. Nay, rather, good my lords, be second to me.
Fear you his tyrannous passion more, alas,
Than the queen's life? a gracious innocent soul,
More free than he is jealous.
   Ant.   That 's enough.
   First Atten. Madam, he hath not slept to-night; commanded
None should come at him.
   Paul.   Not so hot, good sir;
I come to bring him sleep. 'T is such as you,
That creep like shadows by him, and do sigh
At each his needless heavings, such as you
Nourish the cause of his awaking. I
Do come with words as med'cinal as true,
Honest as either, to purge him of that humour
That presses him from sleep.
   Leon.   What noise there, ho?
   Paul. No noise, my lord; but needful conference,
About some gossips for your highness.
   Leon.   How?—
Away with that audacious lady. Antigonus,
I charged thee that she should not come about me:
I knew she would.
   Ant.   I told her so, my lord,
On your displeasure's peril and on mine,
She should not visit you.
   Leon.   What, canst not rule her?
   Paul. From all dishonesty he can: in this,—
Unless he take the course that you have done,
Commit me for committing honour—trust it,
He shall not rule me.
   Ant.   Lo you now, you hear.
When she will take the rein, I let her run;
But she 'll not stumble.
   Paul.   Good my liege, I come,—
And, I beseech you, hear me, who profess
Myself your loyal servant, your physician,
Your most obedient counsellor, yet that dares
Less appear so in comforting your evils,
Than such as most seem yours,—I say, I come
From your good queen.

Leon.   Good queen!
Paul.   Good queen, my lord, good queen: I say, good
          queen;
And would by combat make her good, so were I
A man, the worst about you.
      Leon.   Force her hence.
      Paul.   Let him that makes but trifles of his eyes
First hand me.   On mine own accord I'll off,
But first I'll do my errand.—The good queen,
For she is good, hath brought you forth a daughter:
Here 't is; commends it to your blessing.
                              [*Laying down the Child*
      Leon.   Out!
A mankind witch!   Hence with her, out o' door:
A most intelligencing bawd!
      Paul.   Not so:
I am as ignorant in that, as you
In so entitling me, and no less honest
Than you are mad: which is enough, I'll warrant,
As this world goes, to pass for honest.
      Leon.   Traitors!
Will you not push her out?   Give her the bastard.—
[*To Antigonus*] Thou, dotard, thou art woman-tired,
          unroosted
By thy dame Partlet here.—Take up the bastard:
Take 't up, I say; give 't to thy crone.
      Paul.   For ever
Unvenerable be thy hands, if thou
Tak'st up the princess by that forcéd baseness
Which he has put upon 't!
      Leon.   He dreads his wife.
      Paul.   So I would you did: then 't were past all doubt
You'd call your children yours.
      Leon.   A nest of traitors!
      Ant.   I am none, by this good light.
      Paul.   Nor I; nor any,
But one that 's here, and that 's himself; for he
The sacred honour of himself, his queen's,
His hopeful son's, his babe's, betrays to slander,
Whose sting is sharper than the sword's, and will not—
For, as the case now stands, it is a curse
He cannot be compelled to 't—once remove
The root of his opinion, which is rotten
As ever oak, or stone, was sound.
      Leon.   A callat
Of boundless tongue, who late hath beat her husband
And now baits me!—This brat is none of mine:
It is the issue of Polixenes.
Hence with it; and, together with the dam,

Commit them to the fire.
    Paul.   It is yours;
And, might we lay the old proverb to your charge,
So like you, 't is the worse.——Behold, my lords,
Although the print be little, the whole matter
And copy of the father: eye, nose, lip,
The trick of 's frown, his forehead; nay, the valley,
The pretty dimples of his chin and cheek; his smiles;
The very mould and frame of hand, nail, finger.——
And thou, good goddess Nature, which hast made it
So like to him that got it, if thou hast
The ordering of the mind too, 'mongst all colours
No yellow in 't; lest she suspect, as he does,
Her children not her husband's.
    Leon.   A gross hag!——
And, lozel, thou art worthy to be hanged,
That wilt not stay her tongue.
    Ant.   Hang all the husbands
That cannot do that feat, you 'll leave yourself
Hardly one subject.
    Leon.   Once more, take her hence.
    Paul.   A most unworthy and unnatural lord
Can do no more.
    Leon.   I 'll have thee burned.
    Paul.   I care not:
It is an heretic that makes the fire,
Not she which burns in 't.　I 'll not call you tyrant;
But this most cruel usage of your queen——
Not able to produce more accusation
Than your own weak-hinged fancy——something savours
Of tyranny, and will ignoble make you,
Yea, scandalous to the world.
    Leon.   On your allegiance,
Out of the chamber with her!　Were I a tyrant,
Where were her life? she durst not call me so,
If she did know me one.　Away with her!
    Paul.   I pray you, do not push me; I 'll be gone.
Look to your babe, my lord; 't is yours; Jove send her
A better guiding spirit!——What needs these hands?——
You that are thus so tender o'er his follies
Will never do him good, not one of you.
So, so:——farewell; we are gone.　　　　　[*Exit*
    Leon.   Thou, traitor, hast set on thy wife to this.——
My child? away with 't——even thou, that hast
A heart so tender o'er it, take it hence,
And see it instantly consumed with fire:
Even thou, and none but thou.　Take it up straight.
Within this hour bring me word 't is done——
And by good testimony——or I 'll seize thy life,

With what thou else call'st thine.   If thou refuse,
And wilt encounter with my wrath, say so;
The bastard brains with these my proper hands
Shall I dash out.   Go, take it to the fire,
For thou sett'st on thy wife.
    Ant.   I did not, sir:
These lords, my noble fellows, if they please,
Can clear me in 't.
    First Lord.   We can: my royal liege,
He is not guilty of her coming hither.
    Leon.   You are liars all.
    First Lord.   'Beseech your highness, give us better credit.
We have always truly served you, and beseech
So to esteem of us; and on our knees we beg,
As recompense of our dear services,
Past, and to come, that you do change this purpose;
Which, being so horrible, so bloody, must
Lead on to some foul issue.   We all kneel.
    Leon.   I am a feather for each wind that blows.
Shall I live on, to see this bastard kneel
And call me father?   Better burn it now,
Than curse it then.   But, be it; let it live:—
It shall not neither.—[*To Antigonus*]   You, sir, come you
        hither;
You that have been so tenderly officious
With Lady Margery, your midwife, there,
To save this bastard's life—for 't is a bastard,
So sure as this beard 's grey—what will you adventure
To save this brat's life?
    Ant.   Anything, my lord,
That my ability may undergo,
And nobleness impose: at least, thus much;
I 'll pawn the little blood which I have left,
To save the innocent; anything possible.
    Leon.   It shall be possible.   Swear by this sword,
Thou wilt perform my bidding.
    Ant.   I will, my lord.
    Leon.   Mark and perform it, seest thou, for the fail
Of any point in 't shall not only be
Death to thyself, but to thy lewd-tongued wife,
Whom for this time we pardon.   We enjoin thee,
As thou art liegeman to us, that thou carry
This female bastard hence; and that thou bear it
To some remote and desert place, quite out
Of our dominions; and that there thou leave it,
Without more mercy, to its own protection,
And favour of the climate.   As by strange fortune
It came to us, I do in justice charge thee,
On thy soul's peril and thy body's torture,

That thou commend it strangely to some place,
Where chance may nurse, or end it.   Take it up.
    Ant.   I swear to do this, though a present death
Had been more merciful.—Come on, poor babe:
Some powerful spirit instruct the kites and ravens
To be thy nurses! Wolves, and bears, they say,
Casting their savageness aside, have done
Like offices of pity.—Sir, be prosperous
In more than this deed doth require!—And blessing
Against this cruelty fight on thy side,
Poor thing, condemned to loss!   [*Exit with the Child*
    Leon.   No, I 'll not rear
Another's issue.
    First Atten.   Please your highness, posts
From those you sent to the oracle are come
An hour since: Cleomenes and Dion,
Being well arrived from Delphos, are both landed,
Hasting to the court.
    First Lord.   So please you, sir, their speed
Hath been beyond account.
    Leon.   Twenty-three days
They have been absent: 't is good speed, foretells,
The great Apollo suddenly will have
The truth of this appear.   Prepare you, lords:
Summon a session, that we may arraign
Our most disloyal lady; for, as she hath
Been publicly accused, so shall she have
A just and open trial.   While she lives
My heart will be a burden to me.   Leave me,
And think upon my bidding.   [*Exeunt*

ACT THREE

SCENE I.—Sicily. A Street in some Town

Enter CLEOMENES *and* DION

    Cleo.   The climate 's delicate, the air most sweet,
Fertile the isle, the temple much surpassing
The common praise it bears.
    Dion.   I shall report,
For most it caught me, the celestial habits—
Methinks, I so should term them—and the reverence
Of the grave wearers.   O, the sacrifice,
How ceremonious, solemn, and unearthly
It was i' the offering!
    Cleo.   But, of all, the burst
And the ear-deafening voice o' the oracle,

Kin to Jove's thunder, so surprised my sense,
That I was nothing.
    Dion.   If the event o' the journey
Prove as successful to the queen—O, be 't so!—
As it hath been to us rare, pleasant, speedy,
The time is worth the use on 't.
    Cleo.   Great Apollo,
Turn all to the best! These proclamations,
So forcing faults upon Hermione,
I little like.
    Dion.   The violent carriage of it
Will clear or end the business, when the oracle—
Thus by Apollo's great divine sealed up—
Shall the contents discover, something rare
Even then will rush to knowledge.—Go, fresh horses;—
And gracious be the issue!   *[Exeunt*

SCENE II.—The Same.   A Court of Justice

Enter LEONTES, *Lords, and Officers*

    Leon.   This sessions—to our great grief we pronounce—
Even pushes 'gainst our heart: the party tried,
The daughter of a king, our wife, and one
Of us too much beloved.—Let us be cleared
Of being tyrannous, since we so openly
Proceed in justice, which shall have due course,
Even to the guilt or the purgation.
Produce the prisoner.
    Off.   It is his highness' pleasure that the queen
Appear in person here in court.—Silence!

Enter HERMIONE, *guarded;* PAULINA *and
Ladies attending*

    Leon.   Read the indictment.
    Off.   "Hermione, queen to the worthy Leontes, King
of Sicilia, thou art here accused and arraigned of high
treason, in committing adultery with Polixenes, King
of Bohemia, and conspiring with Camillo to take away
the life of our sovereign lord the king, thy royal husband:
the pretence whereof being by circumstances partly laid
open, thou, Hermione, contrary to the faith and allegiance
of a true subject, didst counsel and aid them, for their
better safety, to fly away by night."
    Her.   Since what I am to say must be but that
Which contradicts my accusation, and
The testimony on my part no other
But what comes from myself, it shall scarce boot me

To say, "Not guilty;" mine integrity,
Being counted falsehood, shall, as I express it,
Be so received.   But thus:—if powers divine
Behold our human actions—as they do—
I doubt not then but innocence shall make
False accusation blush and tyranny
Tremble at patience.—You, my lord, best know
—Who least will seem to do so—my past life
Hath been as continent, as chaste, as true,
As I am now unhappy; which is more
Than history can pattern, though devised
And played to take spectators; for behold me,
A fellow of the royal bed, which owe
A moiety of the throne, a great king's daughter,
The mother to a hopeful prince, here standing
To prate and talk for life and honour 'fore
Who please to come and hear.   For life, I prize it
As I weigh grief which I would spare: for honour,
'T is a derivative from me to mine;
And only that I stand for.   I appeal
To your own conscience, sir, before Polixenes
Came to your court, how I was in your grace,
How merited to be so; since he came,
With what encounter so uncurrent I
Have strained, to appear thus: if one jot beyond
The bound of honour, or in act or will
That way inclining, hardened be the hearts
Of all that hear me, and my near'st of kin
Cry "Fie!" upon my grave!
    Leon.   I ne'er heard yet
That any of these bolder vices wanted
Less impudence to gainsay what they did
Than to perform it first.
    Her.   That 's true enough;
Though 't is a saying, sir, not due to me.
    Leon.   You will not own it.
    Her.   More than mistress of,
Which comes to me in name of fault, I must not
At all acknowledge.   For Polixenes—
With whom I am accused—I do confess,
I loved him as in honour he required,
With such a kind of love as might become
A lady like me; with a love, even such,
So and no other, as yourself commanded:
Which not to have done, I think, had been in me
Both disobedience and ingratitude
To you, and toward your friend, whose love had spoke
Even since it could speak, from an infant, freely,
That it was yours.   Now, for conspiracy,

I know not how it tastes; though it be dished
For me to try how: all I know of it
Is, that Camillo was an honest man;
And why he left your court the gods themselves,
Wotting no more than I, are ignorant.
    Leon. You knew of his departure, as you know
What you have underta'en to do in 's absence.
    Her. Sir,
You speak a language that I understand not:
My life stands in the level of your dreams,
Which I 'll lay down.
    Leon.   Your actions are my dreams:
You had a bastard by Polixenes,
And I but dreamed it.—As you were past all shame,
—Those of your fact are so,—so past all truth,
Which to deny concerns more than avails; for as
Thy brat hath been cast out, like to itself,
No father owning it—which is, indeed,
More criminal in thee than it,—so thou
Shalt feel our justice, in whose easiest passage
Look for no less than death.
    Her.   Sir, spare your threats:
The bug which you would fright me with I seek.
To me can life be no commodity:
The crown and comfort of my life, your favour,
I do give lost; for I do feel it gone,
But know not how it went. My second joy,
And first-fruits of my body, from his presence
I am barred, like one infectious. My third comfort,
Starred most unluckily, is from my breast,
The innocent milk in its most innocent mouth,
Haled out to murder: myself on every post
Proclaimed a strumpet: with immodest hatred,
The childbed privilege denied, which 'longs
To women of all fashion: lastly, hurried
Here to this place, i' the open air, before
I have got strength of limit. Now, my liege,
Tell me what blessings I have here alive,
That I should fear to die? Therefore, proceed.
But yet hear this; mistake me not;—no life,—
I prize it not a straw; but for mine honour,
Which I would free, if I shall be condemned
Upon surmises, all proofs sleeping else
But what your jealousies awake, I tell you,
'T is rigour and not law.—Your honours all,
I do refer me to the oracle:
Apollo be my judge.
    First Lord.   This your request
Is altogether just. Therefore, bring forth,

And in Apollo's name, his oracle.   [*Exeunt several Officers*
  Her. The Emperor of Russia was my father:
O! that he were alive, and here beholding
His daughter's trial; that he did but see
The flatness of my misery,—yet with eyes
Of pity, not revenge!

Re-enter Officers, with CLEOMENES *and* DION

  Off. You here shall swear upon this sword of justice
That you, Cleomenes and Dion, have
Been both at Delphos; and from thence have brought
This sealed-up oracle, by the hand delivered
Of great Apollo's priest; and that, since then,
You have not dared to break the holy seal,
Nor read the secrets in 't.
  Cleo., Dion.   All this we swear.
  Leon. Break up the seals, and read.
  Off. [*Reads*] 'Hermione is chaste; Polixenes blame-
less; Camillo a true subject; Leontes a jealous tyrant;
his innocent babe truly begotten: and the king shall live
without an heir, if that which is lost be not found!'
  Lords. Now, bléssed be the great Apollo!
  Her.   Praised!
  Leon. Hast thou read truth?
  Off.   Ay, my lord; even so
As it is here set down.
  Leon. There is not truth at all i' the oracle.
The sessions shall proceed: this is mere falsehood.

Enter a Servant, hastily

  Serv. My lord the king, the king!
  Leon.   What is the business?
  Serv. O sir, I shall be hated to report it!
The prince your son, with mere conceit and fear
Of the queen's speed, is gone.
  Leon.   How! gone?
  Serv.   Is dead.
  Leon. Apollo's angry, and the heavens themselves
Do strike at my injustice.   [*Hermione faints*
                How now there!
  Paul. This news is mortal to the queen.—Look down,
And see what death is doing.
  Leon.   Take her hence:
Her heart is but o'ercharged; she will recover,—
I have too much believed mine own suspicion:—
'Beseech you, tenderly apply to her
Some remedies for life.—
          [*Exeunt Paulina and Ladies, with Hermione*
             Apollo, pardon

My great profaneness 'gainst thine oracle!—
I 'll reconcile me to Polixenes,
New woo my queen, recall the good Camillo,
Whom I proclaim a man of truth, of mercy:
For, being transported by my jealousies
To bloody thoughts and to revenge, I chose
Camillo for the minister to poison
My friend Polixenes; which had been done,
But that the good mind of Camillo tardied
My swift command, though I with death and with
Reward did threaten and encourage him,
Not doing it, and being done: he, most humane,
And filled with honour, to my kingly guest
Unclasped my practice, quit his fortunes here,
Which you knew great, and to the certain hazard
Of all incertainties himself commended,
No richer than his honour:—how he glisters
Thorough my rust! and how his piety
Does my deeds make the blacker!

Re-enter PAULINA

    Paul.   Woe the while;
O, cut my lace, lest my heart, cracking it,
Break too!
    First Lord.   What fit is this, good lady?
    Paul.   What studied torments, tyrant, hast for me?
What wheels? racks? fires? what flaying? boiling,
In leads, or oils? what old or newer torture
Must I receive, whose every word deserves
To taste of thy most worst? Thy tyranny,
Together working with thy jealousies—
Fancies too weak for boys, too green and idle
For girls of nine—O! think, what they have done,
And then run mad, indeed,—stark mad! for all
Thy bygone fooleries were but spices of it.
That thou betray'dst Polixenes, 't was nothing;
That did but show thee, of a fool, inconstant,
And damnable ingrateful; nor was 't much,
Thou wouldst have poisoned good Camillo's honour,
To have him kill a king; poor trespasses,
More monstrous standing by: whereof I reckon
The casting forth to crows thy baby daughter,
To be or none, or little,—though a devil
Would have shed water out of fire, ere done 't:
Nor is 't directly laid to thee, the death
Of the young prince, whose honourable thoughts—
Thoughts high for one so tender—cleft the heart
That could conceive a gross and foolish sire
Blemished his gracious dam: this is not, no,

Laid to thy answer: but the last,—O lords!
When I have said, cry 'Woe!'—the queen, the queen,
The sweet'st, dear'st creature's dead; and vengeance for 't
Not dropped down yet.
  First Lord.   The higher powers forbid!
  Paul. I say, she 's dead; I 'll swear 't: if word nor
    oath
Prevail not, go and see. If you can bring
Tincture or lustre in her lip, her eye,
Heat outwardly or breath within, I 'll serve you
As I would do the gods.—But, O thou tyrant!
Do not repent these things, for they are heavier
Than all thy woes can stir; therefore, betake thee
To nothing but despair. A thousand knees
Ten thousand years together, naked, fasting,
Upon a barren mountain, and still winter,
In storm perpetual, could not move the gods
To look that way thou wert.
  Leon.   Go on, go on;
Thou canst not speak too much: I have deserved
All tongues to talk their bitterest.
  First Lord.   Say no more:
Howe'er the business goes, you have made fault
I' the boldness of your speech.
  Paul.   I am sorry for 't:
All faults I make, when I shall come to know them,
I do repent. Alas, I have showed too much
The rashness of a woman. He is touched
To the noble heart.—What 's gone, and what 's past help,
Should be past grief: do not receive affliction
At my petition; I beseech you rather,
Let me be punished, that have minded you
Of what you should forget. Now, good my liege,
Sir, royal sir, forgive a foolish woman:
The love I bore your queen,—lo, fool again!—
I 'll speak of her no more, nor of your children;
I 'll not remember you of my own lord,
Who is lost too. Take your patience to you,
And I 'll say nothing.
  Leon.   Thou didst speak but well,
When most the truth, which I receive much better
Than to be pitied of thee. Pr'ythee, bring me
To the dead bodies of my queen and son.
One grave shall be for both: upon them shall
The causes of their death appear, unto
Our shame perpetual. Once a day I 'll visit
The chapel where they lie; and tears shed there
Shall be my recreation: so long as nature
Will bear up with this exercise, so long

I daily vow to use it. Come, and lead me
To these sorrows.   [*Exeunt*

SCENE III.—Bohemia. A Desert Country near the Sea

Enter ANTIGONUS, *with the Babe; and a Mariner*

Ant. Thou art perfect, then, our ship hath touched upon
The deserts of Bohemia?
  Mar.   Ay, my lord; and fear
We have landed in ill time: the skies look grimly,
And threaten present blusters. In my conscience,
The heavens with that we have in hand are angry,
And frown upon 's.
  Ant. Their sacred wills be done!—Go, get aboard;
Look to thy bark: I 'll not be long before
I call upon thee.
  Mar. Make your best haste, and go not
Too far i' the land: 't is like to be loud weather;
Besides, this place is famous for the creatures
Of prey that keep upon 't.
  Ant.   Go thou away:
I 'll follow instantly.
  Mar.   I am glad at heart
To be so rid o' the business.   [*Exit*
  Ant.   Come, poor babe:—
I have heard—but not believed—the spirits o' the dead
May walk again: if such thing be, thy mother
Appeared to me last night, for ne'er was dream
So like a waking. To me comes a creature,
Sometimes her head on one side, some another;
I never saw a vessel of like sorrow,
So filled, and so becoming: in pure white robes,
Like very sanctity, she did approach
My cabin where I lay, thrice bowed before me,
And, gasping to begin some speech, her eyes
Became two spouts: the fury spent, anon
Did this break from her: "Good Antigonus,
Since fate, against thy better disposition,
Hath made thy person for the thrower-out
Of my poor babe, according to thine oath,—
Places remote enough are in Bohemia,
There weep, and leave it crying; and, for the babe
Is counted lost for ever, Perdita,
I pr'ythee, call 't: for this ungentle business,
Put on thee by my lord, thou ne'er shalt see
Thy wife Paulina more:"—and so, with shrieks,
She melted into air. Affrighted much,
I did in time collect myself, and thought

This was so, and no slumber. Dreams are toys;
Yet for this once, yea, superstitiously,
I will be squared by this. I do believe,
Hermione hath suffered death; and that
Apollo would, this being indeed the issue
Of King Polixenes, it should here be laid,
Either for life or death, upon the earth
Of its right father.—Blossom, speed thee well!
                              [*Laying down the Babe*
There lie; and there thy character: there these,
                              [*Laying down a bundle*
Which may, if fortune please, both breed thee, pretty,
And still rest thine.—The storm begins.—Poor wretch,
That for thy mother's fault art thus exposed
To loss, and what may follow!—Weep I cannot,
But my heart bleeds, and most accursed am I,
To be by oath enjoined to this.—Farewell!—
The day frowns more and more:—thou art like to have
A lullaby too rough:—I never saw
The heavens so dim by day. A savage clamour,—
Well may I get aboard!—this is the chase:—
I am gone for ever.   [*Exit, pursued by a bear*

Enter an Old Shepherd

Shep. I would there were no age between ten and
three-and-twenty, or that youth would sleep out the
rest; for there is nothing in the between but getting
wenches with child, wronging the anciently, stealing,
fighting.—Hark you now!—Would any but these boiled-
brains of nineteen and two-and-twenty hunt this weather?
They have scared away two of my best sheep; which, I
fear, the wolf will sooner find than the master: if any-
where I have them, 't is by the seaside, browsing of ivy.
Good luck, an 't be thy will!—What have we here?
[*Taking up the Babe*] Mercy on 's, a barn; a very pretty
barn! A boy, or a child, I wonder? A pretty one; a
very pretty one. Sure, some scape: though I am not
bookish, yet I can read waiting-gentlewoman in the scape.
This has some stair-work, some trunk-work, some behind-
door-work: they were warmer that got this, than the poor
thing is here. I 'll take it up for pity; yet I 'll tarry till
my son come: he hollaed but even now.—Whoa, ho hoa!
  Clo. [*Without*] Hilloa, loa!
  Shep. What! art so near? If thou 'lt see a thing to
talk on when thou art dead and rotten, come hither.

Enter Clown

What ail'st thou, man?
  Clo. I have seen two such sights, by sea and by land

—but I am not to say it is a sea, for it is now the sky: betwixt the firmament and it you cannot thrust a bodkin's point.

Shep. Why, boy, how is it?

Clo. I would you did but see how it chafes, how it rages, how it takes up the shore! but that 's not to the point. O, the most piteous cry of the poor souls! sometimes to see 'em, and not to see 'em; now the ship boring the moon with her mainmast, and anon swallowed with yest and froth, as you 'd thrust a cork into a hogshead. And then for the land-service:—to see how the bear tore out his shoulder-bone; how he cried to me for help, and said his name was Antigonus, a nobleman.—But to make an end of the ship:—to see how the sea flap-dragoned it;—but, first, how the poor souls roared, and the sea mocked them;—and how the poor gentleman roared, and the bear mocked him, both roaring louder than the sea or weather.

Shep. Name of mercy! when was this, boy?

Clo. Now, now; I have not winked since I saw these sights: the men are not yet cold under water, nor the bear half-dined on the gentleman: he 's at it now.

Shep. Would I had been by, to have helped the old man!

Clo. I would you had been by the ship's side, to have helped her: there your charity would have lacked footing.

Shep. Heavy matters! heavy matters! but look thee here, boy. Now bless thyself. Thou mettest with things dying, I with things new-born. Here 's a sight for thee! Look thee, a bearing-cloth for a squire's child! Look thee here:—take up, take up, boy; open 't. So, let 's see. It was told me, I should be rich by the fairies: this is some changeling.—Open 't:—what 's within, boy?

Clo. You're a made old man: if the sins of your youth are forgiven you, you 're well to live. Gold! all gold!

Shep. This is fairy gold, boy, and 't will prove so: up with 't, keep it close; home, home, the next way. We are lucky, boy; and to be so still, requires nothing but secrecy.—Let my sheep go.—Come, good boy, the next way home.

Clo. Go you the next way with your findings: I 'll go see if the bear be gone from the gentleman, and how much he hath eaten. They are never curst, but when they are hungry. If there be any of him left, I 'll bury it.

Shep. That 's a good deed. If thou may'st discern by that which is left of him what he is, fetch me to the sight of him.

Clo. Marry, will I; and you shall help to put him i' the ground.

Shep. 'Tis a lucky day, boy, and we 'll do good deeds
on 't.
                                                        [Exeunt

ACT FOUR

Enter TIME, *as Chorus*

  Time. I,—that please some, try all; both joy and
      terror
Of good and bad; that make, and unfold error,—
Now take upon me, in the name of Time,
To use my wings. Impute it not a crime
To me or my swift passage, that I slide
O'er sixteen years, and leave the growth untried
Of that wide gap; since it is in my power
To o'erthrow law, and in one self-born hour
To plant and o'erwhelm custom. Let me pass,
The same I am, ere ancient'st order was,
Or what is now received: I witness to
The times that brought them in; so shall I do
To the freshest things now reigning, and make stale
The glistering of this present, as my tale
Now seems to it. Your patience this allowing,
I turn my glass, and give my scene such growing
As you had slept between. Leontes leaving,—
The effects of his fond jealousies so grieving
That he shuts up himself,—imagine me,
Gentle spectators, that I now may be
In fair Bohemia; and remember well,
I mentioned a son o' the king's, which Florizel
I now name to you, and with speed so pace
To speak of Perdita, now grown in grace
Equal with wondering;—what of her ensues,
I list not prophecy, but let Time's news
Be known when 't is brought forth;—a shepherd's
      daughter,
And what to her adheres which follows after,
Is the argument of Time. Of this allow,
If ever you have spent time worse ere now:
If never, yet that Time himself doth say,
He wishes earnestly you never may.
                                            [Exit

SCENE I.—Bohemia. A Room in the Palace of POLIXENES

Enter POLIXENES *and* CAMILLO

  Pol. I pray thee, good Camillo, be no more impor-
tunate; 't is a sickness denying thee anything, a death
to grant this.

Cam. It is fifteen years since I saw my country:
though I have, for the most part, been aired abroad, I
desire to lay my bones there. Besides, the penitent king,
my master, hath sent for me; to whose feeling sorrows
I might be some allay, or I o'erween to think so,—which
is another spur to my departure.

Pol. As thou lovest me, Camillo, wipe not out the
rest of thy services by leaving me now. The need I have
of thee, thine own goodness hath made: better not to
have had thee than thus to want thee. Thou, having
made me businesses which none without thee can
sufficiently manage, must either stay to execute them thyself, or take away with thee the very services thou hast
done; which if I have not enough considered,—as too
much I cannot,—to be more thankful to thee shall be
my study; and my profit therein, the heaping friendships.
Of that fatal country, Sicilia, pr'ythee speak no more,
whose very naming punishes me with the remembrance
of that penitent, as thou call'st him, and reconciled king,
my brother, whose loss of his most precious queen and
children are even now to be afresh lamented. Say to
me, when saw'st thou the Prince Florizel, my son? Kings
are no less unhappy, their issue not being gracious, than they
are in losing them when they have approved their virtues.

Cam. Sir, it is three days since I saw the prince. What
his happier affairs may be, are to me unknown; but I
have missingly noted he is of late much retired from court,
and is less frequent to his princely exercises than formerly
he hath appeared.

Pol. I have considered so much, Camillo, and with
some care; so far, that I have eyes under my service
which look upon his removedness: from whom I have
this intelligence, that he is seldom from the house of a
most homely shepherd; a man, they say, that from very
nothing, and beyond the imagination of his neighbours,
is grown into an unspeakable estate.

Cam. I have heard, sir, of such a man, who hath a
daughter of most rare note: the report of her is extended
more than can be thought to begin from such a cottage.

Pol. That 's likewise part of my intelligence, but I
fear the angle that plucks our son thither. Thou shalt
accompany us to the place, where we will, not appearing
what we are, have some question with the shepherd; from
whose simplicity I think it not uneasy to get the cause of
my son's resort thither. Pr'ythee, be my present partner
in this business, and lay aside the thoughts of Sicilia.

Cam. I willingly obey your command.

Pol. My best Camillo!—We must disguise ourselves.
                                                    [*Exeunt*

SCENE II.—The Same.   A Road near the Shepherd's
Cottage

Enter AUTOLYCUS, *singing*

When daffodils begin to peer,—
  With, heigh! the doxy over the dale,—
Why, then comes in the sweet o' the year;
  For the red blood reigns in the winter's pale.

The white sheet bleaching on the hedge,—
  With heigh! the sweet birds, O, how they sing!—
Doth set my pugging tooth on edge;
  For a quart of ale is a dish·for a king.

The lark, that tirra-lirra chants,—
  With heigh! with heigh! the thrush and the jay,
Are summer songs for me and my aunts,
  While we lie tumbling in the hay.

I have served Prince Florizel, and, in my time, wore three
pile; but now I am out of service:

But shall I go mourn for that, my dear?
  The pale moon shines by night;
And when I wander here and there,
  I then do most go right.

If tinkers may have leave to live,
  And bear the sow-skin budget,
Then my account I well may give,
  And in the stocks avouch it.

My traffic is sheets; when the kite builds, look to lesser
linen.   My father named me Autolycus; who being, as
I am, littered under Mercury, was likewise a snapper-up
of unconsidered trifles.   With die and drab I purchased
this caparison, and my revenue is the silly cheat.   Gallows
and knock are too powerful on the highway; beating and
hanging are terrors to me: for the life to come, I sleep out
the thought of it.—A prize! a prize!

Enter Clown

Clo.   Let me see:—every 'leven wether tods; every
tod yields pound and odd shilling: fifteen hundred shorn,
what comes the wool to?
Aut.   [*Aside*] If the springe hold, the cock 's mine.
Clo.   I cannot do 't without counters.—Let me see;

what am I to buy for our sheep-shearing feast? "Three pound of sugar; five pound of currants; rice,"—what will this sister of mine do with rice? But my father hath made her mistress of the feast, and she lays it on. She hath made me four-and-twenty nosegays for the shearers; threeman songmen all, and very good ones, but they are most of them means and bases: but one Puritan amongst them, and he sings psalms to hornpipes. I must have saffron, to colour the warden pies; mace; dates,—none: that 's out of my note: "nutmegs, seven: a race or two of ginger;" but that I may beg:—"four pound of prunes, and as many of raisins o' the sun."

Aut. O, that ever I was born! [*Grovelling on the ground*

Clo. I' the name of me,—

Aut. O, help me, help me! pluck but off these rags, and then, death, death!

Clo. Alack, poor soul! thou hast need of more rags to lay on thee, rather than have these off.

Aut. O, sir, the loathsomeness of them offends me more than the stripes I have received, which are mighty ones, and millions.

Clo. Alas, poor man! a million of beating may come to a great matter.

Aut. I am robbed, sir, and beaten; my money and apparel ta'en from me, and these detestable things put upon me.

Clo. What, by a horseman, or a footman?

Aut. A footman, sweet sir, a footman.

Clo. Indeed, he should be a footman, by the garments he hath left with thee: if this be a horseman's coat, it hath seen very hot service. Lend me thy hand, I 'll help thee: come, lend me thy hand.   [*Helping him up*

Aut. O, good sir, tenderly, O!

Clo. Alas, poor soul!

Aut. O, good sir; softly, good sir. I fear, sir, my shoulder-blade is out.

Clo. How now? canst stand?

Aut. Softly, dear sir [*picks his pocket*], good sir, softly. You ha' done me a charitable office.

Clo. Dost lack any money? I have a little money for thee.

Aut. No, good, sweet sir: no, I beseech you, sir. I have a kinsman not past three-quarters of a mile hence, unto whom I was going: I shall there have money, or anything I want. Offer me no money, I pray you! that kills my heart.

Clo. What manner of fellow was he that robbed you?

Aut. A fellow, sir, that I have known to go about with trol-my-dames: I knew him once a servant of the prince.

I cannot tell, good sir, for which of his virtues it was, but he was certainly whipped out of the court.

Clo. His vices, you would say; there 's no virtue whipped out of the court: they cherish it, to make it stay there; and yet it will no more but abide.

Aut. Vices, I would say, sir. I know this man well: he hath been since an ape-bearer; then a process-server, a bailiff; then he compassed a motion of the Prodigal Son, and married a tinker's wife within a mile where my land and living lies; and, having flown over many knavish professions, he settled only in rogue: some call him Autolycus.

Clo. Out upon him! Prig, for my life; prig: he haunts wakes, fairs, and bear-baitings.

Aut. Very true, sir; he, sir, he: that 's the rogue that put me into this apparel.

Clo. Not a more cowardly rogue in all Bohemia: if you had but looked big and spit at him he 'd have run.

Aut. I must confess to you, sir, I am no fighter: I am false of heart that way, and that he knew, I warrant him.

Clo. How do you now?

Aut. Sweet sir, much better than I was: I can stand, and walk. I will even take my leave of you, and pace softly towards my kinsman's.

Clo. Shall I bring thee on the way?

Aut. No, good-faced sir; no, sweet sir.

Clo. Then fare thee well. I must go buy spices for our sheep-shearing.

Aut. Prosper you, sweet sir: [*Exit Clown*]—Your purse is not hot enough to purchase your spice. I 'll be with you at your sheep-shearing too. If I make not this cheat bring out another, and the shearers prove sheep, let me be enrolled and my name put in the book of virtue!

> *Jog on, jog on, the foot-path way,*
> *And merrily hent the stile-a;*
> *A merry heart goes all the day,*
> *Your sad tires in a mile-a.*

[*Exit*

SCENE III—The Same. A Lawn before a Shepherd's Cottage

Enter FLORIZEL *and* PERDITA

Flo. These your unusual weeds to each part of you
Do give a life; no shepherdess, but Flora
Peering in April's front. This your sheep-shearing
Is as a meeting of the petty gods,

And you the queen on 't.
    Per.   Sir, my gracious lord,
To chide at your extremes it not becomes me:
O, pardon, that I name them.—Your high self,
The gracious mark o' the land, you have obscured
With a swain's wearing, and me, poor lowly maid,
Most goddess-like pranked up. But that our feasts
In every mess have folly, and the feeders
Digest it with a custom, I should blush
To see you so attiréd; swoon, I think,
To show myself a glass.
    Flo.   I bless the time
When my good falcon made her flight across
Thy father's ground.
    Per.   Now, Jove afford you cause!
To me the difference forges dread; your greatness
Hath not been used to fear. Even now I tremble
To think, your father, by some accident,
Should pass this way, as you did. O, the Fates!
How would he look, to see his work, so noble,
Vilely bound up? What would he say? Or how
Should I, in these my borrowed flaunts, behold
The sternness of his presence?
    Flo.   Apprehend
Nothing but jollity. The gods themselves,
Humbling their deities to love, have taken
The shapes of beasts upon them: Jupiter
Became a bull, and bellowed; the green Neptune
A ram, and bleated; and the fire-robed god,
Golden Apollo, a poor humble swain,
As I seem now. Their transformations
Were never for a piece of beauty rarer,
Nor in a way so chaste, since my desires
Run not before mine honour nor my lusts
Burn hotter than my faith.
    Per.   O, but, sir,
Your resolution cannot hold, when 't is
Opposed, as it must be, by the power of the king.
One of these two must be necessities,
Which then will speak,—that you must change this purpose,
Or I my life.
    Flo.   Thou dearest Perdita,
With these forced thoughts, I pr'ythee, darken not
The mirth o' the feast: or I 'll be thine, my fair,
Or not my father's; for I cannot be
Mine own, nor anything to any, if
I be not thine: to this I am most constant,
Though destiny say no. Be merry, gentle;
Strangle such thoughts as these with anything

That you behold the while. Your guests are coming:
Lift up your countenance, as it were the day
Of celebration of that nuptial which
We two have sworn shall come.
   Per.   O Lady Fortune,
Stand you auspicious!
   Flo.   See, your guests approach;
Address yourself to entertain them sprightly,
And let 's be red with mirth.

Enter Shepherd, *with* POLIXENES *and* CAMILLO, *disguised;*
    Clown, MOPSA, DORCAS, *and others*

   Shep. Fie, daughter! when my old wife lived, upon
This day she was both pantler, butler, cook;
Both dame and servant; welcomed all, served all;
Would sing her song, and dance her turn; now here,
At upper end o' the table, now i' the middle;
On his shoulder, and his; her face o' fire
With labour, and the thing she took to quench it,
She would to each one sip. You are retired,
As if you were a feasted one, and not
The hostess of the meeting: pray you, bid
These unknown friends to us welcome; for it is
A way to make us better friends, more known.
Come, quench your blushes, and present yourself
That which you are, mistress o' the feast: come on,
And bid us welcome to your sheep-shearing,
As your good flock shall prosper.
   Per. [*To Polixenes*]   Sir, welcome.
It is my father's will, I should take on me
The hostess-ship o' the day. [*To Camillo*] You 're wel-
          come, sir.—
Give me those flowers there, Dorcas.—Reverend sirs,
For you there 's rosemary and rue; these keep
Seeming and savour all the winter long:
Grace and remembrance be to you both,
And welcome to our shearing!
   Pol.   Shepherdess—
A fair one are you,—well you fit our ages
With flowers of winter.
   Per.   Sir, the year growing ancient,
Not yet on summer's death, nor on the birth
Of trembling winter,—the fairest flowers o' the season
Are our carnations, and streaked gillyvors,
Which some call nature's bastards: of that kind
Our rustic garden 's barren, and I care not
To get slips of them.
   Pol.   Wherefore, gentle maiden,

Do you neglect them?
    Per.   For I have heard it said,
There is an art which in their piedness shares
With great creating nature.
    Pol.   Say, there be;
Yet nature is made better by no mean,
But nature makes that mean: so o'er that art
Which, you say, adds to nature, is an art
That nature makes.   You see, sweet maid, we marry
A gentler scion to the wildest stock,
And make conceive a bark of baser kind
By bud of noble race: this is an art
Which does mend nature,—change it rather; but
The art itself is nature.
    Per.   So it is.
    Pol. Then make your garden rich in gillyvors,
And do not call them bastards.
    Per.   I 'll not put
The dibble in earth to set one slip of them:
No more than were I painted, I would wish
This youth should say 't were well, and only therefore
Desire to breed by me.—Here 's flowers for you;
Hot lavender, mints, savoury, marjoram;
The marigold, that goes to bed wi' the sun,
And with him rises weeping: these are flowers
Of middle summer, and, I think, they are given
To men of middle age.   You are very welcome.
    Cam. I should leave grazing, were I of your flock,
And only live by gazing.
    Per.   Out, alas!
You 'd be so lean, that blasts of January
Would blow you through and through.—Now, my fair'st
      friend,
I would I had some flowers o' the spring, that might
Become your time of day; and yours, and yours,
That wear upon your virgin branches yet
Your maidenheads growing:—O Proserpina,
For the flowers now that, frighted, thou lett'st fall
From Dis's waggon!—daffodils,
That come before the swallow dares, and take
The winds of March with beauty; violets dim,
But sweeter than the lids of Juno's eyes,
Or Cytherea's breath; pale primroses,
That die unmarried ere they can behold
Bright Phœbus in his strength, a malady
Most incident to maids; bold oxlips, and
The crown-imperial; lilies of all kinds,
The flower-de-luce being one.   O, these I lack,
To make you garlands of, and my sweet friend,

To strew him o'er and o'er.
Flo.   What, like a corse?
Per.   No, like a bank, for love to lie and play on,
Not like a corse; or if,—not to be buried
But quick, and in mine arms.   Come, take your flowers.
Methinks, I play as I have seen them do
In Whitsun-pastorals: sure, this robe of mine
Does change my disposition.
Flo.   What you do
Still betters what is done.   When you speak, sweet,
I 'd have you do it ever: when you sing,
I 'd have you buy and sell so; so give alms;
Pray so; and, for the ordering your affairs,
To sing them too: when you do dance, I wish you
A wave o' the sea, that you might ever do
Nothing but that; move still, still so,
And own no other function: each your doing,
So singular in each particular,
Crowns what you are doing in the present deeds,
That all your acts are queens.
Per.   O Doricles,
Your praises are too large: but that your youth,
And the true blood which peeps so fairly through it,
Do plainly give you out an unstained shepherd,
With wisdom I might fear, my Doricles,
You wooed me the false way.
Flo.   I think, you have
As little skill to fear, as I have purpose
To put you to 't.—But, come; our dance, I pray.
Your hand, my Perdita: so turtles pair,
That never mean to part.
Per.   I 'll swear for 'em.
Pol.   This is the prettiest low-born lass that ever
Ran on the green-sward: nothing she does or seems,
But smacks of something greater than herself,
Too noble for this place.
Cam.   He tells her something,
That makes her blood look out.   Good sooth, she is
The queen of curds and cream.—
Clo.   Come on, strike up
Dor.   Mopsa must be your mistress: marry, garlic,
To mend her kissing with!
Mop.   Now, in good time!
Clo.   Not a word, a word: we stand upon our manners.—
Come, strike up.   [*Music*
          [*Here a dance of Shepherds and Shepherdesses*
Pol.   Pray you, good shepherd, what fair swain is this,
Which dances with your daughter?
Shep.   They call him Doricles, and boasts himself

To have a worthy feeding; but I have it
Upon his own report, and I believe it:
He looks like sooth.   He says, he loves my daughter:
I think so too; for never gazed the moon
Upon the water, as he 'll stand, and read,
As 't were, my daughter's eyes; and, to be plain,
I think, there is not half a kiss to choose
Who loves another best.
    Pol.   She dances featly.
    Shep.   So she does anything, though I report it
That should be silent.   If young Doricles
Do light upon her, she shall bring him that
Which he not dreams of.

Enter a Servant

    Serv.   O master! if you did but hear the pedlar at the
door, you would never dance again after a tabor and pipe;
no, the bagpipe could not move you.   He sings several
tunes faster than you 'll tell money; he utters them as he
had eaten ballads, and all men's ears grew to his tunes.
    Clo.   He could never come better; he shall come in.
I love a ballad but even too well; if it be doleful matter
merrily set down, or a very pleasant thing indeed and
sung lamentably.
    Serv.   He hath songs, for man or woman, of all sizes;
no milliner can so fit his customers with gloves.   He has
the prettiest love-songs for maids; so without bawdry,
which is strange; with such delicate burdens of "dildos"
and "fadings," "jump her and thump her;" and where
some stretch-mouthed rascal would, as it were, mean
mischief, and break a foul gap into the matter, he makes the
maid to answer, "Whoop, do me no harm, good man;"
puts him off, slights him with "Whoop, do me no harm,
good man."
    Pol.   This is a brave fellow.
    Clo.   Believe me, thou talkest of an admirable conceited
fellow.   Has he any unbraided wares?
    Serv.   He hath ribands of all the colours i' the rainbow;
points, more than all the lawyers in Bohemia can learnedly
handle, though they come to him by the gross; inkles,
caddisses, cambrics, lawns: why, he sings them over, as
they were gods or goddesses.   You would think a smock
were a she-angel, he so chants to the sleeve-hand, and
the work about the square on 't.
    Clo.   Pr'ythee, bring him in, and let him approach
singing.
    Per.   Forewarn him, that he use no scurrilous words
in 's tunes.   [*Exit Servant*

Clo. You have of these pedlars, that have more in them than you 'd think, sister.

Per. Ay, good brother, or go about to think.

Enter AUTOLYCUS, *singing*

> Lawn, as white as driven snow;
> Cyprus, black as e'er was crow;
> Gloves, as sweet as damask roses;
> Masks for faces, and for noses;
> Bugle-bracelet, necklace-amber,
> Perfume for a lady's chamber;
> Golden quoifs, and stomachers,
> For my lads to give their dears;
> Pins and poking-sticks of steel;
> What maids lack, from head to heel;
> Come, buy of me, come; come buy, come buy;
> Buy, lads, or else your lasses cry:
> Come, buy.

Clo. If I were not in love with Mopsa, thou shouldst take no money of me; but being enthralled as I am, it will also be the bondage of certain ribands and gloves.

Mop. I was promised them against the feast, but they come not too late now.

Dor. He hath promised you more than that, or there be liars.

Mop. He hath paid you all he promised you: may be, he has paid you more, which will shame you to give him again.

Clo. Is there no manners left among maids? will they wear their plackets where they should bear their faces? Is there not milking-time, when you are going to bed, or kiln-hole, to whistle off these secrets, but you must be tittle-tattling before all our guests? 'T is well they are whispering. Clamour your tongues, and not a word more.

Mop. I have done. Come, you promised me a tawdry lace, and a pair of sweet gloves.

Clo. Have I not told thee, how I was cozened by the way, and lost all my money?

Aut. And indeed, sir, there are cozeners abroad; therefore it behoves men to be wary.

Clo. Fear not thou, man, thou shalt lose nothing here.

Aut. I hope so, sir; for I have about me many parcels of charge.

Clo. What hast here? ballads?

Mop. 'Pray now, buy some: I love a ballad in print o' life, for then we are sure they are true.

Aut. Here 's one to a very doleful tune, how a usurer's wife was brought to bed of twenty moneybags at a burden;

and how she longed to eat adders' heads, and toads carbonadoed.

Mop. Is it true, think you?

Aut. Very true; and but a month old.

Dor. Bless me from marrying a usurer!

Aut. Here 's the midwife's name to 't, one Mistress Taleporter, and five or six honest wives that were present. Why should I carry lies abroad?

Mop. 'Pray you now, buy it.

Clo. Come on, lay it by: and let 's first see more ballads; we 'll buy the other things anon.

Aut. Here 's another ballad, of a fish, that appeared upon the coast, on Wednesday the fourscore of April, forty thousand fathom above water, and sung this ballad against the hard hearts of maids: it was thought she was a woman, and was turned into a cold fish, for she would not exchange flesh with one that loved her. The ballad is very pitiful, and as true.

Dor. Is it true too, think you?

Aut. Five justices' hands at it, and witnesses more than my pack will hold.

Clo. Lay it by too: another.

Aut. This is a merry ballad, but a very pretty one.

Mop. Let 's have some merry ones.

Aut. Why, this is a passing merry one, and goes to the tune of 'Two maids wooing a man.' There 's scarce a maid westward but she sings it; 't is in request, I can tell you.

Mop. We can both sing it: If thou 'lt bear a part, thou shalt hear; 't is in three parts.

Dor. We had the tune on 't a month ago.

Aut. I can bear my part; you must know, 't is my occupation: have at it with you.

SONG

Aut. *Get you hence, for I must go,*
        Where it fits not you to know.

Dor. *Whither?*

Mop. *O! whither?*

Dor. *Whither?*

Mop. *It becomes thy oath full well,*
        Thou to me thy secrets tell.

Dor. *Me too: let me go thither.*

Mop. *Or thou go'st to the grange, or mill.*

Dor. *If to either, thou dost ill.*

Aut. *Neither.*

Dor. *What, neither?*

Aut. *Neither.*

Dor.   *Thou hast sworn my love to be.*
Mop.   *Thou hast sworn it more to me:*
          Then, whither go'st? say, whither?

Clo. We 'll have this song out anon by ourselves.
My father and the gentlemen are in sad talk, and we 'll not
trouble them: come, bring away thy pack after me.
Wenches, I 'll buy for you both. Pedlar, let 's have the
first choice.—Follow me, girls.
Aut. [*Aside*] And you shall pay well for 'em.

> *Will you buy any tape,*
> *Or lace for your cape,*
> *My dainty duck, my dear-a?*
> *Any silk, any thread,*
> *Any toys for your head,*
> *Of the new'st and fin'st, fin'st wear-a?*
> *Come to the pedlar;*
> *Money's a meddler,*
> *That doth utter all men's ware-a.*

[*Exeunt Clown, Autolycus, Dorcas, and Mopsa*

Re-enter Servant

Serv. Master, there is three carters, three shepherds,
three neat-herds, three swine-herds, that have made
themselves all men of hair: they call themselves Saltiers;
and they have a dance, which the wenches say is a galli-
maufry of gambols, because they are not in 't; but they
themselves are o' the mind,—if it be not too rough for
some that know little but bowling—it will please plentifully.
Shep. Away! we 'll none on 't: here has been too
much homely foolery already.—I know, sir, we weary you.
Pol. You weary those that refresh us. Pray, let 's
see these four threes of herdsmen.
Serv. One three of them, by their own report, sir,
hath danced before the king; and not the worst of the
three but jumps twelve foot and a half by the squire.
Shep. Leave your prating. Since these good men
are pleased, let them come in: but quickly now.
Serv. Why, they stay at door, sir.   [*Exit*

Re-enter Servant, with twelve Rustics habited like Satyrs.
They dance, and then exeunt

Pol. O father, you 'll know more of that hereafter.—
[*To Camillo*] Is it not too far gone?—'T is time to
          part them.—
He 's simple, and tells much. How now, fair shepherd?
Your heart is full of something, that does take

Your mind from feasting.   Sooth, when I was young,
And handed love as you do, I was wont
To load my she with knacks: I would have ransacked
The pedlar's silken treasury, and have poured it
To her acceptance; you have let him go,
And nothing marted with him.   If your lass
Interpretation should abuse, and call this
Your lack of love or bounty, you were straited
For a reply, at least if you make a care
Of happy holding her.
  Flo.   Old sir, I know
She prizes not such trifles as these are.
The gifts she looks from me are packed and locked
Up in my heart, which I have given already,
But not delivered—O, hear me breathe my life
Before this ancient sir, who, it should seem
Hath sometime loved: I take thy hand; this hand,
As soft as dove's down, and as white as it
Or Ethiopian's tooth, or the fanned snow
That 's bolted by the northern blasts twice o'er.
  Pol. What follows this?
How prettily the young swain seems to wash
The hand, was fair before!—I have put you out.—
But, to your protestation: let me hear
What you profess.
  Flo.   Do, and be witness to 't.
  Pol. And this my neighbour too?
  Flo.   And he, and more
Than he, and men; the earth, the heavens, and all;
That, were I crowned the most imperial monarch,
Thereof most worthy, were I the fairest youth
That ever made eye swerve, had force and knowledge
More than was ever man's, I would not prize them,
Without her love: for her employ them all,
Commend them and condemn them to her service
Or to their own perdition.
  Pol.   Fairly offered.
  Cam. This shows a sound affection.
  Shep.   But, my daughter,
Say you the like to him?
  Per.   I cannot speak
So well, nothing so well; no, nor mean better:
By the pattern of mine own thoughts I cut out
The purity of his.
  Shep.   Take hands; a bargain:—
And, friends unknown, you shall bear witness to 't
I give my daughter to him, and will make
Her portion equal his.
  Flo.   O, that must be

I' the virtue of your daughter: one being dead,
I shall have more than you can dream of yet;
Enough then for your wonder. But, come on;
Contract us 'fore these witnesses.
 Shep.   Come, your hand;
And, daughter, yours.
 Pol.   Soft, swain, a while, 'beseech you;
Have you a father?
 Flo.   I have; but what of him?
 Pol.   Knows he of this?
 Flo.   He neither does nor shall.
 Pol.   Methinks, a father
Is at the nuptial of his son a guest
That best becomes the table. Pray you, once more,
Is not your father grown incapable
Of reasonable affairs? is he not stupid
With age, and altering rheums? can he speak? hear?
Know man from man? dispute his own estate?
Lies he not bed-rid? and again does nothing
But what he did being childish?
 Flo.   No, good sir:
He has his health, and ampler strength, indeed,
Than most have of his age.
 Pol.   By my white beard,
You offer him, if this be so, a wrong
Something unfilial. Reason, my son
Should choose himself a wife; but as good reason,
The father—all whose joy is nothing else
But fair posterity—should hold some counsel
In such a business.
 Flo.   I yield all this;
But for some other reasons, my grave sir,
Which 't is not fit you know, I not acquaint
My father of this business.
 Pol.   Let him know 't.
 Flo.   He shall not.
 Pol.   Pr'ythee, let him.
 Flo.   No, he must not.
 Shep.   Let him, my son: he shall not need to grieve
At knowing of thy choice.
 Flo.   Come, come, he must not.—
Mark our contract.
 Pol.   Mark your divorce, young sir,
         [*Discovering himself*
Whom son I dare not call: thou art too base
To be acknowledged. Thou a sceptre's heir,
That thus affects a sheep-hook!—Thou old traitor,
I am sorry, that by hanging thee I can but
Shorten thy life one week.—And thou, fresh piece

Of excellent witchcraft, who, of force, must know
The royal fool thou cop'st with,—
   Shep.   O, my heart!
   Pol. I 'll have thy beauty scratched with briers, and made
More homely than thy state.—For thee, fond boy,
If I may ever know thou dost but sigh
That thou no more shalt see this knack—as never
I mean thou shalt—we 'll bar thee from succession;
Not hold thee of our blood, no, not our kin,
Far' than Deucalion off—mark thou my words
Follow us to the court. Thou, churl, for this time,
Though full of our displeasure, yet we free thee
From the dead blow of it.—And you, enchantment,
Worthy enough a herdsman; yea, him, too
That makes himself, but for our honour therein,
Unworthy thee,—if ever henceforth thou
These rural latches to his entrance open,
Or hoop his body more with thy embraces,
I will devise a death as cruel for thee
As thou art tender to 't.   *[Exit*
   Per.   Even here undone!
I was not much afeard; for once, or twice,
I was about to speak, and tell him plainly,
The selfsame sun that shines upon his court
Hides not his visage from our cottage, but
Looks on alike.—*[To Florizel]* Will 't please you sir, be gone?
I told you what would come of this. 'Beseech you,
Of your own state take care: this dream of mine,
Being now awake, I 'll queen it no inch further,
But milk my ewes, and weep.
   Cam.   Why, how now, father?
Speak, ere thou diest.
   Shep.   I cannot speak, nor think
Nor dare to know that which I know.—*[To Florizel]* O sir!
You have undone a man of fourscore-three,
That thought to fill his grave in quiet; yea,
To die upon the bed my father died,
To lie close by his honest bones: but now
Some hangman must put on my shroud, and lay me
Where no priest shovels in dust.—*[To Perdita]* O cursed wretch!
That knew'st this was the prince, and wouldst adventure
To mingle faith with him.—Undone! undone!
If I might die within this hour, I have lived
To die when I desire.   *[Exit*
   Flo.   Why look you so upon me?

I am but sorry, not afeared; delayed,
But nothing altered. What I was, I am:
More straining on, for plucking back: not following
My leash unwillingly.
   Cam.   Gracious my lord,
You know your father's temper: at this time
He will allow no speech.—which, I do guess,
You do not purpose to him,—and as hardly
Will he endure your sight as yet, I fear:
Then, till the fury of his highness settle,
Come not before him.
   Flo.   I not purpose it.
I think, Camillo?
   Cam.   Even he, my lord.
   Per.   How often have I told you 'twould be thus!
How often said, my dignity would last
But till 't were known!
   Flo.   It cannot fail, but by
The violation of my faith; and then,
Let nature crush the sides o' the earth together,
And mar the seeds within!—Lift up thy looks:—
From my succession wipe me, father: I
Am heir to my affection.
   Cam.   Be advised.
   Flo.   I am, and by my fancy: if my reason
Will thereto be obedient, I have reason;
If not, my senses, better pleased with madness,
Do bid it welcome.
   Cam.   This is desperate, sir.
   Flo.   So call it: but it does fulfil my vow,
I needs must think it honesty. Camillo,
Not for Bohemia, nor the pomp that may
Be thereat gleaned, for all the sun sees, or
The close earth wombs, or the profound seas hide
In unknown fathoms, will I break my oath
To this my fair beloved. Therefore, I pray you,
As you 've e'er been my father's honoured friend,
When he shall miss me,—as, in faith, I mean not
To see him any more,—cast your good counsels
Upon his passion: let myself and fortune
Tug for the time to come. This may you know,
And so deliver:—I am put to sea
With her whom here I cannot hold on shore;
And, most opportune to our need, I have
A vessel rides fast by, but not prepared
For this design. What course I mean to hold
Shall nothing benefit your knowledge, nor
Concern me the reporting.
   Cam.   O my lord,

I would your spirit were easier for advice,
Or stronger for your need.
  Flo.   Hark, Perdita.—[*Takes her aside*
[*To Camillo*] I 'll hear you by-and-by.
  Cam.   He 's irremovable,
Resolved for flight. Now were I happy, if
His going I could frame to serve my turn,
Save him from danger, do him love and honour,
Purchase the sight again of dear Sicilia,
And that unhappy king, my master, whom
I so much thirst to see.
  Flo.   Now, good Camillo,
I am so fraught with curious business, that
I leave out ceremony.   [*Going*
  Cam.   Sir, I think,
You have heard of my poor services, i' the love
That I have borne your father?
  Flo.   Very nobly
Have you deserved: it is my father's music,
To speak your deeds; not little of his care,
To have them recompensed as thought on.
  Cam.   Well, my lord,
If you may please to think I love the king,
And thorough him, what 's nearest to him, which is
Your gracious self, embrace but my direction,
If your more ponderous and settled project
May suffer alteration,—on mine honour,
I 'll point you where you shall have such receiving
As shall become your highness; where you may
Enjoy your mistress—from the whom, I see,
There 's no disjunction to be made, but by,
As heavens forfend, your ruin;—marry her;
And with my best endeavours, in your absence,
Your discontenting father strive to qualify,
And bring him up to liking.
  Flo.   How, Camillo,
May this, almost a miracle, be done?
That I may call thee something more than man,
And, after that, trust to thee.
  Cam.   Have you thought on
A place whereto you 'll go?
  Flo.   Not any yet;
But as the unthought-on accident is guilty
To what we wildly do, so we profess
Ourselves to be the slaves of chance, and flies
Of every wind that blows.
  Cam.   Then list to me:
This follows:—if you will not change your purpose,
But undergo this flight, make for Sicilia,

And there present yourself and your fair princess,—
For so, I see, she must be,—'fore Leontes:
She shall be habited, as it becomes
The partner of your bed.   Methinks, I see
Leontes, opening his free arms, and weeping
His welcomes forth; asks thee, the son, forgiveness,
As 't were i' the father's person; kisses the hands
Of your fresh princess; o'er and o'er divides him
'Twixt his unkindness and his kindness: the one
He chides to hell, and bids the other grow
Faster than thought or time.

     Flo.   Worthy Camillo,
What colour for my visitation shall I
Hold up before him?

     Cam.   Sent by the king, your father
To greet him and to give him comforts.   Sir,
The manner of your bearing towards him, with
What you, as from your father, shall deliver,
Things known betwixt us three, I 'll write you down:
The which shall point you forth at every sitting
What you must say, that he shall not perceive
But that you have your father's bosom there
And speak his very heart.

     Flo.   I am bound to you.
There is some sap in this.

     Cam.   A course more promising
Than a wild dedication of yourselves
To unpathed waters, undreamed shores, most certain
To miseries enough; no hope to help you,
But as you shake off one to take another;
Nothing so certain as your anchors, who
Do their best office if they can but stay you
Where you 'll be loath to be.   Besides, you know,
Prosperity 's the very bond of love,
Whose fresh complexion and whose heart together
Affliction alters.

     Per.   One of these is true:
I think affliction may subdue the cheek,
But not take in the mind.

     Cam.   Yea, say you so?
There shall not, at your father's house, these seven years,
Be born another such.

     Flo.   My good Camillo,
She is as forward of her breeding as
She 's i' the rear our birth.

     Cam.   I cannot say,
Pity she lacks instructions, for she seems
Mistress to most that teach.

     Per.   Your pardon, sir;

For this I 'll blush you thanks.
    Flo.   My prettiest Perdita!—
But, O, the thorns we stand upon!—Camillo,
Preserver of my father, now of me,
The medicine of our house, how shall we do?
We are not furnished like Bohemia's son,
Nor shall appear so in Sicilia.
    Cam.   My lord,
Fear none of this.   I think, you know, my fortunes
Do all lie there: it shall be so my care
To have you royally appointed as if
The scene you play were mine.   For instance, sir,
That you may know you shall not want,—one word.
                                       [They talk aside

Re-enter AUTOLYCUS

    Aut.   Ha, ha! what a fool Honesty is! and Trust, his
sworn brother, a very simple gentleman!   I have sold all
my trumpery: not a counterfeit stone, not a riband, glass,
pomander, brooch, table-book, ballad, knife, tape, glove,
shoe-tie, bracelet, horn-ring, to keep my pack from fasting:
they throng who should buy first; as if my trinkets had
been hallowed, and brought a benediction to the buyer:
by which means I saw whose purse was best in picture,
and what I saw, to my good use I remembered.   My clown
(who wants but something to be a reasonable man) grew
so in love with the wenches' song, that he would not stir
his pettitoes, till he had both tune and words; which so
drew the rest of the herd to me, with all their other senses
stuck in ears; you might have pinched a placket, it was
senseless; 't was nothing to geld a codpiece of a purse:
I would have filed keys off, that hung in chains: no
hearing, no feeling, but my sir's song, and admiring the
nothing of it; so that, in this time of lethargy, I picked
and cut most of their festival purses; and had not the old
man come in with a whoobub against his daughter and
the king's son, and scared my choughs from the chaff, I
had not left a purse alive in the whole army.
          [Camillo, Florizel, and Perdita come forward
    Cam.   Nay, but my letters, by this means being there
So soon as you arrive, shall clear that doubt.
    Flo.   And those that you 'll procure from King Leontes—
    Cam.   Shall satisfy your father.
    Per.   Happy be you!
All that you speak shows fair.
    Cam.   *[Seeing Autolycus]*   Who have we here?
We 'll make an instrument of this: omit
Nothing, may give us aid.
    Aut.   If they have overheard me now,—why, hanging.

Cam. How now, good fellow? why shakest thou so?
Fear not, man; here 's no harm intended to thee.

Aut. I am a poor fellow, sir.

Cam. Why, be so still; here 's nobody will steal that
from thee: yet, for the outside of thy poverty, we must
make an exchange; therefore, discase thee instantly (thou
must think, there 's a necessity in 't) and change garments
with this gentleman. Though the pennyworth on his side
be the worst, yet hold thee, there 's some boot.

Aut. I am a poor fellow, sir.—[*Aside*] I know ye well
enough.

Cam. Nay, pr'ythee, despatch: the gentleman is half
flayed already.

Aut. Are you in earnest, sir?—[*Aside*] I smell the
trick of it.

Flo. Despatch, I pr'ythee.

Aut. Indeed, I have had earnest; but I cannot with
conscience take it.

Cam. Unbuckle, unbuckle.—

[*Florizel and Autolycus exchange garments*
Fortunate mistress,—let my prophecy
Come home to you!—you must retire yourself
Into some covert: take your sweet-heart's hat,
And pluck it o'er your brows; muffle your face;
Dismantle you, and, as you can, disliken
The truth of your own seeming, that you may—
For I do fear eyes over you—to shipboard
Get undescried.

Per.   I see the play so lies
That I must bear a part.

Cam.   No remedy—
Have you done there?

Flo.   Should I now meet my father
He would not call me son.

Cam.   Nay, you shall have no hat.—
Come, lady, come,—Farewell, my friend.

Aut.   Adieu, sir.

Flo. O Perdita, what have we twain forgot!
Pray you, a word.   [*They converse apart*

Cam. What I do next shall be to tell the King
Of this escape, and whither they are bound;
Wherein, my hope is, I shall so prevail
To force him after; in whose company
I shall review Sicilia, for whose sight
I have a woman's longing.—

Flo.   Fortune speed us!—
Thus we set on, Camillo, to the sea-side.

Cam. The swifter speed, the better.

[*Exeunt Florizel, Perdita, and Camillo*

Aut. I understand the business; I hear it. To have an open ear, a quick eye, and a nimble hand, is necessary for a cut-purse; a good nose is requisite also, to smell out work for the other senses. I see, this is the time that the unjust man doth thrive. What an exchange had this been, without boot! what a boot is here with this exchange! Sure, the gods do this year connive at us, and we may do anything *extempore.* The prince himself is about a piece of iniquity; stealing away from his father, with his clog at his heels. If I thought it were a piece of honesty to acquaint the king withal, I would not do 't: I hold it the more knavery to conceal it, and therein am I constant to my profession. Aside, aside:—here is more matter for a hot brain. Every lane's end, every shop, church, session, hanging, yields a careful man work.

Re-enter Clown *and* Shepherd

Clo. See, see, what a man you are now! There is no other way, but to tell the king she 's a changeling, and none of your flesh and blood.

Shep. Nay, but hear me.

Clo. Nay, but hear me.

Shep. Go to, then.

Clo. She being none of your flesh and blood, your flesh and blood has not offended the king; and so your flesh and blood is not to be punished by him. Show those things you found about her; those secret things, all but what she has with her. This being done, let the law go whistle: I warrant you.

Shep. I will tell the king all, every word, yea, and his son's pranks too; who, I may say, is no honest man, neither to his father, nor to me, to go about to make me the king's brother-in-law.

Clo. Indeed, brother-in-law was the furthest off you could have been to him; and then your blood had been the dearer, by I know how much an ounce.

Aut. [*Aside*] Very wisely, puppies!

Shep. Well, let us to the king; there is that in this fardel will make him scratch his beard.

Aut. [*Aside*] I know not what impediment this complaint may be to the flight of my master.

Clo. Pray heartily he be at palace.

Aut. [*Aside*] Though I am not naturally honest, I am so sometimes by chance:—let me pocket up my pedlar's excrement. [*Takes off his false beard*] How now, rustics? Whither are you bound?

Shep. To the palace, an it like your worship.

Aut. Your affairs there? what? with whom? the con-

dition of that fardel, the place of your dwelling, your names,
your ages, of what having, breeding, and anything that
is fitting to be known? discover.

Clo. We are but plain fellows, sir.

Aut. A lie: you are rough and hairy. Let me have
no lying; it becomes none but tradesmen, and they often
give us soldiers the lie; but we pay them for it with stamped
coin, not stabbing steel: therefore, they do not give us the
lie.

Clo. Your worship had like to have given us one, if
you had not taken yourself with the manner.

Shep. Are you a courtier, an 't like you, sir?

Aut. Whether it like me, or no, I am a courtier. Seest
thou not the air of the court in these enfoldings? hath
not my gait in it the measure of the court? receives not
thy nose court-odour from me? reflect I not on thy baseness court-contempt? Think'st thou, for that I insinuate,
or toze from thee thy business, I am therefore no courtier?
I am courtier, cap-a-pè; and one that will either push
on, or pluck back thy business there: whereupon I command thee to open thy affair.

Shep. My business, sir, is to the king.

Aut. What advocate hast thou to him?

Shep. I know not, an 't like you.

Clo. Advocate's the court-word for a pheasant: say,
you have none.

Shep. None, sir: I have no pheasant, cock, nor
hen.

Aut. How blessed are we that are not simple men!
Yet nature might have made me as these are,
Therefore I 'll not disdain.

Clo. This cannot be but a great courtier.

Shep. His garments are rich, but he wears them not
handsomely.

Clo. He seems to be the more noble in being fan-
tastical: a great man, I 'll warrant; I know by the picking
on 's teeth.

Aut. The fardel there? what 's i' the fardel? Wherefore that box?

Shep. Sir, there lies such secrets in this fardel and box
which none must know but the king; and which he shall
know within this hour, if I may come to the speech of
him.

Aut. Age, thou hast lost thy labour.

Shep. Why, sir?

Aut. The king is not at the palace: he is gone aboard
a new ship to purge melancholy, and air himself: for, if
thou be'st capable of things serious, thou must know, the
king is full of grief.

Shep. So 't is said, sir; about his son, that should have married a shepherd's daughter.

Aut. If that shepherd be not in hand-fast, let him fly: the curses he shall have, the tortures he shall feel, will break the back of man, the heart of monster.

Clo. Think you so, sir?

Aut. Not he alone shall suffer what wit can make heavy, and vengeance bitter; but those that are germane to him, though removed fifty times, shall all come under the hangman: which, though it be great pity, yet it is necessary. An old sheep-whistling rogue, a ram-tender, to offer to have his daughter come into grace! Some say, he shall be stoned; but that death is too soft for him, say I. Draw our throne into a sheepcote! all deaths are too few, the sharpest too easy.

Clo. Has the old man e'er a son, sir, do you hear, an 't like you, sir?

Aut. He has a son, who shall be flayed alive; then 'nointed over with honey, set on the head of a wasp's nest; then stand, till he be three-quarters and a dram dead; then recovered again with aqua-vitæ, or some other hot infusion; then, raw as he is, and in the hottest day prognostication proclaims, shall he be set against a brick wall, the sun looking with a southward eye upon him, where he is to behold him with flies blown to death. But what talk we of these traitory rascals, whose miseries are to be smiled at, their offences being so capital? Tell me —for you seem to be honest plain men—what you have to the king? being something gently considered, I 'll bring you where he is aboard, tender your persons to his presence, whisper him in your behalfs; and, if it be in man, besides the king, to effect your suits, here is man shall do it.

Clo. He seems to be of great authority: close with him, give him gold; and though authority be a stubborn bear, yet he is oft led by the nose with gold. Show the inside of your purse to the outside of his hand, and no more ado. Remember; stoned, and flayed alive!

Shep. An 't please you, sir, to undertake the business for us, here is that gold I have: I 'll make it as much more, and leave this young man in pawn, till I bring it you.

Aut. After I have done what I promised?

Shep. Ay, sir.

Aut. Well, give me the moiety.—Are you a party in this business?

Clo. In some sort, sir? but though my case be a pitiful one, I hope I shall not be flayed out of it.

Aut. O! that 's the case of the shepherd's son. Hang him, he 'll be made an example.

Clo. Comfort, good comfort! We must to the king, and show our strange sights: he must know, 't is none of your daughter, nor my sister; we are gone else. Sir, I will give you as much as this old man does when the business is performed; and remain, as he says, your pawn till it be brought you.

Aut. I will trust you. Walk before toward the sea-side; go on the right hand; I will but look upon the hedge, and follow you.

Clo. We are blessed in this man, as I may say; even blessed.

Shep. Let 's before, as he bids us. He was provided to do us good.

           [Exeunt Shepherd and Clown

Aut. If I had a mind to be honest, I see, Fortune would not suffer me: she drops booties in my mouth. I am courted now with a double occasion—gold, and a means to do the prince my master good? which, who knows how that may turn back to my advancement? I will bring these two moles, these blind ones, aboard him: if he think it fit to shore them again, and that the complaint they have to the king concerns him nothing, let him call me rogue for being so far officious; for I am proof against that title, and what shame else belongs to 't. To him will I present them; there may be matter in it.   *[Exit*

ACT FIVE

Scene I.—Sicilia. A Room in the Palace of Leontes

Enter Leontes, Cleomenes, Dion, Paulina, *and others*

Cleo. Sir, you have done enough, and have performed
A saint-like sorrow: no fault could you make,
Which you have not redeemed; indeed, paid down
More penitence than done trespass. At the last,
Do as the heavens have done, forget your evil;
With them, forgive yourself.

Leon.   Whilst I remember
Her, and her virtues, I cannot forget
My blemishes in them, and so still think of
The wrong I did myself; which was so much,
That heirless it hath made my kingdom, and
Destroyed the sweet'st companion that e'er man
Bred his hopes out of.

Paul.   True, too true, my lord:
If one by one you wedded all the world,
Or from the all that are took something good,

To make a perfect woman, she you killed
Would be unparalleled.
    Leon.   I think so.   Killed!
She I killed! I did so: but thou strik'st me
Sorely, to say I did; it is as bitter
Upon thy tongue, as in my thought. Now, good now,
Say so but seldom.
    Cleo.   Not at all, good lady:
You might have spoken a thousand things that would
Have done the time more benefit, and graced
Your kindness better.
    Paul.   You are one of those
Would have him wed again.
    Dion.   If you would not so,
You pity not the state, nor the remembrance
Of his most sovereign name: consider little,
What dangers, by his highness' fail of issue,
May drop upon his kingdom, and devour
Incertain lookers-on. What were more holy
Than to rejoice the former queen is well?
What holier than for royalty's repair,
For present comfort, and for future good,—
To bless the bed of majesty again
With a sweet fellow to 't?
    Paul.   There is none worthy,
Respecting her that 's gone. Besides, the gods
Will have fulfilled their secret purposes;
For has not the divine Apollo said,
Is 't not the tenor of his oracle,
That King Leontes shall not have an heir,
Till his lost child be found? which, that it shall,
Is all as monstrous to our human reason,
As my Antigonus to break his grave,
And come again to me; who, on my life,
Did perish with the infant. 'T is your counsel
My lord should to the heavens be contrary,
Oppose against their wills.—[*To Leontes*] Care not for
        issue;
The crown will find an heir; great Alexander
Left his to the worthiest, so his successor
Was like to be the best
    Leon.   Good Paulina,—
Who hast the memory of Hermione,
I know, in honour,—O, that ever I
Had squared me to thy counsel!—then, even now,
I might have looked upon my queen's full eyes,
Have taken treasure from her lips,—
    Paul.   And left them
More rich for what they yielded.

Leon.   Thou speak'st truth.
No more such wives: therefore, no wife: one worse,
And better used, would make her sainted spirit
Again possess her corse, and on this stage—
Where we offend her now—appear, soul-vexed,
And begin "Why to me?"
    Paul.   Had she such power,
She had just cause.
    Leon.   She had; and would incense me
To murder her I married.
    Paul.   I should so:
Were I the ghost that walked, I 'd bid you mark
Her eye, and tell me for what dull part in 't
You chose her; then I 'd shriek, that even your ears
Should rift to hear me, and the words that followed
Should be "Remember mine."
    Leon.   Stars, stars,
And all eyes else dead coals.—Fear thou no wife:
I 'll have no wife, Paulina.
    Paul.   Will you swear
Never to marry, but by my free leave?
    Leon.   Never, Paulina: so be blessed my spirit!
    Paul.   Then, good my lords, bear witness to his oath.
    Cleo.   You tempt him overmuch.
    Paul.   Unless another
As like Hermione as is her picture,
Affront his eye.
    Cleo.   Good madam,—
    Paul.   I have done.
Yet, if my lord will marry,—if you will, sir,
No remedy, but you will,—give me the office
To choose you a queen.   She shall not be so young
As was your former; but she shall be such
As, walked your first queen's ghost, it should take joy
To see her in your arms.
    Leon.   My true Paulina,
We shall not marry, till thou bidd'st us.
    Paul.   That
Shall be when your first queen's again in breath:
Never till then.

Enter a Gentleman

    Gent.   One that gives out himself Prince Florizel,
Son of Polixenes, with his princess (she
The fairest I have yet beheld), desires access
To your high presence.
    Leon.   What with him? he comes not
Like to his father's greatness; his approach,

So out of circumstance and sudden, tells us
'T is not a visitation framed, but forced
By need and accident.   What train?
   Gent.   But few,
And those but mean.
   Leon.   His princess, say you, with him?
   Gent.   Ay, the most peerless piece of earth, I think,
That e'er the sun shone bright on.
   Paul.   O Hermione!
As every present time doth boast itself
Above a better, gone, so must thy grace
Give way to what's seen now.   Sir, you yourself
Have said and writ so, but your writing now
Is colder than that theme,—"She had not been,
Nor was not to be equalled;"—thus your verse
Flowed with her beauty once; 't is shrewdly ebbed,
To say you have seen a better.
   Gent.   Pardon, madam:
The one I have almost forgot,—your pardon;—
The other, when she has obtained your eye,
Will have your tongue too.   This is a creature,
Would she begin a sect, might quench the zeal
Of all professors else, make proselytes
Of whom she but bid follow.
   Paul.   How! not women?
   Gent.   Women will love her, that she is a woman
More worth than any man; men, that she is
The rarest of all women.
   Leon.   Go, Cleomenes;
Yourself, assisted with your honoured friends,
Bring them to our embracement.—Still 't is strange,
              [*Exeunt Cleomenes, Lords and Gentleman*
He thus should steal upon us.
   Paul.   Had our prince—
Jewel of children—seen this hour, he had paired
Well with this lord: there was not full a month
Between their births.
   Leon.   Pr'ythee, no more: cease: thou know'st,
He dies to me again, when talked of: sure,
When I shall see this gentleman, thy speeches
Will bring me to consider that which may
Unfurnish me of reason.—They are come.—

Re-enter CLEOMENES, *with* FLORIZEL, PERDITA, *and others*

Your mother was most true to wedlock, prince;
For she did print your royal father off,
Conceiving you.   Were I but twenty-one,
Your father's image is so hit in you

His very air, that I should call you brother,
As I did him; and speak of something, wildly
By us performed before.   Most dearly welcome!
And your fair princess, goddess!—O, alas,
I lost a couple, that 'twixt heaven and earth
Might thus have stood, begetting wonder as
You, gracious couple, do.   And then I lost—
All mine own folly—the society,
Amity too, of your brave father; whom,
Though bearing misery, I desire my life
Once more to look on him.
    Flo.   By his command
Have I here touched Sicilia; and from him
Give you all greetings that a king at friend
Can send his brother: and, but infirmity,
Which waits upon worn times, hath something seized
His wished ability, he had himself
The land and waters 'twixt your throne and his
Measured to look upon you, whom he loves—
He bade me say so—more than all the sceptres
And those that bear them living.
    Leon.   O my brother,
Good gentleman, the wrongs I have done thee stir
Afresh within me; and these thy offices
So rarely kind are as interpreters
Of my behind-hand slackness.—Welcome hither,
As is the spring to the earth.   And hath he too
Exposed this paragon to the fearful usage—
At least ungentle—of the dreadful Neptune,
To greet a man not worth her pains, much less
The adventure of her person?
    Flo.   Good my lord,
She came from Libya.
    Leon.   Where the warlike Smalus,
That noble, honoured lord, is feared and loved?
    Flo.   Most royal sir, from thence; from him, whose
              daughter
His tears proclaimed his, parting with her, thence,
A prosperous south-wind friendly, we have crossed,
To execute the charge my father gave me,
For visiting your highness.   My best train
I have from your Sicilian shores dismissed,
Who for Bohemia bend, to signify
Not only my success in Libya, sir,
But my arrival, and my wife's, in safety
Here, where we are.
    Leon.   The blessèd gods
Purge all infection from our air, whilst you
Do climate here!   You have a holy father,

A graceful gentleman, against whose person,
So sacred as it is, I have done sin;
For which the heavens, taking angry note,
Have left me issueless; and your father's blessed,
As he from heaven merits it, with you,
Worthy his goodness.   What might I have been,
Might I a son and daughter now have looked on,
Such goodly things as you!

Enter a Lord

Lord.   Most noble sir,
That which I shall report will bear no credit,
Were not the proof so nigh.   Please you, great sir,
Bohemia greets you from himself by me;
Desires you to attach his son, who has—
His dignity and duty both cast off—
Fled from his father, from his hopes, and with
A shepherd's daughter.
    Leon.   Where 's Bohemia? speak.
    Lord.   Here in your city; I now came from him:
I speak amazedly, and it becomes
My marvel, and my message.   To your court
Whiles he was hastening—in the chase, it seems,
Of this fair couple—meets he on the way
The father of this seeming lady, and
Her brother, having both their country quitted
With this young prince.
    Flo.   Camillo has betrayed me,
Whose honour, and whose honesty, till now
Endured all weathers.
    Lord.   Lay 't so to his charge:
He 's with the king your father.
    Leon.   Who? Camillo?
    Lord.   Camillo, sir: I spake with him, who now
Has three poor men in question.   Never saw I
Wretches so quake: they kneel, they kiss the earth,
Forswear themselves as often as they speak:
Bohemia stops his ears, and threatens them
With divers deaths in death.
    Per.   O my poor father!—
The heaven sets spies upon us, will not have
Our contract celebrated.
    Leon.   You are married?
    Flo.   We are not, sir, nor are we like to be;
The stars, I see, will kiss the valleys first:
The odds for high and low 's alike.
    Leon.   My lord,
Is this the daughter of a king?

Flo.   She is,
When once she is my wife.
   Leon.   That once, I see, by your good father's speed,
Will come on very slowly.   I am sorry,
Most sorry, you have broken from his liking,
Where you were tied in duty; and as sorry,
Your choice is not so rich in worth as beauty,
That you might well enjoy her.
   Flo.   Dear, look up:
Though Fortune, visible an enemy,
Should chase us with my father, power no jot
Hath she to change our loves.—'Beseech you, sir,
Remember since you owed no more to time
Than I do now; with thought of such affections,
Step forth mine advocate: at your request,
My father will grant precious things as trifles.
   Leon.   Would he do so, I 'd beg your precious mistress,
Which he counts but a trifle.
   Paul.   Sir, my liege,
Your eye hath too much youth in 't: not a month
'Fore your queen died, she was more worth such gazes
Than what you look on now.
   Leon.   I thought of her,
Even in these looks I made.—[*To Florizel*] But your
        petition
Is yet unanswered.   I will to your father:
Your honour not o'erthrown by your desires,
I am friend to them and you; upon which errand
I now go toward him.   Therefore, follow me,
And mark what way I make: come, good my lord.
                                              [*Exeunt*

SCENE II.—The Same.   Before the Palace

Enter AUTOLYCUS *and a Gentleman*

   Aut.   'Beseech you, sir, were you present at this relation?
   First Gent.   I was by at the opening of the fardel,
heard the old shepherd deliver the manner how he found
it: whereupon, after a little amazedness, we were all commanded out of the chamber; only this, methought I
heard the shepherd say he found the child.
   Aut.   I would most gladly know the issue of it.
   First Gent.   I make a broken delivery of the business;
but the changes I perceived in the king and Camillo, were
very notes of admiration: they seemed almost, with staring
on one another, to tear the cases of their eyes; there was

speech in their dumbness, language in their very gesture; they looked, as they had heard of a world ransomed, or one destroyed. A notable passion of wonder appeared in them; but the wisest beholder, that knew no more but seeing, could not say, if the importance were joy or sorrow, but in the extremity of the one it must needs be.

Enter another Gentleman

Here comes a gentleman, that, haply, knows more. **The** news, Rogero?

Second Gent. Nothing but bonfires. The oracle is fulfilled; the king's daughter is found; such a deal of wonder is broken out within this hour, that ballad-makers cannot be able to express it. Here comes the Lady Paulina's steward: he can deliver you more.

Enter a third Gentleman

How goes it now, sir? this news, which is called true, is so like an old tale, that the verity of it is in strong suspicion. Has the king found his heir?

Third Gent. Most true, if ever truth were pregnant by circumstance: that which you hear you'll swear you see, there is such unity in the proofs. The mantle of Queen Hermione;—her jewel about the neck of it;—the letters of Antigonus found with it, which they knew to be his character;—the majesty of the creature, in resemblance of the mother;—the affection of nobleness, which nature shows above her breeding, and many other evidences proclaim her with all certainty to be the king's daughter. Did you see the meeting of the two kings?

Second Gent. No.

Third Gent. Then you have lost a sight which was to be seen, cannot be spoken of. There might you have beheld one joy crown another; so, and in such a manner, that it seemed, sorrow wept to take leave of them, for their joy waded in tears. There was casting up of eyes, holding up of hands, with countenance of such distraction, that they were to be known by garment, not by favour. Our king, being ready to leap out of himself for joy of his found daughter, as if that joy were now become a loss, cries, "O thy mother, thy mother!" then asks Bohemia forgiveness; then embraces his son-in-law; then again worries he his daughter with clipping her; now he thanks the old shepherd, which stands by like a weather-bitten conduit of many kings' reigns. I never heard of such another encounter, which lames report to follow it, and undoes description to do it.

Second Gent. What, pray you, became of Antigonus, that carried hence the child?

Third Gent. Like an old tale still, which will have matter to rehearse, though credit be asleep, and not an ear open. He was torn to pieces with a bear: this avouches the shepherd's son, who has not only his innocence, which seems much, to justify him, but a handkerchief, and rings of his, that Paulina knows.

First Gent. What became of his bark, and his followers?

Third Gent. Wracked, the same instant of their master's death, and in the view of the shepherd: so that all the instruments, which aided to expose the child, were even then lost, when it was found. But, O, the noble combat, that 'twixt joy and sorrow was fought in Paulina! She had one eye declined for the loss of her husband, another elevated that the oracle was fulfilled: she lifted the princess from the earth, and so locks her in embracing, as if she would pin her to her heart, that she might no more be in danger of losing.

First Gent. The dignity of this act was worth the audience of kings and princes, for by such was it acted.

Third Gent. One of the prettiest touches of all, and that which angled for mine eyes—caught the water, though not the fish—was, when at the relation of the queen's death, with the manner how she came to 't, bravely confessed and lamented by the king, how attentiveness wounded his daughter, till, from one sign of dolour to another, she did, with an alas! I would fain say, bleed tears, for, I am sure, my heart wept blood. Who was most marble there, changed colour; some swooned, all sorrowed: if all the world could have seen it, the woe had been universal.

First Gent. Are they returned to the court?

Third Gent. No; the princess hearing of her mother's statue, which is in the keeping of Paulina,—a piece many years in doing, and now newly performed by that rare Italian master, Julio Romano; who, had he himself eternity, and could put breath into his work, would beguile Nature of her custom, so perfectly he is her ape: he so near to Hermione hath done Hermione, that, they say, one would speak to her, and stand in hope of answer: thither, with all greediness of affection, are they gone; and there they intend to sup.

Second Gent. I thought she had some great matter there in hand, for she hath privately, twice or thrice a day, ever since the death of Hermione, visited that removed house. Shall we thither, and with our company piece the rejoicing?

First Gent. Who would be thence that has the benefit

of access? every wink of an eye, some new grace will be born; our absence makes us unthrifty to our knowledge. Let's along.   [*Exeunt Gentlemen*

Aut. Now, had I not the dash of my former life in me, would preferment drop on my head. I brought the old man and his son aboard the prince; told him I heard them talk of a fardel, and I know not what; but he at that time, over-fond of the shepherd's daughter—so he then took her to be—began to be much sea-sick, and himself little better, extremity of weather continuing, this mystery remained undiscovered. But 't is all one to me; for had I been the finder-out of this secret, it would not have relished among my other discredits.—Here come those I have done good to against my will, and already appearing in the blossoms of their fortune.

Enter Shepherd *and* Clown

Shep. Come, boy: I am past more children; but thy sons and daughters will be all gentlemen born.

Clo. You are well met, sir. You denied to fight with me this other day, because I was no gentleman born: see you these clothes? say, you see them not, and think me still no gentleman born: you were best say, these robes are not gentlemen born. Give me the lie, do, and try whether I am not now a gentleman born.

Aut. I know you are now, sir, a gentleman born.

Clo. Ay, and have been so any time these four hours.

Shep. And so have I, boy.

Clo. So you have;—but I was a gentleman born before my father, for the king's son took me by the hand, and called me, brother; and then the two kings called my father, brother; and then the prince my brother, and the princess, my sister, called my father, father; and so we wept: and there was the first gentleman-like tears that ever we shed.

Shep. We may live, son, to shed many more.

Clo. Ay, or else 't were hard luck, being in so preposterous estate as we are.

Aut. I humbly beseech you, sir, to pardon me all the faults I have committed to your worship, and to give me your good report to the prince my master.

Shep. 'Pr'ythee, son, do; for we must be gentle, now we are gentlemen.

Clo. Thou wilt amend thy life?

Aut. Ay, an it like your good worship.

Clo. Give me thy hand: I will swear to the prince, thou art as honest a true fellow as any is in Bohemia.

Shep. You may say it, but not swear it.

Clo. Not swear it, now I am a gentleman? Let boors and franklins say it, I 'll swear it.

Shep. How if it be false, son?

Clo. If it be ne'er so false, a true gentleman may swear it in the behalf of his friend:—and I 'll swear to the prince, thou art a tall fellow of thy hands, and that thou wilt not be drunk; but I know, thou art no tall fellow of thy hands, and that thou wilt be drunk; but I 'll swear it, and I would thou wouldst be a tall fellow of thy hands.

Aut. I will prove so, sir; to my power.

Clo. Ay, by any means prove a tall fellow: if I do not wonder how thou darest venture to be drunk, not being a tall fellow, trust me not.—Hark! the kings and the princes, our kindred, are going to see the queen's picture. Come, follow us: we 'll be thy good masters.   *[Exeunt*

SCENE III.—The Same. A Chapel in PAULINA's House

Enter LEONTES, POLIXENES, FLORIZEL, PERDITA, CAMILLO, PAULINA, *Lords, and Attendants*

Leon. O grave and good Paulina, the great comfort
That I have had of thee!

Paul.   What, sovereign sir,
I did not well, I meant well. All my services
You have paid home; but that you have vouchsafed
With your crowned brother, and these your contracted
Heirs of your kingdoms, my poor house to visit,
It is a surplus of your grace which never
My life may last to answer.

Leon.   O Paulina!
We honour you with trouble. But we came
To see the statue of our queen: your gallery
Have we passed through, not without much content
In many singularities, but we saw not
That which my daughter came to look upon,
The statue of her mother.

Paul.   As she lived peerless,
So her dead likeness, I do well believe,
Excels whatever yet you looked upon,
Or hand of man hath done; therefore I keep it
Lonely, apart. But here it is: prepare
To see the life as lively mocked as ever
Still sleep mocked death: behold; and say, 't is well.

          [Paulina undraws a curtain, and discovers
                    Hermione as a statue
I like your silence: it the more shows off
Your wonder; but yet speak:—first you, my liege.

Comes it not something near?
    Leon.   Her natural posture!—
Chide me, dear stone, that I may say, indeed,
Thou art Hermione; or, rather, thou art she
In thy not chiding, for she was as tender
As infancy and grace.—But yet, Paulina,
Hermione was not so much wrinkled; nothing
So agéd, as this seems.
    Pol.   O, not by much.
    Paul. So much the more our carver's excellence;
Which lets go by some sixteen years, and makes her
As she lived now.
    Leon.   As now she might have done,
So much to my good comfort, as it is
Now piercing to my soul.   O, thus she stood,
Even with such life of majesty—warm life,
As now it coldly stands—when first I wooed her.
I am ashamed: does not the stone rebuke me,
For being more stone than it?—O royal piece!
There 's magic in thy majesty, which has
My evils conjured to remembrance, and
From thy admiring daughter took the spirits,
Standing like stone with thee.
    Per.   And give me leave,
And do not say it 's superstition, that
I kneel, and then implore her blessing.—Lady,
Dear queen, that ended when I but began,
Give me that hand of yours to kiss.
    Paul.   O, patience!
The statue is but newly fixed, the colour 's
Not dry.
    Cam. My lord, your sorrow was too sore laid on,
Which sixteen winters cannot blow away,
So many summers dry: scarce any joy
Did ever so long live; no sorrow,
But killed itself much sooner.
    Pol.   Dear my brother,
Let him that was the cause of this have power
To take off so much grief from you as he
Will piece up in himself.
    Paul.   Indeed, my lord,
If I had thought, the sight of my poor image
Would thus have wrought you—for the stone is mine—
I 'd not have showed it.
    Leon.   Do not draw the curtain.
    Paul. No longer shall you gaze on 't, lest your fancy
May think anon it moves.
    Leon.   Let be, let be!
Would I were dead, but that, methinks, already—

What was he that did make it?—See, my lord,
Would you not deem it breathed, and that those veins
Did verily bear blood?
    Pol.   Masterly done:
The very life seems warm upon her lip.
    Leon.   The fixture of her eye has motion in 't,
As we are mocked with art.
    Paul.   I 'll draw the curtain.
My lord 's almost so far transported, that
He 'll think anon it lives.
    Leon.   O sweet Paulina!
Make me to think so twenty years together:
No settled senses of the world can match
The pleasure of that madness. Let 't alone.
    Paul.   I am sorry, sir, I have thus far stirred you: but
I could afflict you further.
    Leon.   Do, Paulina;
For this affliction has a taste as sweet
As any cordial comfort.—Still, methinks,
There is an air comes from her: what fine chisel
Could ever yet cut breath? Let no man mock me,
For I will kiss her.
    Paul.   Good my lord, forbear.
The ruddiness upon her lip is wet:
You 'll mar it, if you kiss it; stain your own
With oily painting. Shall I draw the curtain?
    Leon.   No, not these twenty years.
    Per.   So long could I
Stand by, a looker-on.
    Paul.   Either forbear,
Quit presently the chapel, or resolve you
For more amazement. If you can behold it,
I 'll make the statue move indeed, descend
And take you by the hand; but then you 'll think—
Which I protest against—I am assisted
By wicked powers.
    Leon.   What you can make her do,
I am content to look on; what to speak,
I am content to hear; for 't is as easy
To make her speak, as move.
    Paul.   It is required,
You do awake your faith. Then, all stand still;
Or those that think it is unlawful business
I am about, let them depart.
    Leon.   Proceed:
No foot shall stir.
    Paul.   Music, awake her, strike!—   [*Music*
'T is time; descend; be stone no more: approach;
Strike all that look upon with marvel. Come;

I 'll fill your grave up: stir; nay, come away;
Bequeath to death your numbness, for from him
Dear life redeems you.—You perceive, she stirs.
                    [*Hermione descends from the pedestal*
Start not: her actions shall be holy, as
You hear my spell is lawful: do not shun her
Until you see her die again, for then
You kill her double.   Nay, present your hand:
When she was young you wooed her; now, in age,
Is she become the suitor.
      Leon.   [*Embracing her*]   O, she 's warm!
If this be magic, let it be an art
Lawful as eating.
      Pol.   She embraces him.
      Cam.   She hangs about his neck.
If she pertain to life, let her speak too.
      Pol.   Ay; and make 't manifest where she has lived,
Or how stolen from the dead.
      Paul.   That she is living,
Were it but told you, should be hooted at
Like an old tale; but it appears she lives,
Though yet she speak not.   Mark a little while.—
Please you to interpose, fair maiden: kneel,
And pray your mother's blessing.—Turn good lady;
Our Perdita is found.
                    [*Perdita kneels to Hermione*
      Her.   You gods, look down,
And from your sacred vials pour your graces
Upon my daughter's head!—Tell me, mine own,
Where hast thou been preserved? where lived, how found
Thy father's court? for thou shalt hear, that I,
Knowing by Paulina that the oracle
Gave hope thou wast in being, have preserved
Myself to see the issue.
      Paul.   There 's time enough for that,
Lest they desire, upon this push, to trouble
Your joys with like relation.—Go together,
You precious winners all: your exultation
Partake to every one.   I, an old turtle,
Will wing me to some withered bough, and there
My mate, that 's never to be found again,
Lament till I am lost.
      Leon.   O, peace, Paulina!
Thou shouldst a husband take by my consent,
As I by thine a wife: this is a match,
And made between 's by vows.   Thou hast found mine;
But how, is to be questioned: for I saw her,
As I thought, dead, and have in vain said many
A prayer upon her grave: I 'll not seek far—

For him, I partly know his mind—to find thee
An honourable husband.—Come, Camillo,
And take her by the hand: whose worth and honesty
Is richly noted, and here justified
By us, a pair of kings.—Let 's from this place.—
What!—Look upon my brother:—both your pardons,
That e'er I put between your holy looks
My ill suspicion.—This' your son-in-law
And son unto the king, whom heavens directing
Is troth-plight to your daughter. Good Paulina,
Lead us from hence, where we may leisurely
Each one demand, and answer to his part
Performed in this wide gap of time, since first
We were dissevered: hastily lead away.

                                     [Exeunt

THE PEEBLES CLASSIC LIBRARY